TENNIS COURSE
VOLUME 2

Lessons and Training

BARRON'S

TENNIS COURSE

VOLUME 2
Lessons and Training

English language edition published in 2000 by Barron's Educational Series, Inc.

Original Title of the Book in German is *Tennis Lehrplan, Band 2: Unterricht & Training*

© 1996 BLV Verlagsgesellschaft GmbH, München/GERMANY

Written by:
Rüdiger Bornemann
Hartmut Gabler
Gerhard Glasbrenner
Jock Reetz
Richard Schönborn
Peter Scholl
Karl Weber

Photo Credits
German Tennis News Archive: p. 213
Baader: p. 9, 92, 95, 102, 182, 197 (right), 216
Collmann: p. 64
Exler: p. 2/3, 21, 22, 41, 49, 52, 53, 108, 111, 122, 123, 125, 127, 128, 129, 130, 151, 160/161, 191, 192, 197 (left), 198, 200, 208, 220, 247, 249
Jakobs: p. 172, 173, 174, 175, 176, 177, 178, 179, 180
Reetz: p. 12, 31, 56, 57, 68, 69, 74, 75, 115
Weber: p. 232

ISBN: 0-7641-1486-7

Library of Congress Catalog Card No.: 99-069379

Illustrations: Jörg Mair
Cover Photo: Duomo Photography/Chris Trotman
Cover Design: Werbeagentur Sander & Krause

Layout: Bücherwerkstatt A. v. Ertzdorff

BLV Publishing, Inc.
Munich Vienna Zurich
80797 Munich

All inquiries should be addressed to:
Barron's Educational Series, Inc.
250 Wireless Boulevard
Hauppauge, New York 11788
http://www.barronseduc.com

Printed in Hong Kong
9 8 7 6 5 4 3 2 1

Contents

Introduction

This tennis manual, *Tennis Course, Volume 2: Teaching and Training*, supplements the first volume of the curriculum, *Techniques and Tactics*.

This book organizes instruction into themes, and the main objective of the first section is to provide practical help, advice, and information regarding the teaching of tennis. The opinions on methods concerning specific problems and questions about teaching and learning are based on practical pedagogical and methodological experiences and the findings of sports medicine.

The intended audience is everyone engaged in any way with teaching and learning tennis. This includes tennis instructors and trainers in clubs, associations or tennis schools, and also teachers and students in schools and colleges, as well as beginners or advanced tennis players who want to improve their own game or that of others. We also have in mind parents who want to give their children concrete help as they learn to play tennis.

The curriculum library of the German Tennis Association is organized so that the individual volumes treat specific aspects of tennis and the ways they function together; they also supplement one another. Thus, the curriculum presented in our previous Volume 1, *Techniques and Tactics*, forms a basis for the current book, where

the tennis techniques are pictured as well as described. The first volume can be used to teach and learn these techniques in instruction sessions. The methods section does not try to provide a strict recipe; situations in tennis instruction are much too varied and complex. Instead, it sketches methods and procedures that have been proven successful, and it gives numerous practical examples.

Obviously, the best training for competition is practicing and participating in the greatest possible number of tournaments. On the other hand, world-class tennis demands a goal-oriented and systematic training program in techniques and coordination, tactics, and conditioning. Such a program will incorporate the best ideas from training science and sports medicine.

There are a number of themes covered in the second part of this book. The selection and scope of topics consider the state of the art and the practical needs of readers.

Space limitations meant that some topics were excluded, or treated briefly. For more detail, we recommend interested readers consult their local tennis association for additional literature.

Curriculum plans of this type always have the problem of combining theory and practice. Here, we will try to present only

as much of the theoretical concepts as necessary to support the practical examples, allowing trainers some fundamentals on which they can develop their own types of exercises. Therefore, the examples are not considered recipes, but they are to be taken as examples that should be used flexibly, paying particular attention to skill level and gender-specific considerations in training children, teens, and adults.

The main focus of the second part of this volume is trainers and sports instructors. However, this book should provide information and encouragement to everyone interested in training and competition. Suggestions throughout are meant to be considered critically and developed further in practice because training and playing both change constantly.

Finally, we would like to note that this curriculum is envisioned as a handbook, in the sense of a reference work, which can be used to find help for particular areas and to answer specific questions on instruction and training.

Rüdiger Bornemann
Hartmut Gabler
Gerhard Glasbrenner
Jock Reetz
Richard Schönborn
Peter Scholl
Karl Weber

Features of Tennis: The Starting Point for Instruction and Training

Grouping Sports According to Performance Standards

One of the important ways sports differ from one another is in the different expressions of the factors that influence performance. If we look at various sports with this in mind, we note that they fall into various groups. For example, we can readily identify five groups:

- Combat sports, such as boxing and wrestling;
- Strength and elasticity sports, such as weight lifting, diving, and sprinting;
- Endurance sports, such as cross-country running and rowing;
- Composite sports, such as apparatus gymnastics and figure skating;
- Games, such as soccer and tennis.

In each of these groups, certain factors (for example, stamina or speed) are necessary to a certain degree, in order to be able to perform well. Nevertheless, each group will have a number of significant factors such as various expressions of individual factors and their relationship to one another.

Reaching international world-class levels may take a player up to 10 years. If he or she reaches this level—which very few can—it may take another 2–4 years until the competitor reaches his or her personal best. This relatively long time (approximately 10–14 years) emphasizes that the development of performance-related factors in tennis requires a significant time commitment.

Because tennis involves a variety of factors that determine performance—these will be treated individually later—it becomes clear how difficult this sport is, even at beginning competitive levels.

Specific Features of Tennis

Ball and Racket

In tennis, one has to master not one, but two, objects—the ball and the racket. The ball, approaching at speeds up to 120 mph must be precisely directed by a racket, whose inertia must be overcome and which itself may reach speeds up to 90 mph!

Return Play

Unlike many team sports, opponents in tennis are separated by the net and never come in contact. Instead, in tennis and other racket sports, opponents interact by playing the ball back and forth.

Various Scorekeeping Methods and Regulations

The traditional way of keeping score in tennis is unique to the sport. The peculiarity of the scorekeeping method and regulations is principally that each game in each set begins anew, fresh, thus never allowing a player to be sure of winning, even if he or she had a very good lead in a set or match.

No Time Limit for a Match

Most sports have a specific, or at least an approximate time limit. A tennis match can last between 30 minutes and 3 1/2 hours over two sets. A five-set match can last more than 5 hours. These varied match lengths impose on the players the need for a range of abilities that are not important in other sports or are important only in a limited way.

Pressure Occurs Intermittently

Volleys consume 20 to 25 percent of the length of play (on sand). The rest of the match consists of pauses.

Tournament Features and a Year-round Season

Competition tennis consists of tournaments and team competitions. As a rule, tournaments are played as elimination matches. Generally, in this type of play, the player must complete at least one match per day. International tournaments usually last a week, with the "Grand Slam" running for two weeks. But there are also three-day events (Friday through Sunday), in which a competitor might have to play several games

in a day. Almost all tournaments also include doubles competitions. This means particular requirements for the players. Often, whole tournament series are played in which, for the individual events, there is a switch from continent to continent or in which competitors alternate between outdoor and indoor courts. The increasing professionalism of tournament tennis and the related independence of ranking list results leads to an almost year-round playing season for the players.

Play and Competition Readiness at Various Age and Ability Levels

In contrast to most other sports, organized competitive tennis can be carried on in almost every age group and on every ability level. Many who had been top athletes in other sports turned to tennis at the ends of their careers and even tried to play tennis competitively into advanced age. In hardly any other sport are there so many active participants in every age group.

Tennis as a Popular Sport

Tennis is primarily a popular sport. One can play tennis with friends, associates, and family members; with younger people and with older people; and in twos in fours,

and in a group as a class. Tennis accommodates various needs such as:

● Socialization and communication,
● Motivation to achieve,
● Social recognition,
● Health and fitness,
● Exertion and relaxation,
● Athletic activity,
● Personal challenge.

Tennis can be played outdoors or indoors as a year-round sport—and for a lifetime. In this sense, tennis is a so-called lifetime sport: This results from the fact that personal effort in playing can be easily varied. One can play tennis with limited exertion, one can keep it going with a much weaker partner, and one can shorten the length of play significantly. However, one can also play flat out in a heated match against an equally strong opponent. Finally, a major factor favoring tennis is that it does not require a high level of organization. Compared with many other sports, one can pursue tennis as a hobby to fit one's schedule relatively flexibly, since the only necessity is a partner.

These features of tennis—its specific capabilities, its particular requirements (ball and racket, return play, rules, etc.) and its status as a popular sport—have a major influence on instruction and training of the sport.

Basics of Tennis Instruction

Tennis instruction, like all teaching, is a series of planned and organized lessons toward educational goals.

The pedagogy deals with the question: How can the development of growing people (children and young people) be positively influenced by education? However, it is also increasingly concerned with the life-styles of adults, seniors, and persons with disabilities.

Sports pedagogy is a division of general educational science and a subdivision of sports science. It is concerned with the inter-relationships between athletics and education.

For tennis instruction in particular, it provides the theoretical and—as far as possible—scientifically grounded fundamentals for teaching. It also aids instructors, enabling them to be pedagogically responsible for their instructional activities. The pedagogical responsibility of instructors requires that they gear all their instructional activities to the development of their students, and not, as is often experienced, to the ambitions of officials and parents. To accept pedagogical responsibility also means caring for the whole development of the student and not just succeeding in tennis as a goal. This can be a real problem for the trainer, especially when she must decide whether to encourage a student to leave school early to pursue a lucrative career.

The introduction emphasized that tennis instruction is a body of planned and organized learning that is linked to educational goals. Components of tennis instruction can therefore be identified:

- Educational objectives and content of the instruction (pedagogy);
- Requirements of the instruction;
- Planning, organizing, and executing the instruction (methodology).

Pedagogy deals mainly with the goals and content of the instruction. Educational objectives are technical, tactical, conditioning, and physical skills, but they also include knowledge of the rules and structures of tennis as well as social competencies such as fairness and collegiality.

The content of instruction consists of practice in the areas of technique, tactics, and conditioning. However, there can also be conversations in order to get to know particular attitudes of the students and to develop them. At the center of instructional content is tennis technique (hitting techniques, footwork) with its various ways of carrying out tactical exercises—independent of the venue where the instruction takes place (whether in a club, in school or in a commercial establishment). It is therefore important that the instructor teaches technique in an integrated format, that is, for example, putting particular value on hitting the ball correctly (in conjunction with footwork, backswing, shifting one's weight, and follow-through).

As the most important subdivision of sports science, teaching movement provides the basics (see *Tennis Course, Volume 1: Techniques and Tactics*). The more often the goals in tennis instruction are directed to learning the game and to raising skills levels, the more the areas of training overlap. In every course of instruction, conditions of the instruction must be considered. Therefore it makes a difference whether the instruction takes place under bad or good institutional conditions (i.e., space, funding, personnel). Differences also arise, for example, when comparing instruction in a club or a commercial tennis facility or in the context of a tennis course while on vacation. Instructional conditions influence the student-instructor relationship as well as the student-student relationship. But there are other key factors: What motivates the students? How receptive are they? Is the group homogeneous? What is the instructor's leadership style? How can the results be checked? Sports psychology is concerned with these and other questions.

The methodology of tennis instruction is teaching the teaching-and-learning process (methods), the "how" of formulating educational teaching-and-learning processes. General methodology deals with common aspects of all types of sports, for example, the principle of "from easy to difficult," whereas specific methodology tries to transfer the knowledge of the general methodology to individual sports, in this case, to tennis.

According to these explanations, it becomes clear that the methodology of tennis instruction is supported primarily by sports pedagogy, the teaching of movement, training theory, and sports psychology. Therefore it is concerned with the questions: How can individual concrete progress be attained quickly? How are comprehensive abilities developed on a long-term basis? How can lessons be constructed? How should the instruction be organized? How can the effects be monitored?

The following will be treated as basics of tennis instruction:
- Aspects of instructional activity (as an overview),
- Learning (by the student),
- Teaching (by the instructor),
- Differences between individual and group instruction,
- Aspects of methodology,
- Strategies for individual instruction (such as correction, demonstration, tossing the ball to the student),
- Planning and executing the instruction (on the principle of the aforementioned points).

Aspects of Instructional Activity

According to these introductory conceptual remarks, tennis instruction can be considered an activity in which the student is central in the learning process and the instructor tries to explain to the student particular content using appropriate methods, based on the fundamentals of envisioning goals. In other words, the instruction can also be seen as an interactive activity in which teacher and student work on the aspects of instructional activity, goals, content, and methods, where all these factors depend on one another. To clarify, the factors can be differentiated more finely. We might add the following conditions and qualities to the individual essential factors:

The Student
General athletic ability includes:
- Ability in tennis,
- Willingness to learn,
- Ability to learn,
- Interest,

each depending on level of development.

The Goals
- Acquire and improve skills such as serving, forehand, and lobbing;
- Acquire and improve tactical knowledge and rules of behavior;
- Improve abilities such as strength, speed, and stamina;
- Acquire knowledge of rules and competition protocol;
- Develop attitudes and motivations;
- Be able to participate in competition at a particular level.

Content
Forms of practice, playing, and training include:
- Technical aspects,
- Tactical aspects,
- Conditioning aspects,
- Psychological aspects.

Instructor
- External appearance,
- Manner,
- Pedagogical know-how,
- Knowledge and ability specific to tennis,
- Ability to motivate and create enthusiasm.

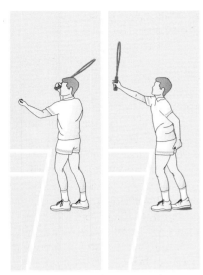

Fig. 1 Easier serve movement. Raise the racket in front of the body (left), hit with a forward overhand movement (right).

controlled manner toward the ball (Fig. 1).

This measure can be learned quickly and offers a relatively high level of safety. Moreover, it excludes balls hit fast with spin, which would be recommended only in competition at the mid- and advanced levels, and therefore is a technique not generally recommended.

The instructor also concerns himself with structuring this material when he chooses his methods of teaching the material. Therefore, in this case, he gives preference to the methodical activities of presenting, explaining, and correcting.

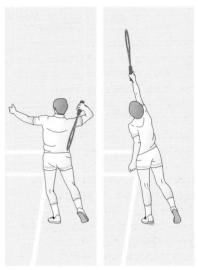

Fig. 2 Best serve movement. Accelerate the racket from a deep loop (left), moving it steeply forward and upward until you reach the point of impact at the highest possible point of reaching.

The specific course of instruction depends on all these factors; therefore, it depends on the student, the goals, the content, and the instructor. Two examples illustrate how these factors influence one another.

Example 1: An adult beginner would like to learn fast enough and well enough to be able to play with friends. First the instructor gears the educational objectives to the interests and expectations of the student. Then, the material is structured in such a way that it suits the educational objectives. When serving, for example, the educational objective could be directed mainly at developing confidence. This essentially leads to simplifying the main and auxiliary actions of the serve (see *Tennis Course, Volume 1*), so that the student holds the racket with a forehand grip, brings it upward in front of the body, and finally accelerates it in a

Example 2: A talented nine-year-old boy would like to learn tennis well enough to eventually compete as a good player. There are specific goals for this, mainly oriented to the structures of competitive tennis. The instructor pays special attention to the physical and psychological development of her student in order to encourage him appropriately (but also, not to overdo it). She therefore structures the material in such a way that, even years later, the student will be able to use it optimally in competition. In particular, she teaches a serve in which the student uses the backhand grip in the main action, so the racket is accelerated steeply upward and forward to the point of impact with the ball (Fig. 2). In this way, fast balls can be hit with spin. This requires specific auxiliary actions such as swinging the racket in a low point in the loop behind the back, among

others. Such a technique is more difficult to learn and requires well-developed motor skills. Therefore the instructor will cover this material in a long-term plan and will present exercise sequences, assign movement tasks, etc. The goals and requirements of the student, as well as the methods chosen to present the material, therefore affect her teaching style.

These two examples show that there can be no exact recipe for practical instruction. It is essential that instructors recognize the effect of the various factors and adjust for them in the practical teaching situation. In this context, it should be noted that the techniques treated in *Tennis Course, Volume 1* relate only to general, basic situations. Individual circumstances and the specific setting of goals can be treated only occasionally because the variety of available techniques that result when one greatly varies goals, situations, and individual circumstances could not be able to be presented as an overview. Because the course of instruction depends on the various factors of the teaching situation (student, instructor, goals, etc.), these factors are treated individually in the next chapter. Before that, learning and the students' individual requirements will be dealt with. This will be followed by a description of general requirements for the tennis instructor.

The next section is dedicated to the various methodological concepts—depending on instructional goals (play-oriented or technique-oriented concept, holistic or partial method, deductive or inductive process). This is followed by a description of the practical educational activities, such as demonstrating techniques, tossing the ball to the student, correcting and organizing. To finish the discussion of these basics, viewpoints on planning and execution of tennis basics will be described. This section begins with a comparison of the pro's and con's of individual and group instruction.

Learning

A tennis instructor who conducts a tennis course with a group of children, teenagers, or adults will be able to recognize changes in each student's performance after a short time. A movement that was originally not known (for example, topspin forehand) an appropriate tactical move (for example, attack shot with the

backhand), or even the ability to lose become apparent. These are clear cases showing that the students have learned something.

Learning is a central goal of the instruction. First, we should define what is understood by the term *learning* and how forms of learning differ from one another. In addition, then, we will discuss the learning process and describe the individual phases. The final section of this chapter will deal with individual learning.

What Is Learning?

Learning is a process that, through receiving and processing information, causes relatively permanent changes in behavior, attitudes, habits, and abilities.

Short-term changes in behavior, which are caused by fatigue, injury, alcohol, effects of drugs or swings in motivation, are not considered as learning. Learning should also be differentiated from behavioral changes that are related to processes such as maturing, growth, and aging. These processes are principally due to endogenous events, and behavioral changes within the scope of learning processes are due mainly to external information and experiences.

What Is the Difference Between Learning and Training?

The difference between learning and training can be explained as follows: Learning concerns itself

primarily with the acquisition of knowlegde, attitudes, motor abilities or tactical patterns. Training concerns itself with the planned and systematic maintenance/promotion or continuation of athletic ability.

Learning Technique

Learning a forehand topspin means, for example, relearning the basics of this technique and using it. This means being able to execute a tactical task (for example, to hit the ball in such a way that it bounces high and fast) and to use the technique in play.

Learning Tactics

Learning and using tactics and tactical patterns are analogous to the individual techniques that form patterns for executing movement tasks. Tactical patterns are typical and promising solutions for particular situations, such as a down-the-line attack shot with a backhand slice and concluding crosscourt volley. Using this tactical approach principally requires that there are opportunities (possible position for the down-the-line attack shot and the height of the point of impact for the crosscourt volley). The player, therefore, must evaluate the situation to decide if there are opportunities, and act accordingly. When learning tactics (executing and establishing tactical patterns), therefore, the opponent's conduct doesn't matter.

Training for Techniques

Training for techniques means using the techniques already learned under more difficult conditions and using them to play cooperatively. This does <u>not</u> mean that learning has stopped because learning always involves change in behavior in the sense of adapting to new situations. At any rate, during training, learning is not the primary goal; rather, using techniques under more difficult conditions is essential.

Forehand Topspin Training

- For the backhand, the student runs around tossed balls and plays with forehand topspin into various target areas (down the line, crosscourt).
- Balls tossed relatively high should fall immediately after the bounce and then be hit in an ascending arc. With these forms of technique training, the situation (type of stroke, direction, etc.) is preplanned to the greatest possible extent. Although there is always a tactical setting of goals, players and trainers concentrate mostly on technique. Corrections depend on the effective and "correct" execution of the movement.

Training for Tactics

Training for tactics means using the tactical pattern already learned under more difficult circumstances in situations similar to those in a match. Ability and the position of the opponent are incorporated into the processes of observation, judgment, and decision. The player can also choose from a variety of possibilities (direction, hitting technique, etc.) according to which solution seems best for the situation and also fits the ability of the player. With respect to training for tactics, the important thing is playing competitively.

Training the Tactics of the Attack Shot with Concluding Volley

- Player B has the task of putting A under such pressure that she herself can attack with a backhand stroke. She is then free to decide on attacking crosscourt or down the line and playing the volley crosscourt or down the line, or as a stop volley. The choice depends mainly on the appropriate observation and judgment of the opponent's behavior and his possibilities; therefore, it depends on the interactive situation.

So far, the forms of learning and training have concerned particular types of volleying. But being successful in tennis means fitting many volleys into a general tactical concept and match strategy. Therefore training for tactics also implies training for match strategies and playing in simulated matches.

What Is Practice?

Practice means taking what is already learned and stabilizing it through repeated execution or through use under various conditions (for example, varying the height and speed of the approaching ball). Practice can take place in the context of learning as well as in training; therefore, exercises should be assigned in training as well as learning.

The differences between learning and training as well as the concomitant assignment of practice for learning and training should be taken into consideration; however, it should be noted that the transition between learning and training is fluid. The differences that were noted should help to clarify the goals of the individual training and instruction exercises, so that students can learn more deliberately. Because there are also fluid transitions between training techniques and tactics in practice, it is advisable to make it clear to the students what the focus of the training unit is (more technique or more tactics).

Forms of Learning

Learning processes in tennis depend to a great extent on learning movement skills (motor skills), as well as, for example, on learning the serve. Learning motor skills is a central goal in tennis instruction. To achieve comprehensive capability in tennis, other skills in addition to motor skills must be mastered (see Table 1, p. 18): The development of a promising tactic is possible only when the player has learned how he has to act in certain play situations, that is, how he has to decide between different playing strategies and which strategic plans are appropriate. Such learning processes depend on the powers of observation,

	Types of Motor Learning	Types of Cognitive Learning	Types of Emotional Learning	Types of Social Learning
General	Walking Running Cycling	Calculating Reading	Self-control	Tolerance
Tennis-specific (or sport-specific)	Hitting techniques Footwork	Rules, tactical behavior	Dealing with losses	Cooperating with partners Fairness

Table 1 Examples of learning processes

imagination, and the ability to reason and are called <u>cognitive forms of learning</u>.

The right tactic leads to success only when the player has—besides the appropriate motor skills—emotional/motivational skills. For example, the player must learn to make a persistent effort to control himself when angry and to remain calm in the face of external influences. Such forms of learning are called <u>emotional learning</u>.

Playing cooperatively or competitively is then meaningful only when specific social conventions are observed. This includes observing rules of play and competition, informal rules (fairness), and collegiality.

The forms of learning can be separated from one another only theoretically. In practice, they are closely bound to one another. Thus, learning a specific stroke technique can also be linked with emotional, cognitive, and social learning. During the learning process, the student tries to picture for herself the structure of the stroke technique involved; she needs the ability to concentrate and to practice persistence, and she should be able to position herself within a group. Finally, it should be noted that learning does not always happen in a planned and goal-oriented educational situation (but can also

happen incidentally) and that learning results do not always have to be positive. Often, uneconomical movements are learned this way, or negative emotional reactions of world-class players (for example, throwing the racket) are imitated.

How Does Learning Happen?

The variety of forms of learning, of learning situations, and of individual requirements of the learner indicates that learning comes about in various ways. So it is not surprising that there is as yet no general learning theory that explains what happens during the learning process. Instead, there are numerous models with a more or less narrow explanatory value. Four of the best-known learning models will be described briefly, and their significance for teaching tennis will be discussed.

Learning by Success
Learning by success, characterized by learning by trial and error, reinforcement learning, or learning by operational conditioning, is based on the following assumptions. If a reinforced stimulus (success) follows a reaction, the result is an increase in probability that this reaction

will occur again under similar circumstances. If, for example, a tennis player frequently plays the topspin stroke successfully with a particular grip as he envisions it, he will probably continue with this grip. Conversely, if he frequently fails using a particular movement, he will try to change his technique. Thus, in practice, learning by success occurs when the tennis instructor praises or criticizes (increased stimulus) his students' execution of particular strokes or social behaviors (reactions).

A further form of learning by success is so-called <u>shaping</u>. With shaping, each mode of behavior that points in the direction of the desired targeted behavior is reinforced; therefore, it is not expected until the overall targeted behavior occurs. This makes it possible to learn even complex modes of behavior, which are not usually learned spontaneously, using incremental steps.

At any rate, the area of application of shaping (and that of the "simple" learning by success) is limited to simple learning processes. It can hardly be expected that the complex requirements in tennis, and particularly all the stroke techniques, could be developed only through learning by success. To explain such learning processes, therefore, we need to investigate theories of learning further.

Learning by Model

Behind the theory of learning by model is the assumption that new modes of behavior arise by observing the behavior of others. Such modeling, developed in connection with the phenomenon of social learning, can often be seen in the practice of learning movement. Children in particular are able to learn relatively quickly solely by observing what someone else does (for example, an athletic movement). (In connection with this, we also speak of learning intuitively). Here, an observed behavior is not simply copied, but rather it is judged and finally imitated or not. For the most part, in the area of motor learning, only the movements of successful athletes or recognized trainers are imitated in this way.

In instruction, instructors try to exploit the theory of learning by model by demonstrating the desired mode of behavior (for example, showing correct technique) or by using media (for example, film or photo sequences).

Cognitive Learning

With cognitive learning theories (for example, learning by insight), the processes of perception, imagination, memory, and thinking are most important. During the learning process, students try to solve a current problem by linking previous experiences and knowledge with current conditions; that is, they approach the problem on an intellectual level. For example, if a tennis player decides to play a ball with strong forward spin and has an intellectual model, she can still have a clear picture, as long as she has the necessary experience

and knowledge that a steep forward-upward movement of the racket head is necessary. And this allows her to devise an appropriate plan of action (oriented to tactical concepts and strategies) and to execute it deliberately. Because more or less comprehensive previous experiences are necessary for structuring problem situations, cognitive learning theories are especially important for older youths and adults. This also results in instruction in which frequent explanations of movement allow for quicker and more goal-oriented learning.

Learning as an "Internal Game"

Lately it has been recommended that learning be based not so much on success using models, with the help of cognitive processes, but rather on processes of experience—feeling and "just doing it." From this, one can see that thoughts (for example, on the individual parts of the movement or on things that have nothing to do with the lesson) disturb the movement sequence and should therefore be eliminated. One should concentrate rather on the "here and now." It is assumed that the connection between perception and action should be experienced as a unit that should not be disturbed by any deliberate intrusions in individual components of the movement sequence; rather, the movement sequence should be experienced as a whole. An important characteristic of this type of learning, practicing, and playing is "letting it happen."

Phases of Learning Athletic Movement

The process of mastering athletic movement is often subdivided into characteristic phases. Therefore, in the course of the learning process, we can differentiate three learning phases:

- First phase—development of rough coordination (basic form).
- Second phase—development of fine coordination (refined form).
- Third phase—stabilization of fine coordination (stabilization).

The learner goes through these phases according to this sequence. On the other hand, these phases do not represent a rigid pattern. The transitions are fluid; the time frame of each phase is individual and can be diversified, depending on the level of difficulty of the task.

First Learning Phase— Basic Form

The first learning phase encompasses the course of learning from the initial attempts in the new movement to a stage in which the learner can execute the movement in the basic form under good conditions. In this phase there is still no—or only one—vague sense of the movement. The sequence of movements improves mainly because of the orientation that results from the action of the movement, repeated attempts, and, of course, new information from the instructor.

Basics of Tennis Instruction

Characteristics of the Basic Form
- Basic technique.
- Unnecessary, auxiliary movements.
- Tense auxiliary movements.
- Faulty linking of movement components.
- High expenditure of concentration.
- High expenditure of energy.

Implications for Instruction
- Frequent and clear demonstration.
- Short explanatory information so that the first try is successful.
- Relationship to familiar movements (for example, leading off, serving, throwing).
- Main attention concentrated on the main action.
- Concentrated but short exercise of the simplified whole movement.
- First attempt under easier conditions (for example, hitting a resting ball).

Second Learning Phase— Refined Form
The second learning phase covers the transition from the basic form to a stage in which the learner, under favorable conditions, can execute the movement almost flawlessly (refined form). In this phase a better sense of the movement is gradually developed. This brings an increase in self-control during the movement sequence. The increased sense of the movement is associated with intensely visualizing the image of the movement.

Through new feedback and correction by the instructor this vivid visualizing gets more comprehensive and more exact. Consequently, the movement sequence constantly improves in coordinating time and space. In this phase, the significance of the movement sequence as a part of a comprehensive play approach should become increasingly clear.

At this point, the player's attention is increasingly given to observing both opponent and ball, and she is ready to use the movement sequences appropriate for the situation. In this way, one can promote the understanding of the tactical importance of the new techniques. Because practice is extended and unfamiliar movement sequences cannot always be mastered using the prescribed physical requirements, in the transition from practice to training the instructor must encourage exercises that promote strength, speed, stamina, flexibility, and coordination.

Characteristics of Refined Form
- Exact execution.
- Consistent performance.
- Good linking of movement components.
- Adequate increase in concentration.
- Adequate increase in energy.
- However, continued uncertainty and inaccuracy with extreme changes in circumstances.

Implications for Instruction
- Intensive and diversified visual information on the movement sequence (demonstration, video, photo sequences).
- Exact description.
- Intensive practice under generally consistent conditions.
- Systematic correction (from basic- to refined-form errors).
- Mental practice.
- Reference to the sense of the movement (muscle tension, feel for the swing, etc.) when describing movement components.
- Advice regarding conscious observation of movement components when hitting (for example, checking the angle between the hand and the racket before the backswing).
- Recommendations when practicing with the ball, regarding awareness of movement components that would not normally be located in the field of vision (observing, lowering the the racket head during transition from the backswing to the hitting phase).
- Rechecking the rehearsed movement; that is, direct questions about details.
- Agreed-upon variations of the toss in terms of height, direction, length, and speed in connection with accurate observation of the ball-tosser's movements, of the flight of the ball, and of its bounce.
- Practice in gamelike situations (tactics).
- Instruction in tactics.
- Work with film and video material (structuring the observation of playing situations).
- Technically oriented exercises for conditioning and coordination.

Third Learning Phase—Stabilization

The action stabilizes when the student constantly improves in matching movement skills to ever-changing play situations. This means that:

- Using tactics, he can use his skills to strengthen the play situation and can carry out the action as before or completely revamp it;
- He can judge the approaching ball exactly and can automatically react to the flight and bounce of the ball.

Attaining this goal depends on timely and, of course, practical information and correction by the instructor.

Critiquing and correcting the sequence of movements are most successful when one has a sense of the movement. Stabilization achieved in this way allows one to focus attention on changing the play situation and on key aspects of the movement. This promotes increasingly faster and more precise reactions to changing conditions and sudden surprises.

If basic motor skills (strength, speed, endurance, and agility) are improved in this way, the sequence of movements becomes more automatic, optimal, and more dependable over time.

Characteristics of Stabilization

- Dependable and precise execution (even in high-speed play).
- Optimal linking of movement components.
- Stable performance in the presence of changing conditions.
- Stable performance in the case of sudden disturbances.
- Diminished requirements on concentration.

Implications for Instruction

- Explaining components.
- Refined correction of particulars.
- Practicing under changing conditions (for example, practicing returns with a continuous variety of serves).
- Mental practice of key aspects of movement (for example, mentally visualizing of the upper arc during the backswing for topspin with forehand).
- Advice on sense of movement acquisition (for examples, see the refined form).

- Training by observation (video and film).
- Tactical training (theory and practice).
- Special exercises for conditioning and coordination.

Personal Prerequisites for Learning, Practice, and Training

The instructional processes described so far do not apply at the same pace to all students. Moreover, students have differing results on the way to achieving various goals, which depend on the various skills that individual students bring with them to the game. The most important personal characteristics which the instructor should consider in the course of instruction are:

- Constitutional characteristics such as height, weight, and physical proportions;
- Condition-related characteristics such as stamina, strength, speed, and agility;

Fig. 3   Enthusiastic children practice their game.

- Coordination (see chapter entitled "Training Coordination";
- Ability to acquire motor skills;
- Mental abilities such as play anticipation and assessment;
- Past experience related to the instructional material.

Personal characteristics are markedly different in the various developmental stages.

Expression of Personal Characteristics in Various Developmental Stages

In the following section, we will briefly describe personal traits related to constitution and conditioning, as well as the ability to learn motor skills, as it is expressed especially in seven developmental stages beginning with age 6–7 up to late adulthood at 60–70 years. It should be particularly noted that calendar years do not always correspond exactly with biological years, and the wide range of developmental skills in children should be kept clearly in mind. Rather, it should be assumed from a relatively large distribution of developmental events (that is, for example, when compared with the cross section) that the development of one set of children is accelerated, while the development of another is slowed down.

Younger School Children (approximately 6–7 years old)

During elementary school years, boys as well as girls experience a significant growth in breadth, and they acquire a favorable change in physical proportions, especially an improvement of the power-weight relationship. These changes cause a rapid increase in the ability to learn motor skills, accompanied by

Fig. 4 Learning a forehand volley instinctively.

a significant increase in eagerness to learn.

Children learn holistically and in play situations. Detailed explanations of movement are of little value, compared to varied movement exercises and frequent demonstration, because children learn movement sequences mostly by observation (learning by model) and by trying things out (in the sense of learning from success). Children of this age are particularly resilient considering performance factors such as strength, stamina, speed, agility, and coordination. Therefore, demands on maximum strength and anaerobic endurance should be avoided because aerobic endurance loads, as well as requirements of speed, agility, and coordination, are generally unwise. Training for coordination is acceptable, but strength and stamina training is inappropriate. As a result, coordinative movement exercises should take priority, with a broad emphasis on motor skills, not just limited to tennis.

Fig. 5 Same age, but differing physical development.

Older School Children (approximately 10–13 years old)

Until about age 10, constitutional features have changed so much that we can assume harmonious physical proportions and a very good power-weight relationship. Children have a great urge to move and a marked eagerness to learn. The ability to learn motor skills is excellent at this age, which in fact many call the phase of the best motor skills learning.

At this age, simpler movements are learned holistically and often instinctively (learning by model). In addition, we can assume an increase in cognitive processes—and this is especially important for learning difficult movement sequences. Accordingly, the later elementary school years are suited to learning new movement sequences as well as to refining movements the child can do in the basic form. The remarks on resilience and trainability in reference to younger children also apply for the most part to the 10–13 year olds. Therefore, it is advisable to stress coordination skills in various ways (general and tennis-specific) in older elementary school children. The goal of instruction and training at this age should therefore be the general motor skills and the refinement of the varied (tennis-specific) technical and tactical fundamentals. Measures to improve the physical performance factors of strength and stamina complete the instruction; they should be treated predominantly as games.

Early Adolescents (girls approximately 12–14 years old and boys approximately 13–15 years old)

In this first stage of puberty, in which we see the onset of considerable sex-specific and individual differences, we can also observe a significantly increased lengthening of the limbs, resulting in unharmonious proportions between the trunk and the extremities. Movement coordination of youths, who in childhood could command only limited and not-yet-stabilized activity in the motor area, is delicate in this stage of puberty. The particularly special learning advantages of the previous phase are now gone. Learning new movement sequences brings about greater problems. Holistic learning happens less often. The goal of the instruction should therefore be principally to review and solidify the movement skills learned in childhood. In spite of these greater or lesser limitations in the coordinative area, we should not speak of a time of crisis. Rather, the trainability and resilience in the area of conditioning increase considerably. Hormonal changes in this age result in a higher trainability in stamina and strength, but because their joints have not yet solidified, maximum strength training should be avoided. If we consider the developmental circumstances of youths in puberty, then we can draw the following guideline for instructions: Focus on stabilization and refinement of what has already been learned in the coordination and increased training of aspects of conditioning, especially strength and stamina.

Later Adolescents (girls approximately 14–17 years old and boys approximately 15–18 years old)

In the second phase of puberty (adolescence), limb growth slows down and an increased breadth growth starts. This brings positive changes in physical proportions (especially the relationship of trunk and extremities) and the power-weight relationship, again causing favorable circumstances for learning new coordination skills and motor skills. Learning is less often holistic and instinctual as in late elementary school age; on the other hand, youths are now ready to support learning processes on the intellectual level (cognitive learning), in which learning complex movement sequences is more favorable.

Because there is a great deal of demand for resilience, especially in intensive training (for example, for anaerobic endurance and maximum strength), we should be careful that the training level is sufficient. The trainability of all conditioning points is well established (and considerably better for boys in the area of strength and speed than for girls, so that they can reach a high level of physical skills). These requirements positively affect learning of certain difficult movement sequences (for example, backhand and smash), which require a high degree of coordination and of conditioning, and thus can be learned only to a limited degree in childhood.

Young Adults (approximately 17/18 years old to 30/35 years old)

Compared with children and youth, there is a much greater range of proficiency between proficient and trained young-adult players and people who have never played tennis.

In competitive sports, the young-adult years can be considered a phase of greatest motor ability. In most sports, as in tennis, people of this age reach their highest performance levels. This holds true for coordination as well as for conditioning. With out-of-practice and untrained players at this age, one cannot assume a stable working motor activity; however, when considering motor activity related to sports, even at age 30 there are not insignificant losses of potential, in particular because of inadequate movement in everyday activity. However, a relatively high technical level based on cognitive learning techniques can be achieved through intensive practice even

with beginners (in particular, late starters who come from other sports). This is also true for the conditioning area, where a very good trainability and resilience can be assumed in all areas, especially stamina.

Adults in Middle Age (approximately 30/35 years old to 45/50 years old)

In this level of development, there are even stronger differences in motor activity in the context of sports between people who have been active in sports and those who have not.

With proficient and trained players the mid-adult years can be seen as a period of maintainable, relatively high motor skills. Both the coordination and the conditioning skills are generally not significantly less than in those years with the highest skills. Therefore, we should keep in mind that not all performance factors are age-related (although stamina is particularly dependent on age) to the extent that the absolute

skills level diminishes. Even with out-of-practice and untrained players a level of maintenance can be assumed in the area of everyday motor skills. However, with the demands of motor skills for sports—as well as of coordination and conditioning—increasingly significant losses of potential become apparent.

The ability to learn motor skills decreases significantly, so that new learning of automatic diverse forms of movement becomes increasingly difficult. Automatic actions are much more effective. In any case, motor activity declines. An increasing tendency toward economizing, expediency, and limiting motor skills is evident. But at this age, despite the more seriously limited ability to learn, a medium level in technique and conditioning is still attainable through appropriate practice for beginners.

Table 2 Typical periods of development (adapted from Winter)

Developmental period	Characteristics	Age span
Younger school children	Phase of rapid progress in learning motor skills	0–app. 6–10
Older school children	Best phase for learning motor skills in childhood	app. 10–12/13
Early Adolescents	Phase of restructuring motor skills and capabilities	Girls app. 12–14 Boys app. 13–15
Later Adolescents	Phase of gender-specific differentiation of progressive individualization and increasing stabilization	Girls app. 14–17 Boys app. 15–18
Young adults	Years of relative maintenance of motor skills	app. 17/18–30/35
Middle-aged adults	Years of gradual diminution of motor skills	app. 30/35–45/50
Older adults	Years of accelerated diminution of motor skills	app. from 45/50

Older Adults
(approximately 45/50 years old to 60/70 years old)

With increasing age, there is an even greater difference between those who engage in sports regularly and those who are inactive. In coordination as well as in conditioning, people of this age who train on a regular basis succeed in maintaining a higher skills level, which gradually but consistently increases, compared with the general population and those who no longer train regularly. Deficits in everyday motor skills are almost nonexistent in these people.

On the other hand, the diminution of skills in those who do not engage in sports is also evident in the area of everyday motor skills. A sharp decrease in existing automatic actions accompanied by difficulty in learning new movements is typical. However, even at this age, one can learn tennis-specific movement skills if only in basic form through appropriate practice, even if this requires long-term practice. However, the age-related drop-off in conditioning level can be slowed down considerably through an appropriate training program. Concerning resilience in the physical area at this age, it should be noted that preexisting medical conditions frequently cause a higher risk in athletic activities and that the pressures should also be age-appropriate from a quantitative standpoint. Therefore, tennis instructors should encourage their students of this age to have themselves checked regularly by a sports medicine specialist.

Teaching

What makes a good tennis instructor? The question is very difficult to answer because observation shows that tennis instructors operate in various ways and still show similar success rates, where success is primarily measured by attainment of teaching goals and generally satisfied students.

If you ask students for characteristics of a good tennis instructor, you get answers such as the following:
– "He can explain well."
– "He tosses the ball well."
– "He can analyze and correct well."
– "He understands how to motivate me."
– "He is patient."
– "I can trust him."
– "He treats everyone the same."

Some of the students' negative comments include, for example:
– "He only criticizes."
– "He is moody."
– "He hardly makes an effort."
– "He asks too much of me."
– "He doesn't say anything at all."
– "He's unfair."
– "He often arrives late."
– "He doesn't have a plan."

Prerequisites for the Tennis Instructor

Such positive and negative comments indicate that tennis instructors have various approaches, and they may also have correspondingly various expectations. Such expectations of behavior are considered in terms of social roles. By social role, we mean the totality of the expectations of behavior that are carried over to those in certain positions (for example, positions in a club, such as president, treasurer, tennis instructor) within a given social system (as in our example in the club structure). According to this, we cannot assume that there is <u>the</u> personality of the tennis instructor, nor <u>the</u> personality of the tennis player. However, it is much more important to describe the social role of tennis instructors. For example, we should consider role conflicts, and therefore differences, between the expectations carried over to tennis instructors along with their own expectations and abilities. In considering such, four emerge as most important.

The Tennis Instructor as a Professional

The tennis instructor should have not only professional knowledge but also practical ability. Her professional knowledge relies mainly on teaching movement, methodology, and training. The practical ability and personal experiences make it possible for her to demonstrate so that students understand, to toss the ball appropriately to them, and now and then to play along with the students and to substitute for her students. And finally, she must be accepted by the students on the basis of her practical ability.

The Tennis Instructor as an Educator

In training children and teenagers, the tennis instructor not only has the task of teaching tennis but also must be effective as an educator. In reference to tennis, she must be able to motivate and assure that winning and losing are handled appropriately and that self-discipline, responsibility for health, fairness, and collegial behavior are considered highly valued. The educational responsibility for the comprehensive development of the young person extends beyond playing tennis. As a result, all these expectations and requirements must be considered, so that young tennis players distinguish themselves in training and competition on and off the tennis court. Such expectations and demands come mainly from parents, other tennis students and trainers, club and association officials, sometimes from sponsors and representatives of the media, and finally from school. They have an effect on children and young people who have quite general needs, for example, the need for:

- varied experiences and adventures,
- appropriate praise and recognition,
- emotional warmth,
- responsibility for their own actions as they mature.

Besides the relationships between instructor and student, we should consider that students form relatively stable relationships among themselves, especially in the course of group instruction. Students not only get to know themselves but they also develop emotional relationships with one another. Such relationships underlie the structure of the group. The individual student has a place in this structure: for example, as "star," "loner," or "team player." Many group members take on particular roles, such as "spokesperson," "leader," or "clown." Regarding group structure, it is also important to know whether the group as a whole is homogeneous or heterogeneous, considering level of ability, and whether there are cliques and conflicts, or other problems. All these factors comprise the group dynamic. For the instructor, it is therefore important to be aware of the kind of relationship the students have with him (and vice versa), and those relationships students have among themselves, so that he can take this into consideration when planning instruction.

The Tennis Instructor as a Coach

The tennis instructor also often gets the job of assuming the function of coach for his students at tournaments, when traveling, or in training camp.

The Tennis Instructor as Organizer

And finally, the tennis instructor is also expected to develop and carry out an overarching concept for the training program, to set up and conduct tournaments, and to organize and direct a training camp.

Leadership Styles (Instructor–Student Relationship)

As borrowed from educational theory, three different leadership styles are often also applied to tennis instruction: the autocratic, the laissez-faire, and the democratic.

The more a tennis instructor teaches in a group, the more her approach toward teaching, especially from the viewpoint of leadership style, can be observed.

In the autocratic leadership style, the instructor dominates. He determines the instructional activities, explains, demonstrates, evaluates, gives directions and orders, scolds, and praises those who completely conform to the instruction.

In the laissez-faire leadership style, the activities are, for the most part, left up to the student. In a narrow sense, this teaching style should not be considered as a "leadership" style and is unimportant in the practice of tennis instruction.

In the democratic leadership style, the instructional activities are discussed and decided upon jointly by instructor and student, who act as partners. The instructor suggests; the students are supposed to find their own solutions for their tasks as far as possible. This instructional style is therefore characterized by open planning of tasks and the sympathetic influence of the instructor on the individual students.

In practice, it is not wise to choose strictly between the autocratic and the democratic leadership style. Style is much more dependent on the particular situation. Thus in the course of instruction, especially with children or young people, it can be entirely appropriate to be relatively strict (autocratic). The democratic leadership style, on the other hand, is useful mainly when, the instruction is planned jointly and problems are discussed on the sidelines during instruction. The choice of leadership style should not be the only criterion considered when evaluating the instructor. It is much more important that he meets the criteria described in the section on the tennis teacher as educator using his own exemplary characteristics. This includes:

- external appearance (clothing, personal hygiene)
- behavior in his own tennis game (vis-à-vis himself, his partner/opponent, the referee)
- behavior (langauge, imitation, and gestures) vis-à-vis his students, which should be considerate, that is, ready to help with details, fair, trustworthy and above all committed.

Methodological Concepts

When the tennis instructor has a clear understanding of the goals and content of his instruction, then he must consider the methodology. In particular, he must decide:

- what should be the sequence and scope of the content (technique, playing, etc.),
- which instructional measures (demonstration, explanation, aids, organizational forms) are most suited to attaining these goals.

Choice of the Correct Procedure

Independent of possible supplemental educational or social objectives of the instruction, ability to play should always be foremost. There are two basic schools of thought on teaching this: respectively, more play-oriented or more technique-oriented. (Fig. 6).

How strong the amount of focus on one or the other schools of thought is depends on the tennis instructor himself, the students, and the external conditions and circumstances. We do not recommend adherence to a one-sided procedure either for the play- or technique-oriented approach (see also p. 28).

The Play-Oriented Approach

Here, there is a central focus on the play idea, allowing playing to be greatly simplified. These simplifications depend on the court (minicourt), the equipment (short rackets, foam balls), and the rules (at first, the ball bounces twice, no service line area, etc.).

Playing ability gets progressively better throughout a continuing, carefully planned practice regimen in which the simplifications are removed. Techniques and tactics thus develop while playing. The simplified games begin to approximate a regulation tennis

Fig. 6 Methodological concepts and processes.

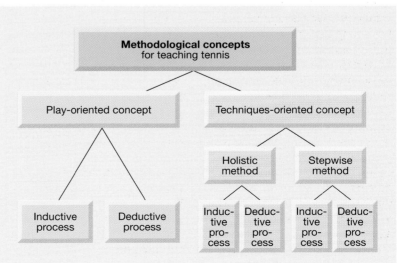

match, and, overall, they approximate a *series of games*. Here, the instructor can choose to proceed either deductively or inductively. Deductively means that, in the context of the play-oriented approach, the instructor precisely prescribes games and types of play. On the other hand, inductively means that, in the context of the prescribed external conditions, he lets the student try games, find himself, and vary activities.

The Technique-Oriented Approach

The central interest here is teaching the components of the game as well as the technical skills step by step, from a tactical perspective.

It is assumed that the quality of the game is also improved through introducing, refining, and expanding the individual techniques step by step. Necessary skills can be taught holistically or in parts (see Fig. 6, p. 27).

We speak of a holistic method when a technique is learned without intermediary steps. For the tennis instructor that means that she either:

– Demonstrates the technique to be learned as a complete unit and has the student acquire it afterward in measured practice sessions;
– Repeatedly demonstrates the technique and at times has the student copy it in shorter segments (10–20 seconds) (learning by imitation, learning instinctively, see pp. 18–19); or
– Assigns a task without previous demonstration and has the student figure out the

technique holistically in a measured practice phase.

By a stepwise approach, we mean a procedure in which the tennis instructor organizes and teaches a skill via a series of intermediate steps. First the individual parts of the targeted skill are mastered, and then they are integrated. The sequence of exercises needs to be properly designed for such a procedure.

The holistic skill as well as partial movements can be presented to the students in a prescribed way (deductively) or for them to try out (inductively). Using the example of an exercise series for learning the serve, this is the process according to the stepwise method:

1. Throw the ball high with the left hand: Stand with your left hip close to a wall or a fence. Indicate the height of the throw with a marker. The ball should be thrown with the left hand straight up in the air as high as the mark. Set a small target area (newspaper, tire, tennis racket, racket cover) at a distance of approximately 12 in. (30 cm) in front of your left foot. The ball should fall onto this surface after being thrown upward.
2. Sequence of movements of the right arm without a racket: From the starting position with your right hand, throw the ball over the net or into the opposite service line area.
3. Sequence of movements with the right arm with racket: The student stands in the starting position behind a line ("T" or baseline) and, with the racket in the right hand, using a fluid and rhythmic sequence, he

practices the backswing, hitting, and follow-through movements.
4. Coordination of throwing and hitting movements: Throw the ball upward with the left hand and hit it forward with the racket using the form described in step 3.

Play-Oriented or Technique-Oriented Approach

As a rule, the competing approaches should be combined so that they complement each other. For the practical instructional situation, these combinations have to be established independent of the group, goal setting, and content. Because all tennis instruction has the capacity for play as its goal, whether oriented toward competition or not, games similar to tennis should always be used. These games must be suited to the level of the players, that is, they must have continuity with previously learned techniques. Tennislike games that become increasingly complex therefore represent the sequence, and simultaneously develop the idea that the play-oriented approach is the "fast lane" of instruction. In this case, we still have to teach in the "slow lanes" and always technical and tactical skills (Fig. 7). On the other hand, the instructor who prefers to focus on technique should also consider letting the techniques mastered be used in the context of a game. Only in the following exceptional cases should the tennis instructor decide on a purely play-oriented or a

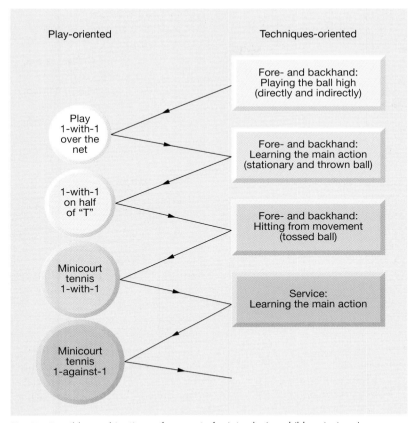

Fig. 7 Possible combinations of concepts for introducing children to tennis.

purely technique-oriented approach:
- A student expresses the wish that the instructor teaches him or corrects only specific techniques (technique-oriented).
- A student requests an instructor to have her play only (play-oriented).
- Even over a long period of time, weak students are not in a position to use what they have learned in a game (technique-oriented).
- Students have reliable techniques and they should improve their tactical use of these techniques in a game (play-oriented).

Holistic Versus Stepwise Method

The tennis instructor should set priorities and operate **holistically** when teaching techniques. The following cases, however, call for a **stepwise method**:
- The technique to be mastered is too difficult for the student (for example, serving).
- The tennis instructor has students with learning difficulties for whom holistic learning does not work.
- Because the student has not been able to master components of the movement in techniques that she has tried

holistically, they must be taught and corrected to some extent (for example, loop behind the back when serving).

Deductive Versus Inductive Procedure

Choosing one or the other method (see Table 3) depends on:
- Available practice time,
- Age of the students,
- Degree of difficulty of the skill to be learned,
- Importance of superior (nonmotor) educational objectives.

It is well known that inductive presentation and learning take longer and do not always lead to the desired goal. For this reason, the deductive procedure is typically recommended.

Nevertheless, the tennis instructor should proceed inductively occasionally in order to develop and foster independence, creativity, and insight.
- In particular, children could be allowed to learn inductively now and then. Independent trial excites the imagination and motivates the student to practice.
- When introducing new techniques, one could begin inductively and continue working deductively after an appropriate time. With a simplified assignment of tasks, students recognize the tactical necessity of technique and making progress.

	Deductive process: *Instructor demonstrates*	Inductive process: *Student tries things out*
Steps	1. Description and demonstration of the movement 2. Instruction of the movement (organizing practice) 3. Perhaps, helping with the moves 4. Correcting the movement 5. Perhaps, further instruction of movement 6. Situational use of the movement	1. Movement task is assigned 2. Direct the trial and the test 3. Emphasize good opportunities to succeed at the task 4. Demonstrate favorable solutions and explain movements
Characteristics	– Goal is prominent – Instructor is guide – Practical visualization of the movement – Goal is reached quickly through economical process – Motivation is possible only from the outside, through the instructor point of contact	– Learning process is prominent – Independent testing – Practical setting of tasks – Goal is reached in a roundabout way – Student is mostly motivated by the task
Example: Introducing the Smash	1. Explain the situation and intent 2. Demonstrate 3. Determine the point of contact (ball guide) 4. Stretch the hitting arm to the point of contact 5. Assume the sideways-on hitting position 6. The teacher throws the ball — Hit it over the net with a very short hitting movement (main action only) 7. Perhaps, correct	1. Station the student at the net. Play a lob to him. Task: Play the ball into the court. 2. "Try to play the ball quickly and to the side." 3. "See how Monica plays the ball—try to imitate her." 4. "I'll show you and explain again how Monica smashed." 5. "Peter, you have problems meeting the ball well; let's do the preliminary exercises again. . . "

Table 3   Comparison of deductive and inductive processes

Summary
The following recommendations can be made:
1. Play- and technique-oriented procedures should be combined as much as possible; that is, learned techniques are always practiced afterward and used in play.
2. If the tennis instructor teaches in the minicourt and uses beginners' rackets and balls, play-oriented procedures should be the preferred method; that is, students should play as much as possible and techniques and tactics should be acquired while playing.
3. Hitting techniques should be taught holistically.

4. An inductive procedure is particularly recommended for children. The tennis instructor may begin inductively and continue deductively if difficulties arise.

Of course, these points are only recommendations; many roads lead to Rome. In fact, there are many situations where another procedure could be better. This was explained earlier in a series of exceptions. The deciding factor is to inspire the students through the instruction.

Instructional Activities

The practical activities of the tennis instructor's teaching are to:
- Demonstrate,
- Describe movements,
- Explain movements,
- Teach movements,
- Assign movement exercises,
- Correct movements,
- Exercise students through ball tosses,
- Organize,
- Use media and teaching aids.

Demonstration

Demonstration by the instructor is the most important—and as a rule always the first—source of

Principle	Reason	Example
Pay attention to the optimal position of the student.	The part of the movement to be observed must be clearly visible.	Stand with your back to the student, in order to demonstrate the movement of the racket in the loop while serving.
Demonstrate correctly on a technical level.	Create an optimal visualization of the movement for the student.	Clearly maintaining the sideways-on hitting position for the backhand volley.
Note the reason for observing.	Direct attention to specific components of the movement.	Observe the left hand during the backhand ground stroke.
Make immediate comprehension of the demonstration possible.	Information is absorbed within approximately 20 seconds and can be used immediately.	Allow for immediate understanding of volley technique through use of the ball machine.
Repeat the demonstration often.	To create a complete and precise visualization of the movement.	Show the hitting movement during the volley several times in succession.
Demonstrate in a way appropriate to the student.	To suit the spatial and temporal structures to the student's performance level.	Spatial: deep knee-bend to the half-volley. Temporal: slowed-down service movement.
Make the relationship of the demonstration and tactics clear.	To make the student aware of situations and goals for using types of strokes.	When and to where does one play a stop?
Also demonstrate without a ball (dry-run).	To avoid having the student be distracted by the ball's trajectory.	Show forehand ground stroke as holistic movement.
If necessary, demonstrate sub-movements as a preliminary step.	To emphasize essential details of movement.	Show the backswing movement for the smash.

Table 4 Principles and forms for an optimal demonstration

information for the student. It fulfills the following important functions:

- The students get quick, exact, first-hand information about what they need to learn.
- The instructor shows mastery what he wants to teach and enforces the idea that he takes it seriously.

- The instructor motivates the students by his personal example.
- The students can learn holistically under these circumstances.
- Direct learning is made possible when the instructor and student execute the demonstrated movement together (imitation).

Incorporating Demonstration into the Learning Process

The technique to be learned should first be explained in its tactical context and then demonstrated. In this way, the students can learn the skill and judge its value in terms of their own abilities. Finally, there is the actual student-oriented demonstration in order to provide a visual impression that is followed by a spatial idea of the movement and then a temporal one. Table 4 summarizes the most important elements for an optimum demonstration.

Fig. 8 The instructor demonstrates.

The Role of Language and Speaking in Instruction

In teaching, language includes all of the instructor's utterances that he uses to facilitate and organize learning. However, it also includes all of the student's utterances, as well as conversation between instructor and student.
Speaking allows the instructor to:
- Describe movements,
- Explain movements,
- Give instructions for movements,
- Assign movement exercises,
- Correct movements.

Essential demands on language of the instructor are summarized in Table 5.

The Verbal Factor: Adjusting Language to the Students

If the tennis instructor uses the language of the lesson plans, it will surely be correct. However, children will not always understand this language. Lesson plans have been written primarily for the instructor and are an important source of information for her.

However, for instruction, language should motivate the students. It should develop and help improve the student's image of the movement and plan of action. To do this, the language of instruction very often must be different from the language of the lesson plans. In this way, one can, for example, tell the students who are practicing the ground stroke with the forehand that they might "lead" the ball with the racket in the direction of the stroke, although the contact between the ball and the strings lasts only a few thousandths of a second. At any rate, in many cases this information will help students meet the ball more precisely because they shift their weight forward during the hitting phase while rotating their upper body.

Therefore, language in instruction must be oriented to:
- The structure of the material to be taught;
- The students' ability to understand, depending on their age, intelligence, and previous experience.

In particular, it is important to know that the instructor reacts to the movement that she sees, that is, the external perspective. She orients herself mainly to the spatial-temporal movement sequence. For that reason, her language is oriented toward the visual observation. But students more often perceive movement by way of the internal perspective (so-called kinesthetic perception). They "feel" that they hit the ball too late and "sense" that they swung the racket too little. Therefore they also need from the instructor information that addresses this internal perspective. This is not always easy because any phenomena of internal perspective of movement can be captured only partially by language, which is demonstrated by the fact that students often cannot fully describe their internal experiences using language.

When speaking, the instructor should also be careful to address the students before, during, or after the action.
- <u>Before the action</u>, the instructor should ask herself how she can help the students construct their plan of action; she should not give the students too much information in order not to overwhelm them.
- <u>During the action</u>, students can hardly take in and process detailed information. For this reason, oral utterances must be focused on accentuation of the sequence of movements or rhythms.
- <u>After the action</u>, the instructor must be careful that the students have observed the movement and use it. Therefore, it depends on supporting this use in such a way that it improves the development of the plan of action.

Table 5 Demands on the language (verbal information) of the instructor

Basic correctness	Effective flow of information	Comprehensibility		Speaking qualities	Tone	Coordination with body language
– Coordinated with curriculum (taught according to situational needs) – Methodically correct	– Pace – Pauses	– Logical organization – Simplicity – Brevity – Lively speech	– Appropriateness to age and experience of the student	– Loudness – Clarity	– Modulation – Pitch – Clarity – Appropriateness	– Friendliness – Appropriate gestures

Describing Movements

Describing movements serves to prepare and complete the visual information and thus also serves to improve the student's image of the movement. It is a well-ordered representation of the spatial, temporal, and dynamic sequence of the particular skill.

Describing movements has the following functions:
- It summarizes the goal (for example, on serving: "the racket is increasingly accelerated behind the back").
- It can direct the student's attention to what is essential (for example, on topspin: "Pay attention to the steep and quick upward movement of the racket").
- It can link with what is already known: ("Take the racket back as you would when backswinging for a volley" as a description of the backswing movement for a backhand return on a twist-service).

The description of movements accompanies and completes the demonstration. That means:
- It can bring order to the image of the movement (for example, when serving: "Your left knee was already extended when the racket face was still swinging downward to the turning point behind your back").
- It can clearly differentiate what is essential from what is not (for example, in the case of a topspin with forehand: "It is important to swing the racket quickly and steeply, no matter in what direction and how far you follow through").

Explaining Movements

Explaining movements can supplement and justify the description of movements whenever it is considered necessary or required by students. Functional links should be provided along with the explanation of movements. In that way, the students can learn the function of the main action of a technique in a tactical exercise and to what extent particular expressions of the auxiliary actions prepare, support, or obstruct. It helps here to teach the movement by explaining how it works and the rationale behind it.

The movement explanations should:
- Be short and concise if they take place on the tennis court,
- Lead to conversation and discussion after the lesson if the students want it or consider it necessary,
- Be reinforced by a simultaneous demonstration.

Giving Instructions for Movements

The instructor gives instructions for a movement to organize, practice, and teach the student. He makes it concise but explains as specifically as possible how the next step and the corresponding preparation for it should look. This makes the movement instruction a type of deductive instruction (see p. 29).

Assigning Movement Exercises

In contrast, movement exercise represents the essential part of an inductive approach (see p. 29). If the student's space is not limited, it is called a *free movement exercise*. If information is given ahead of time in order to reach a goal more quickly or to increase the student's understanding, then it is a *controlled movement exercise*.

Correcting Movements

Mistakes always occur in the course of learning new skills. Movements are to be corrected when:
- They lead directly to errors such as not meeting the ball or hitting into the net or out of bounds;
- They lead to disadvantageous situations such as hitting the ball too short;
- They impede the student's long-term development (for example, the semi-continental grip impedes extreme forward spin).

Diagnosing Errors
Depending on the functional movement analysis (see *Tennis Course, Volume 1*, p. 20 ff.), the tennis instructor should aim his correction to achieving the tactical (movement) goal. This means that he determines to what extent the technique in question is suited to carrying out the tactical task, and to what extent the student is in a position to perform it.

Basics of Tennis Instruction

With this in mind, the following approach is recommended for the instructor when diagnosing errors.

- Observe the technique in question during play if at all possible, or under conditions corresponding to tossing the ball to the player.
- Determine if
  - the ball was not met,
  - the ball landed in the net or out of bounds,
  - the tactical task was not completed.
- Evaluate the main component of the technique in terms of the type of error noted.
- Evaluate the auxiliary actions—perhaps as cause for a faulty main action (error/consecutive error).
- Evaluate the physical area of the auxiliary actions as contributing to errors and deficiencies.
- Evaluate the movements of the head, the left arm, or footwork as components that are often not described as auxiliary actions.

Causes of Errors

Errors occur principally because of coordination problems when learning new techniques. Because what we see and what we hear are transformed into movement in different ways, a variety of errors can occur with different students. If the instructor is patient and repeats his instructions, allowing sufficient time for practice, many errors disappear by themselves. In addition to coordination problems, there is a series of further causes:

- Errors as a result of errors in judging the ball's timing and distance;
- Errors as a result of inappropriate intentions (for example, the ball is played

much too quickly) and tactical misjudgments;
- weaknesses in conditioning;
- general weaknesses of coordination, including lack of athletic preparation;
- inadequate feel for the ball;
- poor motivation.

If the instructor has not countered these inadequacies by appropriate practice programs and specific measures, his movement corrections will remain relatively ineffective.

Basics of Correction of Movement

The following basic principles should be observed when correcting:

- Determine the cause of the fault.
- Wait before making corrections, because the student must have time to acquaint herself with the movement; in this way, wrong movements sometimes right themselves during practice, or the student may consciously correct herself.
- Correct as soon as possible after incorrect execution of the movement if this self-correction does not succeed.
- Start with corrections that help meet the ball and hit it into the court; for example, correct faults in the main action or in the auxiliary action that impairs the main action.
- Orient correction first to the tactical task and not to the movement sequences; that is, it should be used only if the function of the technique can not be completed in the situation.
- Address only one error at a time.

- Associate corrections with encouragement rather than with criticism.
- Do not formulate the correction negatively (for example, "Point of impact is too late"), but try to offer as much help as possible (for example, "Swing forward earlier").
- Make corrections appropriate to the student, that is, corresponding to the level of ability (no fine correction at the basic-form stage).
- Do not insist on correcting, if it will not lead to success; offer other help, otherwise the student will get discouraged.
- Work on individual partial movements when possible, and then incorporate the correct partial movement into the total movement (for example, teach only the backswing movement for the volley).
- Be careful with demonstrating mistakes; you might disrupt the correct image of the movement.

How to Correct

The following measures can be taken to correct errors:

- Provide movement instruction (for example, "Stretch your arm when you hit the ball" or "Play longer at the baseline").
- Give repeated demonstration of parts of the technique or the total movement, also using videos, photo sequences, and the like.
- Assign tasks:
  - Achieve good tactical solutions via appropriate assignment of tasks (for example, "Play higher" and therefore longer).
  - Simplify tasks (for example, use less swing on shorter distances).

- Use vivid images to describe tasks (for example, explain weight transfer when volleying in terms of going down a step).
- Provide tasks that are in tune with the feeling (for example, using a heavy tennis racket to perform the hitting movement so that the swing is felt on the serve).
- Introduce tasks with a comparison (for example, to execute the service movement *like* a throwing movement).
- Present tasks with conscious exaggeration (for example, begin the backswing motion in a straight line behind and downward with too large a loop for forehand ground stroke).
- Toss the ball to the player (for example, a short toss can help correct an early point of impact).
- Use rhythmic shouts to support the motion.

Tossing the Ball to the Player

Tossing the ball precisely makes it easier for the student to hit it:
- Under constant or systematically varied conditions and
- At the ideal point of impact.

An instructor, a partner, or even a ball machine can toss the ball.

As opposed to the ball machine, tossing by the instructor has the advantage that it can be adjusted to the student more quickly, allowing it to be adapted at the player's performance level. In addition, the ball machine does not give the student any prediction of the flight of the ball as she would experience in a game.

Fig. 10 Overhand toss.

Fig. 9 Underhand toss, slightly diagonal to the point of impact. Instructor stands precisely opposite the student.

Basics of Tennis Instruction

As a rule, the instructor's toss (also throw) should be underhanded (Fig. 9, p. 35) so that the student can prepare better for his stroke. However, if the student must hit the ball on the upswing (slice, stop), the instructor can also throw overhand (Fig. 10, p. 35).

You should pay attention to the following factors when tossing:

- Direction,
- Length,
- Height,
- Speed,
- Frequency,
- Type of spin.

Direction of the Toss

The "Stationary" Ball

The ball is dropped (Fig. 11) or tossed (Fig. 12) precisely vertically over the intended point of impact; it then bounces to the height where its culmination point is situated exactly at the height of the point of impact; thus the ball "pauses" in the point of impact.

When the instructor tosses the ball, the student learns to recognize the flight rhythm of the ball. It also promotes the sense of a hitting rhythm. Just letting the ball fall is not as effective because it puts increased demands on the student's reaction and coordination. The student can also toss the ball. When tossing for the backhand ground stroke, the racket is gripped in the hitting position with the <u>left</u> hand at the neck of the racket. The ball is tossed with the right hand (hitting hand), and then the racket is grasped by the right hand in the backhand grip and the stroke is completed.

Tossing Accurately from the Student's Hitting Direction

The person tossing stands precisely opposite the point of impact, but for safety considerations the student may only return the ball gently so that the tosser can catch it without difficulty (Fig. 13, p. 37). Beginners are most successful with this.

Tossing from a Slightly Shifted Direction

The student should be able to hit without worrying about hitting the tosser with the ball (Fig. 14, p. 37). It must be guaranteed that the student doesn't have difficulties keeping the lateral distance from the point of impact. Therefore, the ball can travel back to the player or be tossed in a diagonal direction.

Tossing from Behind

The tosser stands behind the student (Fig. 15, p. 37) and throws the ball in the hitting direction. Of course, this situation never occurs in tennis games, but the tennis instructor can teach a point of impact clearly located in front of the body and a good weight transfer into the hitting direction.

Fig. 11 Ball is dropped from above the planned point of impact.

Fig. 12 Ball is tossed vertically above the planned point of impact.

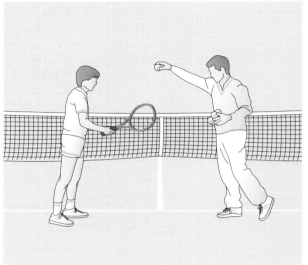

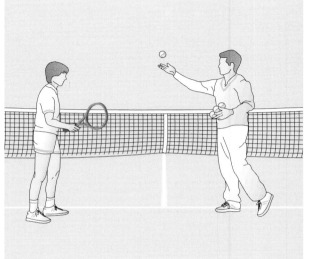

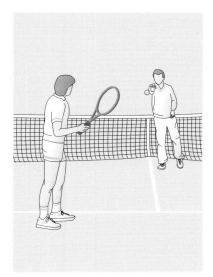

Fig. 13 Toss precisely from the student's hitting direction.

Fig. 14 Toss from the laterally shifted position to the hitting direction; after the landing, the ball bounces away from the student.

Fig. 15 Toss from behind.

Length of the Toss

The ball should be tossed in such a way that the student can hit it as easily as possible at the ideal desired point of impact. This means that the ball is not to be tossed too long or too short.

Height of the Toss

The desired point of impact is located at various heights depending on type of stroke, for example:

- At knee height for a low volley,
- At chest height for a topspin-lob,
- Above head level for a smash.

The ball must be tossed in such a way that it can be hit at the desired height. When there are various body sizes in a group, using a ball machine has disadvantages because it cannot be set for any individual.

Speed and Frequency of the Toss

Speed as well as frequency must be chosen in such a way that the students have enough time to prepare for and execute the stroke according to their level of ability.

Spin of the Toss

When tossing the ball with forward or backward spin, the trajectory and bounce behavior must be calculated, and the student must be made aware not to overestimate them. Balls should not be just hit one way but, so far as it fits the method used, they should also be returned by the instructor (volley).

Success in tennis instruction depends largely on a good toss that is suited to the student.

Organization

Planning the individual units of instruction must include a selection of meaningful and suitable forms aimed at the particular objective.

The tennis instructor must establish ahead of time:

- <u>Where</u> the students should stand and practice (somewhat close to the net, behind the "T," behind the baseline, sometimes in front of a wall, etc.)—depending on the particular tasks assigned and the ability level of the student;
- <u>How</u> the students should line up—independent of the available court and the planned sequence;
- <u>In what sequence</u> the tasks should be completed (procedures and exercise sequences).

Typical Formats for Larger Groups	Activities
Free format with great enough distance between partners	Exercises to get used to the ball; gymnastics, stretching
Circle format with appropriate distance between players	Exercises to get used to the ball and racket; simple games
Semi-circle format	Gymnastics, stretching, explanations for all
Line format; also two parallel lines, perhaps shifted	Gymnastics, stretching, running, sprinting, hitting movements without the ball, footwork (step combinations, running rhythm)
Circular run; players are divided equally on each side of the net	Running in a circle; with an uneven number of participants, the group with the extra player puts the ball into play; prescribed hitting direction
Players are divided equally on both sides of the net and form two or three sub-groups that stand behind designated positions (lines, markings, etc.)	Running in a circle with 2 or 3 balls simultaneously; prescribed hitting direction
Alley format	Throwing and hitting to partners
Line-up format (2–4 players only)	Play against the wall; hit balls played by the instructor or ball machine; after one or more hits, also from various positions, the player returns to the end of the line

Table 6 Presentation formats and processing for exercise sequences

Lining up and executing the exercise sequence (Table 6) must guarantee that
- The teacher has a good chance to observe all of the students,
- All students are meaningfully busy,
- The safety of the students is guaranteed.

Use of Media and Movement Aids

When goals and methods of the instruction have been established and the tennis instructor knows where her instruction will take place (outdoors or indoors), then she can decide whether to use media and educational aids. This means that she must weigh whether the practical value for learning makes the necessary expenditure for and setting up and taking down of equipment worthwhile.

Media
By *media*, we mean:
- Images:
  - Pictures and photo sequences,
  - Film and video;
- Print media:
  - educational charts and guides.

The most important advantages of media (see Table 7) are:
- Best possible information,
- Particular motivation,
- Intensified individual work by students,
- Releasing the instructor for individual coaching.

Movement Aids
Movement aids support learning and make it easier; they also motivate the student. There is a difference between equipment support (Table 8, p. 39) and personal support (Table 9, p. 39). Movement aids that have only one intended use lead to a forced situation; for example, they can

limit the breadth of the backswing when volleying by holding the racket back (Fig. 18, p. 40).

Using movement aids has the following individual goals:
- Making the student aware of the movement sequence,
- Making the instructional organization easier,
- Guaranteeing safety and accuracy,
- Supporting the consistency of instruction,
- Supporting motivation.

Aids to Make the Student Aware of the Movement Sequence
The student should be made aware of the spatial course of movement and the feel of it. In particular, the main action and location of the point of impact should be emphasized.
Examples:
Main action of the volley:
- Force the stroke direction with the aid of a cord drawn through the strings of the racket and tied to the net.

	Visual Aids	Advantages	Disadvantages
Static Images	Sequence of sketches	– essential information only – student can study pictures as often and as long as desired – instructor can stress particular methods	– impersonal (no imitation via model) – no dynamic sequence
	Sequence of photographs	– as above, motivation via model	– stressing methods is hardly possible – no dynamic sequence
	Individual pictures (photos/sketches)	– concentration on essentials	– significance of individual picture for the overall movement sequence is not clear
Moving Images	Video (normal speed)	– optimal overall impression with dynamic sequence – opportunity to analyze the student's performance	– much information in a short period (high density) – great expenditure of time and organizational effort
	Video (slow-motion)	– limited density of information, details	– distorted dynamic sequence

Table 7   Visual media

Equipment		Applications
Rackets Balls	wooden board, various types of rackets, fishing net softballs, learner's balls	devices to teach techniques (esp. point-of-contact technique) according to student's expertise, body size, and strength
Ball machine		precisely playing the ball with the chance of adjusting frequency, speed, ball height, distance, direction, and spin
Ball wall	Paraboloid walls of stone, straight stone walls, angled stone walls, frame net, and trampoline walls	training techniques, precision and reaction
Hitting aid	Ball angle, ball pendulum, fixed balls	training techniques
Goal posts, tires, caps, ropes		training trajectory height and precision; orientation aids for running

Table 8   The most important training devices in tennis instruction (see also Fig. 20, p. 41)

Table 9   Examples of personal aids in tennis instruction

	Description of the Aid	Function of the Aid
Tactile Aids	Accelerating the movement of the upper arm by thrusting the elbow while swinging the racket at the return point of the loop when serving	Teaching the accelerating dynamics of the serve, reducing possible hesitations
	Keeping the left arm firm and pulling it slightly to the rear on the backhand stroke	Establishing the sideways-on position
	Instructor leads the student's hitting hand on the half-volley (Fig. 17, p. 40).	Emphasizing awareness of—and feeling for—the movement
Acoustic Aids	Call: "Bend and hop!" ("Bend" for bending the knee during the back-and-forth movement, "and" on extending the knee, and "hop" for extending the elbow.)	Correcting the sequential movements of knee- and arm-extension on the serve
	Call: "and now"	Supporting the beginning of the forward swing, in order to meet the ball at the right time
Visual Aids	Have the student do footwork at the same time.	Imitating the instructor's example ("shadowing")
	Student begins the backswing movement when the instructor's racket moves forward to play the ball to him.	Supporting correct timing

Basics of Tennis Instruction

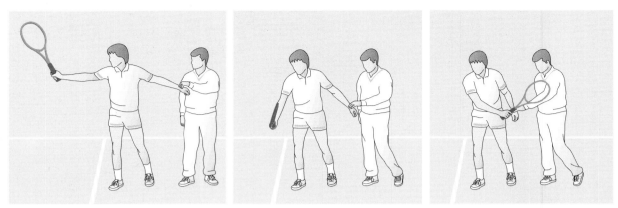

Fig. 16 Instructor guides the student's left hand on a backhand stroke in order to maintain the sideways-hitting position.

Fig. 18 Backswing movement for the forehand volley ends at the instructor's racket.

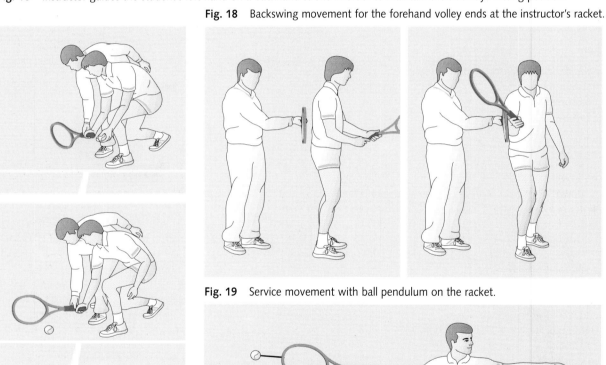

Fig. 19 Service movement with ball pendulum on the racket.

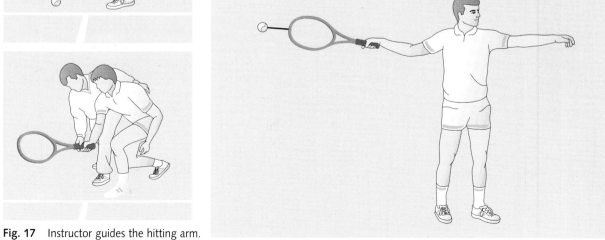

Fig. 17 Instructor guides the hitting arm.

Point of impact for all types of strokes:
- Keep ball at an angle in the ideal point of impact.

Sense of swing for the service:
- Force a vigorous serve motion with the ball guide on the racket (Fig. 19, p. 40)—ball may not touch the racket.

Aids to Make Organization Easier
Caps, racket covers, jumping ropes, and the like help mark the starting positions and paths and thus support the organizational sequence of the lesson.

Aids for Safety and Accuracy
Auxiliary equipment is used for goal orientation.
Examples:
- Enhanced net to improve confidence in hitting, trajectory of topspin, and twist service).
- Towel hung on the net to check stroke direction.
- Innertubes, racket covers, ropes used as auxiliary lines, and so on to mark areas of impact.

Aids for Consistency of Conditions
Relatively consistent trajectories can be created by ball-throwing machines and tennis walls. This can make learning new techniques easier for the student.

Motivational Aids
Auxiliary equipment, ball-throwing machines, and the like provide variety and thus enrich the educational experience. These allow the instructor to motivate his students even further, if necessary. However, it is very important not to overdo the use of auxiliary equipment.

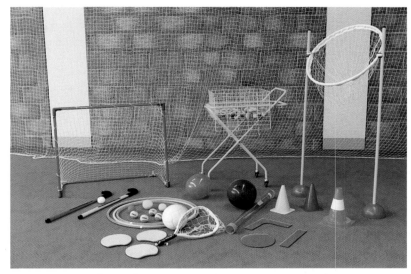

Fig. 20   Training devices for tennis instruction.

Planning and Implementing Tennis Instruction

The requirements of teaching and the suggested instructional activities for tennis instruction were presented in the previous chapter. Based on those fundamentals, this chapter will deal with the necessary steps in planning actual instruction.

Lesson planning, that is, preparing for the instructional situation at hand, should assure that, in the end, the students will have learned something and that the goals set by the students and instructor at the beginning will have been achieved as far as possible.

Individual and Group Instruction

In addition to the traditional individual instruction, which was previously the most popular form of instruction, group instruction is gaining in popularity. In schools and colleges, group instruction has gained prominence because of space and personnel limitations. Most types of play, practice, and competition described in this volume are especially suited for group instruction. Experience has shown that both individual and group instruction have advantages and disadvantages; the most important of these will be discussed in this chapter.

On the whole, group instruction still has more advantages than disadvantages. It has also been proven in practice because all

Basics of Tennis Instruction

groups of students—beginners, advanced, tournament players, children, teenagers, and adults—like it and profit from it. Still, it must be noted that there are limitations to group instruction when the number of participants is too large or the group is too diverse in performance level (heterogeneity).

The most important goal of all educational activities is teaching and optimizing of competency. Group instruction seldom focuses on technique-oriented approaches, but rather on play-oriented ones.

The tennis instructor must organize events in such a way that all participating students can learn to play tennis as partners, depending on their personal ability level. Students take on mutual responsibility for making progress, and they become more competent in controlling and correcting with help from the tennis instructor.

The instructor must take care to have the best instructional conditions (courts, instructional aids, and organization) and to foster the student's initiative. Group instruction demands a lot from the tennis instructor in the area of organization and methods.

In comparison with individual instruction, the instructor must also consider the following factors when planning and teaching his lessons:
- Number of students and courts,
- Homogeneity or heterogeneity of the group,
- Structure of the group (age, sex, etc.),
- Various interests within the group.

In order to achieve the goals in group instruction and to guarantee the success of each individual student, the following principles should be guaranteed and assured:
- Effectiveness: optimum use of the court, sufficient supply of balls, individual coaching and correction;
- Intensity: frequent ball contact and appropriate pressure;
- Safety: appropriate organization and aids for orientation and monitoring by the instructor;
- Variability: switching partners and tasks;
- Functionality: assigning specific tasks such as ball tosser, "ball retriever," and referee;
- Appropriateness: forms of play and practice appropriate for the students, as well as varied activities.

Advantages of Individual Instruction
- The instructor can intensively foster the individuality of the student.
- The student has a partner, ball tosser, or opponent with whom she can train and work on all tactical situations.
- The instructor is a model for the student.

Disadvantages of Individual Instruction
- Performance cannot be compared directly with others of the same age or strength.
- Some important goals cannot be achieved (for example, group work, fairness, tolerance, helpfulness).
- Learning, playing, and practicing with the same instructor or partner can become one-sided and monotonous in the long run, resulting in decreased motivation.

- The student cannot practice at playing doubles.
- Support and reinforcement by others in the group is missing.
- Individual instruction is usually more expensive than group instruction.
- Social integration of beginners and newcomers into a club is hindered.

Advantages of Group Instruction
- Changing partners and diversified tasks allow for more variety and new motivation.
- The student gets experience with different types of partners, techniques, and play from the start.
- Direct performance comparison with others of the same age or strength.
- Many tennis-specific types of play, practice, and competition are possible only in small groups (for example, drill training or line-up format and stroke combinations for doubles.
- People often learn more easily in groups because they can identify with their fellow players and can usually find a suitable partner or opponent.
- The individual student is not always directly monitored and observed by the instructor.
- The tennis facility can be used more effectively with regard to court requirements.
- Social qualities such as team spirit, camaraderie, tolerance, helpfulness, and independence are promoted.
- Social integration into the club for beginners and newcomers is developed.
- Group instruction is generally more economical than individual instruction.

Disadvantages of Group Instruction

- Individual and intensive coaching by the instructor is seldom possible.
- Sometimes there is no good ball tosser.
- Match play is sometimes too brief.

Levels of Instructional Planning

It is wise to plan each individual instructional unit within a broader context, while keeping in mind the overarching objectives. The following levels of instructional planning (Fig. 21) are therefore recommended:

- Investigating the general prerequisites,
- Comprehensive planning,
- Planning the individual instructional units.

Considerations for the Preconditions

The individual instructional unit is usually part of an integrated course. That means that the applicable prerequisites for comprehensive planning should be considered. These are a function of the qualifications of the students and external factors.

The educational topic does not always have to be analyzed when formulating a comprehensive plan.

The premise of all instructional course planning is knowledge of the factors that affect performance, along with the technical and tactical demands of tennis, while conveying this effectively to the students.

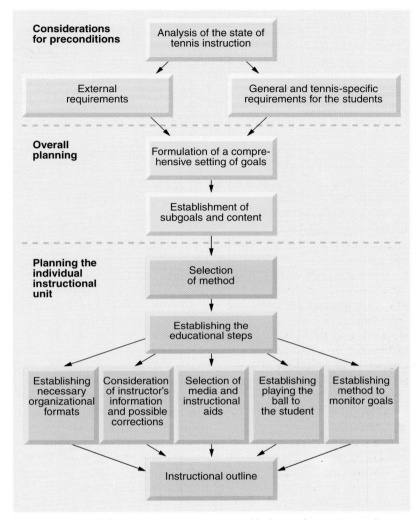

Fig. 21 Levels of planning tennis instruction, modified according to HEYMEN/LEUE.

Qualifications of the Students

Based on these factors, the teaching goals can be tailored to the students, and the pressure and possible reactions of the students can be predicted more precisely.

General Factors

- Age.
- Physical size.
- Ability to learn motor skills.
- Basic motor skills.
- Motivation, interests.
- Social behavior (cooperative attitude).

Tennis-Specific Factors

- Analysis of tennis-specific ability.

Basics of Tennis Instruction

External Factors

External factors influence the organizational structures in particular, as well as the use of educational aids. Under certain circumstances they can also limit goal setting. Thus, the following factors should be taken into consideration:

Space Factors

- Indoor or outdoor courts
- Number, size, and layout of courts
- Media room, electrical outlets

Equipment

- Number of balls and ball baskets
- Rental, training, or substitute rackets
- Auxiliary equipment media

Organizational Factors

- Total number and distribution of instructional units
- Length of a single unit
- Number of students

Comprehensive Planning

Comprehensive planning requires the establishment of preconditions. Thus, the fundamentals of analysis of the educational situation are used to formulate a comprehensive establishment of goals and to choose a methods-based approach with its corresponding subgoals and content.

Establishing Educational Goals

Because instruction will take place over an extended period, goals for comprehensive planning must be set. They should be selected on the basis of the external factors, depending on the learner's qualifications, along with his interests and expectations.

Based on the establishment of comprehensive goals and the time and space requirements, the tennis instructor must choose either a play-oriented or a technique-oriented approach. Then subgoals (elements of playing ability and skills) and content (techniques and play sequences) can be determined for each instructional unit in the learning sequence.

Planning the Individual Instructional Units

Preparation of each lesson is at the heart of instructional planning, and it should be followed by a written outline.

Establishing the Instructional Pace

The tennis instructor decides whether skills and types of play are to be presented holistically or stepwise, deductively or inductively.

Depending on this, she determines the instructional pace required to reach the established stepwise goals. That can be:

- Levels of a methodical sequence,
- Information on a skill to be presented holistically,
- Alternating play and exercise.

Information for the Instructor

The tennis instructor should be prepared to integrate demonstration and oral instruction, as well as to correct typical errors.

In this context, she should consider:

- The planned approach,
- The difficulties of the skills and capabilities to be taught,
- The age and level of the students.

Media and Educational Aids

Supplementing instruction with educational aids or media basically depends on:

- The difficulty of the learning situation,
- The motivational needs of students,
- The time available.

Ball Tossing

Considerations of ball tossing or throwing by the instructor or students as an educational aid depend on:

- The size of the group,
- The techniques and tactics to be learned,
- The level of the students.

Organization

The tennis instructor must establish protocols for lining up and changing places, as well as setting up running and hitting areas, depending on:

- The size of the group,
- The space available,
- The variations in ability in the group (similar or different tasks),
- The independence of the students,
- Safety considerations (flying balls and so on).

Monitoring Educational Goals

Monitoring educational goals should always be included in the plan when:

- A new educational step depends heavily on the quality of what has been learned,
- The students need a review of their progress for renewed motivation,
- The success of the total instructional unit needs to be confirmed in order to continue or even to change the plan.

We have, therefore, the following possibilities:

- Monitoring by objective: playing within marked areas and the like and perhaps standardized ball tossing (using ball-throwing machines);
- Monitoring the execution of the movement (also using video);
- Reviewing performance in competition: observing play and analyzing matches;
- Evaluation using conditioning tests: assessing basic motor skills;
- Having a conversation focusing on instruction: determining if the students have understood everything, if their desires have been met, if they think they were appropriately encouraged, and so on.

Instruction Outline

The planned course of instruction should follow the sequence of the educational steps and should be included, if at all possible, in a lesson plan. This can be a comprehensive work or a short outline. Possible alternative planning could be included.

The educational steps are based on methodology and do not take time constraints into account. Instructional units can emphazise ball tossing, media and instructional aids, organization, possible errors and correction of them, and monitoring (see Table 10).

Teaching Tennis

The tennis instructor has planned his instructional unit and has gone over it in his mind. Now it is time to put this planning into practice. For this, the following factors should be considered.

Before the Lesson Begins
- Be there on time, before the beginning of the lesson.
- Check court, equipment, and so on.
- Plan activities for students who arrive too early, if there are any.

At the Beginning of the Lesson
- Greet, introduce students, if necessary (instructor–students and student–student).
- Check attendance, if applicable.
- Present the objectives of the lesson.
- Answer any student questions and establish their expectations (possibly altering the plan).
- Organize setup of equipment.
- Emphatically point out safety factors (balls, equipment, ball machines, and the like).

During the Lesson
- Carry out the planned sequence.
- Check the sequence conscientiously in order to achieve the following:
  - work on changes (in the case of demanding too much or too little, learning problems, concentration deficiencies, changes in the weather);
  - assign various tasks in groups (diversification);
  - be able to react quickly to safety problems.
- Announce and demonstrate for everyone together.
- Do not simply explain but demonstrate with a part of the group.
- When necessary, motivate students continually to join in.
- Encourage weak students and give them extra help if possible.

At the End of the Lesson
- Finish on time, if possible without abruptly breaking off the last exercise.
- Give "homework": What should be practiced for next time?
- If at all possible, end with a positive experience.
- Finish with a short review and preview of the next lesson.

Table 10   Excerpt from a detailed instructional outline for "Introduction to the forehand ground shot"

Time	Learning step	Didactic method	Media/ instructional aids	Organizational format	Possible correction of errors	Monitoring progress
...	...	...	...	...	...	...
15 mins.	Play a stationary ball	TOM Holistic-deductive	Newspaper as goal	Groups of two	Racket should not be forward and upward: let it drop to the rear	Meet the ball at the "T" behind the net
...	...	...	...	...	...	...

Assessment of the Lesson

Assessment of the lesson (that is, the subjective evaluation of the course and success of the lesson) serves to:

- Confirm the long-term instructional plan or to change it,
- Improve one's own teaching skills.

The tennis instructor should check her own observations periodically by asking her students pertinent questions or by asking colleagues to observe her teaching and to comment. The instructor can ask herself the following questions:

- Have the objectives been met?
- Was the choice of subject matter appropriate?
- Were the students over- or undertaxed in terms of physical and motor skills?
- Were the demonstrations successful?
- Were the spoken directions understood?
- Were the locations of instructions and demonstrations always favorable?
- Were the corrections predominantly successful or unsuccessful?
- Did the movement aids work?
- Were the media accepted, or did they lead to delays in the lesson?
- Was the ball tossing successful?
- Did the students toss/throw well?
- Did the organization follow a smooth sequence?
- Was the space used efficiently?
- Did people play enough, too little, or too much?
- Could differences in skills be accommodated?

- Could unexpected problems be dealt with?
- Did the checks on instructional goals measure what they were supposed to?
- Were the students motivated to participate willingly?

Learning and Training in Groups

In a previous section (see p. 41) the essential requirements, advantages, and disadvantages of group instruction vis-à-vis individual instruction were described. The following section presents types of learning, practice, and training that can be used effectively with various numbers of students and increase the joy of learning, practicing, and training.

Group Instruction with Large Groups

Size of the Group
8 to 24 students on the tennis court. The group size is always oriented to the ability level of the students and the planned instructional content. In the large group, the basics for ability to play are about the same on the large court as they would normally be on the minicourt.
Area of Application
Tennis in the schools, beginners.
Requirements
The students already have experience dealing with ball and racket through exercises to acquaint them with the ball and to improve coordination and agility.

Defining Goals for Group Instruction
The students should (and want to) become familiar with the basics of tennis technique. Because the instructor cannot keep all the students in view, success is always monitored via the tasks required in the lesson, which can be evaluated by the student himself or by his partner. Ways of lining up are described earlier in this volume (see p. 38). This section will deal with exercises using practice walls, ball machines, and other auxiliary equipment; we will consider only those items that are available everywhere.

Learning Simple Stroke Techniques for Forehand, Backhand, and Volley

The sequence for learning these three basic types of strokes is completely open because it represents an elementary unit in teaching beginners. Organizationally, "team teaching" in which the students are also sometimes used as auxiliary instructors, ball throwers, and judges should be considered most helpful. Using the alley for a lining-up exercise is recommended. Here, partners stand opposite each other with obstacles between them; they play over these (lines, stretched string, nets, etc.). The contact-oriented method is the focus, since at first, students learn only the main action, and the scope of the hitting movement grows with the distance.

Judging the ball using its motion, and the corresponding footwork to various points of impact, are the most important central elements for improving competency and should be at the center of group instruction.

Methodology

1. The main action is described by the instructor and imitated by the students first as a dry-run and then with the ball. At first, the stationary ball is played from a side-on position; later the partner throws it under-hand, face-on to an ideal point of impact, contact. In both cases the task is completed if the ball is tossed to the partner at chest height and she can catch the ball. If the approaching ball is first played by the student with the racket slightly tipped up, and then played back to the partner, we speak of a "control shot" to judge the ball. At the beginning, the focus is on playing with one another, and the number of successful tries or faultless ball contacts are counted and compared.

2. When students are achieving a high success rate when hitting from the service position, it is wise to vary the hitting position and the pitches. In partner play, it works very well if the variation of the throw is systematically increased (in regard to direction, length, height, and speed).

In addition, if the students master the throw and toss variations from different court positions and can return the ball to various targeted areas, the foundation for playing tennis has been laid and can be confirmed as the student continues to play.

Examples:

With the circular run using one ball, the clockwise or counter-clockwise running direction is around a net, close to the net with increasing distance from the "T," depending on the abilities of the group. Dividing the larger group into several minicourts (up to eight minicourt nets per court) is especially beneficial. Assigned types of hitting can provide opportunities for variation in play (straight, diagonal, over obstacles).

With the circular run with two or three simultaneously played balls, one ball is played in the "T" between the two outside sidelines, and one ball is played over the center line (also twice crosscourt and straight over the middle). After each ball contact, players move one position in clockwise or counterclockwise direction. Gentler and slower balls, shorter and lighter rackets, and assignment of tasks for individuals (such as a control shot for each ball contact) can make things easier for beginners. Everyone should be included because the circular run primarily helps weak students, who need practice most. It is better to count points and include all students in competition. The instructor can also set up partner- and team-scoring systems, in which the points of the weaker and stronger students are added together. Further, it is also wise to give better students handicaps (keep left hand in shorts pocket, carry a backpack, or other such things).

With the accordion-format there is a continuous change from shorter to greater distances and back again with and without control shot. After successfully playing a certain number of ball contacts, the distance is increased by a specific amount (for example, 1 meter). Which pair will reach the baseline first? Partners can be alternated until everyone has played with everyone else and at the end the best ball tosser is recognized. The forehand, backhand, and volley strokes can be combined in different ways. All these contain the basic building blocks of tennis. And now, only the service stroke is missing.

Learning the Service Stroke

The service can be learned easily and efficiently as partners work according to the following proposal. The main problem with serving is in coordinating the movement of the hitting arm and throwing arm. First, the instructor demonstrates the stroke movement slowly and with the correct timing. It can be imitated well by all the students almost instinctively as a dry-run. Many students are immediately able to combine the stroke movement with the movement of the hand leading the ball, especially if they have experience from other sports, such as volleyball.

If that is not the case, help from partners can lead to surprisingly quick success. The partner throws the ball vertically at the correct point in time into the ideal point of impact, and the learner plays it diagonally into the service line area. At the same time, the partner stands to the side in front of the learner and first throws the ball high into the air with his throwing hand and later with the other hand; in this way he is already practicing throwing the ball with his nonthrowing hand for his own service stroke practice which will follow. Very soon, the student is able to play the ball first from the "T" and later from the baseline into the opposite service line area. The stroke movement by the learner and tossing the ball high into the air by the partner begin simultaneously as a verbal signal accompanies the movement, for example, "and back and forth" or "one, two, three." After several successful attempts with the aid of a partner, the ball is given to the student to toss up himself, so he can serve using the rhythm he practiced (without having to think about the throw). Alternating with successful tries with the aid of a partner and direct tries by oneself, success is not long in coming. Enthusiasm over the first successful serve gives the student so much self-confidence that he soon masters the correctly coordinated serve. Using a type of volley ball in which the ball is allowed to bounce is very good as a practice and playing form. In this game, partners take turns bumping the ball with a racket; the ball should be met over their heads (service point of impact), and then bounce between the partners (count the ball exchanges).

With practice and playing forms for serves and overhead shots, particular attention should be given to safety and ball direction, and the student should concentrate on keeping an eye on the ball. This means that either

- All the students hit in one direction at the same height, or
- With partner work, where they stand opposite each other, the sideways distance has to be large enough.

Readiness to Play

With the basic form of the hitting movements for fore- and backhand, along with calculating the ball and footwork, all the basic requirements concerning readiness to play are covered. A systematic and methodical transition from restricted play on minicourts (see "Minicourt Tennis," p. 53) and half- and whole "T" areas to regular play can be made by moving back step by step from the "T" to the baseline.

The transition to the full court can be made with groups of up to six students.

Group Instruction with Small Groups (3 to 6 students)

With small groups, the instructor takes on the role of principal ball tosser. She must also use her expertise to counter minor differences in the capabilities of the students and to assign tasks that are suited to each individual.

At the beginning, precision and rhythm of the instructor's toss contribute much to the motivation and success of the student. The primary objective for instructor and student, however, is always volleying. That can be done with individual types of strokes and also with multiple variations of different types of strokes. The instructor is free to choose from the selection of instruction and

practice alternatives, and there is a large number of possibilities.

The following can be varied:
- Student's running to both sides, to front and back, diagonally forward and back in two directions, lined up next to each other, and combined;
- Instructor's ball tossing (speed, direction, spin, frequency, and variety);
- Types of strokes (simply, in regular and irregular rotation, combined from the point of view of considering safety, accuracy, speed, spin, and rhythm);
- Varied tasks assigned individually within the group.

The well-prepared group lesson can approach individual instruction with regard to putting pressure on the individual student, but it has clear advantages because of the effect of group dynamics, motivation, and the competitive spirit of the students among one another. Because of considerations of cost and space, group instruction is surely the way of the future. Learning and practicing the elements of tennis clearly come first here.

Group Training
(3 to 4 players)

Group training on the large court is best with only three or four players, which can be increased to double that number (for example, team and replacements) if two courts are available.

The transition to group training can be completed fluidly using techniques and tactics as judged from the viewpoint of pressure.

Group training is particularly wise and effective in groups of three or four, so the instructor or trainer can join the group as the fourth player.

Fig. 22   Group instruction with beginners.

Tennis Instruction with Various Target Groups

This section will deal with methodological viewpoints vis-à-vis various groups in tennis. Themes that were discussed in a general way in the previous section will now be presented more specifically aimed at various audiences.

Audience can be defined by criteria of age, ability, goals, and requirements. The following chapters elaborate on this:

- Tennis for beginners: This discusses minicourt and children's tennis.
- Elementary school: It is directed toward beginners from childhood to advanced age.
- Tennis instruction with advanced adults in recreational tennis: This is directed toward adults who have more or less comprehensive tennis experience. They want to improve their game but have no athletic ambitions in the organized competitive system.
- Tennis instruction with talented children and teenagers: Methods and tips are oriented toward the goal of reaching a high skills level in tournament tennis.
- School tennis: To teach tennis in school, pedagogical and organizational factors must be considered.

- Tennis instruction with the disabled: This final section addresses a small audience, one that has been long overlooked, but very important for social reasons.

Beginners' Tennis/ Minicourt Tennis/ Children's Tennis

The beginner category extends through all age groups. There are three- to four-year-old children, but there are also older people who are beginning with tennis. In spite of various individual assumptions about learning, they can soon be able to carry out simple volleys because of favorable external factors (rackets, balls, court size, net height, etc.).

Today we can say almost without reservation that tennis can be learned at any age. Decisive factors at the outset include a fascination for the equipment as well as fun and excitement in learning to play tennis.

In teaching, the tennis instructor has to develop in his

students not only movement sequences of the techniques but also competency. Here, observational skills are very important. This means that students must:

- First learn to judge the speed, the trajectory, and the bounce behavior of the ball;
- Learn to adjust their footwork and hitting movements to these;
- Then later learn to observe the hitting movements of their partners and to anticipate their effects.

The diversity of groups of tennis beginners was never so great as today. The question arises whether people in all groups of either sex (children, teenagers, young adults, and seniors) can respond to similar teaching and learning patterns or whether specific differentiations are necessary.

Just a few years ago, tennis instructors were working with adults almost exclusively in individual instruction. Group instruction was originally offered for children and teenagers in schools, clubs, and commercial facilities mainly to save money.

Meanwhile, views have changed, and today tennis is taught mostly in groups for all audiences. The fact that well-organized group instruction has become popular for all tennis beginners is undisputed, mainly because learning in groups is more fun and participants motivate one another.

General Comments on Tennis Instruction for Beginners

Setting Goals

Every participant wants to know *why* she should do something. The sense or purpose that is associated with the task (tactical background) must always be done consciously. There are various technical solutions for similar situations. The student should be in a position to see the situation and the solution to the task from the point of view of the participant.

Safety

In all exercises, especially in larger groups, the tennis instructor must pay attention to the safety of the participant (position and use of auxiliary equipment, balls lying around and direction of strokes, distance from other players). If there is a doubt, always interrupt the exercise.

Instruction on Various Skills Levels

With larger groups there is most often a difference in skills level. Because each participant wants to profit from the instruction, it is often necessary to offer various tasks, goals, or ways of keeping score in order to fit the ability levels of the participants. Particular attention should be paid to ball tossing. In these situations, teaching is especially challenging for the instructor, but is all the more satisfying when he has mastered the situation.

Organization

The participants must understand the sequence of the task. For each new exercise, a specific time must be calculated wherein each player needs to be aware of his or her personal task (tossing, hitting, returning, catching balls).

When new rules or other ways of scoring are introduced, the tennis instructor must be sure that the participants have understood everything before the exercise begins. Questions by the participants are always a signal that the explanation was unclear or incomplete.

For instruction with beginners, the following factors are important:
1. The sequence of the task at hand with every stroke technique is:
   - meeting the ball,
   - playing the ball over the net (relatively high),
   - placing the ball (left, right),
   - playing the ball fast.

2. At the beginning, there are movements that move within a limited range during the backswing and stroke:
   - Variation of the point of impact depending on the distance from the body (close–far),
   - Variation of the point of impact depending on the distance from the ground (low–high),
   - Variation of the point of impact depending on the direction of the shot (in front–behind).

Note: – With all excercises the whole body should *always* be involved.

3. The distance and direction from which the ball is tossed/thrown is increased:
   - Variation of the toss direction with an established hitting position,
   - Variation of the beginning of preparation of the backswing (early–late) with an established hitting position determined by the length of the ball flight,
   - Variation of the hitting position (legwork),
   - Variation of the speed during the hitting movement.

Note: – Work less with the "stationary" ball.
   – Limited range of movement remains on the backswing and stroke.
   – Follow-through direction and distance can be agreed upon.

4. Only when playing from "T" to "T" should the distance between the players (instructor/student) be increased.

Note: – If the ball cannot be played over the net with the desired <u>limited range of movement</u>, the <u>toss speed</u> must be increased first and then the <u>speed of the hitting motion</u> must be increased.

5. The range of the backswing and hitting movement increases with <u>slowly</u> (gently) tossed balls.

Note: – Increasing the range of movement is *wise* with: forehand, backhand, lob, and smash and *not wise* with volley, half volley, stop.

An important success factor in beginners' tennis is that play equipment (rackets, balls), court size and net height should be suited to the individual and grow with the ability of the learner. Therefore, it should not be difficult for the experienced tennis instructor to support beginners in all age groups individually and to motivate them accordingly. The following practical recommendations are directed toward all beginners.

Tennis Rackets (Beginners' Rackets)

The size of this racket's strung head corresponds to the normal racket; however, the weight of the racket is significantly lighter. The shaft is shorter, and the overall length of the racket is thus shorter. The rackets are more manageable and can be used with less exertion. In spite of this, they allow secure ball control. Racket weight and length increase with the student's progress and should always be suitable to the physical requirements of the learner. If only regular rackets are available, students can move their grip accordingly.

Tennis Balls

Good beginners' tennis balls are lighter than regular balls and travel more slowly. Being of the same size, they look like regular balls and are more readily accepted by students. The slow flight of these balls allows

beginners to judge the trajectory better and gives them more time for stroke preparation and execution. If there are no beginners' balls available, soft, played-out regular balls are also suitable.

Court Size and Net Height

Every beginner would like to begin playing tennis as soon as possible or, at least, to start regular volleys. This works best on a smaller tennis court with a lower net. You can draw such a court on any flat surface, and you can play over taut rope or makeshift nets. However, as soon as one learns the simplest type of playing and keeping score, it is advantageous to play according to established rules and on standard, clearly marked courts with standard, taut nets. Therefore, a minicourt should look like a genuine smaller version of the regulation tennis court.

Fig. 23   Children play with appropriately smaller rackets.

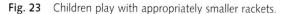

Fig. 24   Minicourt for children within the existing court marking.

Minicourt Tennis–Court and Net Units

For minicourt tennis, we recommend a net 20 ft. (6.10 m) wide and approximately 2.8 ft. (80–85 cm) high. The recommended court width of 20 ft. (6.10 m) can be achieved by putting together two mininets, each approximately 10 ft. (3.05 m) wide. Such mininets are mostly used at home (garage, yard, garden, etc.) and are good for home-training of all students of all ages. However, they are always more important in tennis instruction with large groups (school, popular sports facilities, etc.) because with them the students begin to understand how to play tennis in the first lesson.

Minicourts can be installed on all tennis courts, and even on all somewhat flat hard surfaces (school yards, parking lots). If the net is placed perpendicular to the regulation court, the existing

The minicourt available on every tennis court—between the singles sidelines, "T" and center line—only partially corresponds to the regulation court and therefore can be considered only as an interim measure. The best alternative is a mobile tennis minicourt unit, which divides a regulation tennis court into two, within the existing court markings.

The sidelines that are added to the minicourts can easily be removed after play. Height-adjustable net units can be erected and disassembled in a very short time and can be rolled out of the way after use.

Students can get to play and to compete much sooner on these types of minicourts. Those who have experienced this idea of playing tennis on a minicourt and grasped it can move very easily to playing on the larger regulation court.

Fig. 25   Setting up several minicourts.

markings can be used, and one needs to draw only a few additional lines. You can set up four large or eight small nets on a court, allowing $4 \times 6 = 24$ students or $8 \times 4 = 32$ students to play. If the game is to be played on other sandy, paved, or artificial surfaces (that is, areas that are not made for tennis), you need a surface of 100 feet per minicourt and 200 feet for a competition minicourt. Depending on the surface, the court markings can then be drawn with chalk, tape, rope, or "mobile" lines.

Basic Considerations for Minicourt Tennis

Tennis technique develops during play when the students experience success by fulfilling the various tasks. This represents the play-oriented approach. The tennis instructor takes care that the basic form of an acceptable tennis technique is maintained and continually develops to refined form. Here, there should be no "right" and no "wrong," but only suggestions for executing the assigned tasks and monitoring success, which in most cases, the students can do themselves.

The fast stroke, as opposed to the well-directed and safe shot, plays a totally subsidiary role in minicourt tennis. Therefore, *playing cooperatively* is most important and is linked to the goal of having frequent ball contact during the various volleys. Thus, the overarching question is always: Who had the most ball contacts during the volley and with whom?

After sufficient ball placement accuracy is achieved in hitting techniques—forehand, backhand, volley, and service—*playing competitively* is really fun. Only then is it possible to make use of technical and tactical finesse and to use them in play. Lively, varied tennis is played on the minicourt. The tennis instructor can join in as player in all types of play. However, he can also watch from the sidelines and offer tips if the children can already play together. As a teacher, the tennis instructor will always help the weak ones and encourage the stronger ones. He can accomplish this through appropriately diverse ball tossing.

Building on Play Sequences Is Recommended for Minicourt Tennis

Playing Together

1. The instructor plays the basic strokes of forehand, backhand, and volley with the group offering tips for gripping the racket, placing the shot, point of impact, and timing.
The students play back to the instructor from a standing position and, when moving, quickly achieve a regular volley (for example, circular run). The tasks can be varied in many ways and can be combined (running, type and number of ball contacts, tossing, etc.).
2. The instructor plays long balls using forehand, backhand, and volley face-on, with each student of the group in succession on half of the minicourt. This way, she gets to

know each student, along with his strengths, weaknesses, and qualities. If the volleys with the instructor are successful, it will not take long until the students can play together and will want to engage in long volleys as much as possible.

3. The instructor plays diagonally from the left to right half of the minicourt (or vice versa) with each student in succession. In this way, the stroke types— lob, smash, and stop—as well as the tactically important corner play are introduced and practiced. The student's task can then be to use only forehand or only backhand. This allows for the longest possible volley with the most intense demands.

Playing Competitively

When sufficiently long volleys in the various stroke types and combinations are completed (goal: 10 ball contacts), recommended basic knowledge for playing competitively is established. An introduction to a teacher/student double, as opposed to student/ student, in minicourt tennis has proved to be very advantageous.

In its simplest form, each player is responsible only for her half of the court but may play her balls in the opponent's half, if she wishes. The ball is brought into play underhand diagonally, and the score is kept, one point at a time. The instructor plays first with the weakest student in order to motivate her.

Doubles

At the beginning, the instructor participates, mainly as support for the weaker students. Later, the students play together, and the instructor merely offers tips from the sidelines. They play regular doubles with underhand serves. The ball contacts of the participants are now voluntary, and so standard play situations and diverse tactical strategies soon develop. All the stroke types tried before can now be used in a situational context. The variability of the game becomes very important.

"Table Tennis" Doubles

This game is very important as preparation for singles play. One plays first with the instructor and only later with other students. Ball contacts of the doubles partners rotate regularly after each shot, as in table tennis; each player must find his way around the entire half of the court. The object of the lesson is gaining a feel for the court space and an overall view of the game.

Doubles with Racket Switching

Each player must follow the ball intensely under time pressure (switching rackets) and play closely with his partner. On both sides, one plays with a racket that is taken over by a partner after each ball contact (see Fig. 24, p. 53). Each player takes on the part of a singles player within the doubles game. This type of game is ideally suited to teaching reaction and coordination.

From Doubles to Singles

In singles each player is responsible only for herself, and it is wise to test one's own abilities and strategies carefully. For this reason, the initial singles play should always take place between the instructor and the student. The instructor can build up the weaker ones and can keep the "smart" ones in check.

The transition can be made from the table tennis scoring method to regular tennis rules in which tie-breaker rules and timed play can often be used in minicourt play. In addition, one can serve underhand. If overhand serves are permitted, only one try may be allowed, to avoid any single player dominating. In minicourt tennis there should be long volleys as much as possible, and the play should be lively but not fast.

Minicourt Tennis Tournaments

If tennis students have had fun with competitive play, there should also be possibilities for them to participate in minicourt tennis tournaments. The instructor should be careful that all participants get a chance often. A timed playing situation, such as at a "Gong" tournament with playing times of 10 to 15 minutes, would be very advantageous.

If, at the beginning, people are divided into small groups (of four) that compete and then further divisions are made depending on court space, all participants will have the same amount of playing time, effort, and fun.

Competition on a minicourt should progress according to a plan and should offer a good basis for the transition to tennis competition on the regulation tennis court. Control of ball and body while playing tennis is fun. One learns both the easiest way on the minicourt.

Transition to Regulation Tennis on the Large Court

Depending on the abilities and ambitions of the student, there is a gradual move toward large court tennis assisted by a step-by-step elimination of all of the previously allowed concessions to make play easier. The requirements on rackets, balls, net height, and court size are increased according to the individual's capacity, and depending on his improving competency. In each case, the personal ambitions of the student should be considered. Thus it could well happen that a portion of the beginners (for example, older people) never get to "regular tennis" and have more fun playing the easier way. Therefore today, with the interest in recreational sports, there are also facilities that provide only minicourt tennis as an end in itself and without further advancement. However, things are different with 4- to 6-year-old children; for this group, minicourt tennis serves as an important early stage for talent-searching and as a way to use play to develop skills for standard tennis. The development of a sense of the game and early tactical instruction and development are the basis of all considerations here.

Learning tennis as a beginner happens in diverse ways and in very different conditions: in clubs, in school, on leased courts, in vacation camps, or in special tennis schools. In every case, group instruction has advantages over the traditional individual instruction. In group instruction, students mutually encourage, support, and motivate one another and experience tennis in a relaxed atmosphere. Children's tennis should be introduced and developed inductively through assigning tasks and playing games on minicourts.

Elementary School

The elementary school is a possible venue for beginner's tennis with the slogan "from the minicourt (short distances) to the large court (long distances)." By the end of a systematically constructed 10-hour program, participants should be able to do the following, relatively independent of age:
– play effectively together on the minicourt,
– return the ball tossed by the instructor from the baseline and from the net,
– serve and smash.

The elementary school approach has the following aspects:

- Group instruction, preferably with four players per court.
- Procedures focusing on technique and play.
- Demonstrations and skillful assignment of tasks as prominent activities.
- Bilateral tennis is important. This includes playing with both the right and left hands and also playing two-handed from both sides. This improves general coordination, physical development occurs equally on both sides, and there are not so many injuries due to strain. There is a certain positive transferability in tennis technique; in other words, practicing a stroke with the left hand can improve the execution of the stroke with the right hand. Finally, the variation with the racket is fun for children, so the movement sequences involved with bilateral tennis also helps loosen up the lesson.
- Tasks can be accomplished first with shorter and lighter tennis rackets (or with regular rackets gripped higher) and with special slowly moving beginners' balls.
- For the most part, students practice with a partner. The partner takes on the job of tossing the ball, and then the roles are switched.
- When playing over greater distances, the instructor initially assumes the task of tossing.

Playing the ball indirectly, diagonally over the net.

The Ten-Lesson Program: Overview

Lesson 1: Indirect, vertical tossing of the ball.

Lesson 2: Indirect tossing of the ball high over increasing distances.

Lesson 3: Use of forehand and backhand in the "T"-area.

Lesson 4: First main focus: volley, forehand, and backhand.
Second main focus: forehand and backhand in the "T"-area as a review.

Lesson 5: Use of forehand, backhand, and volley in the "T"-area.

Lesson 6: First main focus: smash.
Second main focus: forehand and backhand at variable distance increases in the direction of the baseline.

Lesson 7: First main focus: service.
Second main focus: forehand and backhand in the direction of the baseline at variable increases in distance; volley from a pitch at various distances.

Lesson 8: Combination of learned stroke techniques.

Lesson 9: Review of all techniques and preparation for the final exam.

Lesson 10: Final exam.

Playing the ball close over the net.

Tennis Instruction with Various Target Groups

Lesson 1

Tasks should be executed with the left hand, the right hand, and also two-handed, sometimes with the forehand and backhand sides. All exercises begin with tossing the ball.

1. Playing alone, play the ball high indirectly vertically.

2. With a partner, alternating, indirect and vertical playing the ball high:
   - Ball bounces in the alley,
   - Players stand outside the alley.

3. Throwing the ball indirectly over the net:
   - Ball should travel high over the net,
   - Ball should bounce just behind the net,
   - Ball should be played high for oneself first in difficult situations (control shot) and only then over the net to the partner.
     a) Players stand in the alley (face-on position to the net).
     b) Players stand outside the single or double lines (sideways-on position to the net).

4. Players stand in a circle and alternate playing the ball indirectly to one another.

5. Play two-on-two, rotating hitting.

Lesson 2

Tasks should be done with the left hand, the right hand, and also two-handed, sometimes with the forehand and backhand sides. The ball comes into play by throwing to the partner or tossing it up for oneself.

1. Pitch the ball indirectly over the net:
   - Position close to net, sideways-on hitting position to the net,
   - Ball should bounce in the corridor.

2. Toss the ball indirectly diagonally over the net (see p. 56):
   - Position close to net, face-on position to the net,
   - Ball should bounce inside or outside of the singles lines (Recommendation for grip).

3. Partners move parallel to the net, one plays diagonally, the other down the line.

4. Partners play diagonally over greater distances.
   - Position: close to the net, face-on position to the net (depending on the direction of the ball, the player stands in a sideways-on hitting position).
   - The student tosses the ball upward for himself (control shot).

5. Play the ball down the line in the alley over the net:
   - Players stand outside the sidelines in the sideways-on hitting position,
   - Increase and decrease distances.

6. Play two-on-two, with partners rotating hitting.

Lesson 3

Tasks should be executed in order with the normal hitting hand or two-handed. Ball comes into play by tossing it for oneself.

1. Play together in the service line area over the net (down the line and crosscourt).

2. Teach lateral distance from the point of impact.
   - Partner stands on the same side of the net as the player and throws the ball to a sideline.
     a) Player hits from a prescribed position.
     b) Teaching of the sideways footwork related to the hitting position (cha-cha-cha rhythm).

3. Volleying in service line area:
   - Teach lateral distance (also with control shot); after the stroke two or three lateral steps toward the middle of the service line area.
   - Play only crosscourt or down the line.

4. Volleying in service line area:
   - Change stroke direction.
   - Catch the ball and start again or play a volley with or without control shot.

5. Play two-on-two, with or against one another.

6. Run around the instructor.

Lesson 4

Lessons 1 through 6 should be executed with the left hand, the right hand, and also two-handed, sometimes with the forehand and backhand sides.

1. Play the ball directly over the net to a partner:
   - Shorter distance to net,
   - Vary distance.

2. Throw the ball over the net to a partner and catch.

3. Let the thrown ball bounce off the racket.
   - Experiment with various positions on the racket face.

4. Return thrown ball gently and high.

5. Toss the thrown ball high over the net two to three times; then hit it back over the net forward and high (partner should catch the ball).

6. Return the ball that has been tossed from the "T" as a volley.
   - Ball tosser: Catch the ball and play it again or continue the volley with or without control shot.

7. Volley back and forth in the sevice line area.

8. Play forehand and backhand in the "T" area as a review of the last lesson.

Lesson 5

Tasks should be done with the normal hitting hand or two-handed. The service line areas are used as courts.

1. Review forehand, backhand, and volley.

2. Combine these three techniques.

3. Deal with tactical tasks with regard to:
   - Stroke direction,
   - Stroke length,
   - Height of the ball trajectory.

4. Play against one another.

Lesson 6

Tasks should be executed with the normal hitting hand.

1. Bounce the ball with the racket.

2. Catch the ball that has been thrown high above head level (not with the normal hand).

3. Play the ball that has been thrown high above head level forward over the net.

4. Play the ball that has been thrown high first at and then above head level downward over the net.
   - Backswing in front of the body, grip, sideways-on hitting position.

5. Run to a point below the expected point of impact of the thrown/played ball:
   a) Catch with nonhitting hand,
   b) Smash,
   c) Smash into target area.

6. Play forehand and backhand with variable increases in distance to the baseline, with the instructor tossing; later, also partner-play; retrieve balls that have been played too far and replay them after a control shot, or return as a volley.

Lesson 7

Tasks should be executed with the normal hitting hand.

1. Throw the ball over the net from the "T" in a high arc.

2. Play the ball forward with the partner tossing.

3. Toss the ball for yourself and play forward.

4. Gradually increase the distance from the net (to the baseline) and play the ball:
   a) In a higher arc,
   b) In a flatter arc over the net into the service line area.

5. Play forehand and backhand with variable increases in distance in the direction of the baseline.

6. Play volley from a pitch at an increasing distance.

Lesson 8

Tasks should be executed with the normal hitting hand or two-handed.

1. Forehand and backhand from the baseline, with the instructor tossing, from the net.

2. Volley, forehand, and backhand, with the instructor pitching, from the baseline.

3. Partner-play, with forehand and backhand from the baseline and play at the net.

4. Service and return.

5. Play two-on-two from the baseline, rotating hitting:
   a) Play together.
   b) Play against one another.

Lesson 9

Tasks should be executed with the normal hitting hand or two-handed.

1. Review all stroke techniques, focusing on each key point.

2. Run through test exercises.

3. Teach "etiquette" (rules of behavior).

Lesson 10

Tasks should be executed with the normal hitting hand or two-handed.

1. Play together:
   - Court: two opposite service line areas.
   - Start: both partners behind the "T."
   - Procedure: Each player has nine tries. The ball must travel over the net ten times on each turn.

2. Serving:
   - Out of ten tries, three must land in the service line area.

3. From the baseline, return balls pitched by the instructor using forehand and backhand:
   - Instructor in net position alternately pitches ten times with forehand and ten times with backhand; student must play five forehand and backhand strokes to the singles court.

4. Return balls pitched by the instructor as volley and smash:
   - From the "T," instructor tosses six times in a row.
   - Six times for a forehand volley, six times for a backhand volley, and ten times for a smash; student must play three forehand volleys, three backhand volleys, and five smashes into the singles court.

All requirements must be met.

Advanced Adults in Recreational Tennis

Description of Target Groups

After beginners in all age groups, one of the largest student groups for tennis instructors are adults who have more or less comprehensive playing experiences, and therefore reasonably developed techniques. These "adult recreational players," have no particular ambitions for athletic achievement. They are mainly tennis players who have been playing for a long time and do not participate in the organized competitive system; they may also be players who first learned the game very late or who have not played for a long time. Adult recreational players have quite varied motives for playing tennis and for wanting to improve their game. As a result, their desires and their expectations of the tennis instructor are quite varied.

The differences in this audience result from:

- The range of age (from early teen years through adults to seniors),
- The basic advantage of athletic activity (camaraderie, fitness, social awareness),
- The recreational environment (club, tennis school, vacation),
- The social relationships (tennis with family, friends, business partners, new associates).

The tennis instructor must engage the student in conversation in order to learn her expectations, and then to:

- Plan her instruction,
- Anticipate the special needs of his students,
- Reduce or expand the expectations of the students as necessary to a realistic level,
- Be able to separate the students into suitable groups.

Despite the recreational player's different expectations and requirements, they all share a common desire to be able to play tennis better. This goal can be satisfied in two ways:

- Playing tennis cooperatively in pairs or in groups,
- Playing competitively as singles or doubles.

Even for individuals, playing tennis can include other goals, such as those described earlier.

"Playing Cooperatively"

Proceeding from an overarching approach, there are internal consequences. Partners want to play tennis in pairs or possibly in groups. Generally that doesn't mean competition, but rather merely enjoying playing the game (under some circumstances with different rules).

Specific Goals

- Longer volleys in baseline play.
- Types of play: development of an individually realistic concept, volley at medium height and speed.

- Principal techniques: the basic forehand and backhand strokes, service, and other techniques for variety and as instruction in coordination.
- Agility and stamina on the tennis court.
- If needed, exercises to develop the supporting musculature (trunk).

"Playing Competitively"

Partners want to play opposite one another competitively, in singles or doubles. In singles, they play mainly from the baseline.

Specific Goals

- Tactic: Develop a personal growth approach; that is, use the techniques primarily with regard to their confidence and placing the ball (avoiding mistakes), doubles training.
- Improve basic strokes and become increasingly more confident using spin.
- Work on individual serves with spin.
- Work on topspin-forehand and slice-backhand.
- Teach the return in connection with teaching perception.
- In connection with doubles training, improve volleys and smashes and offer other techniques as desired and for teaching coordination.
- Develop warm-up and agility program almost as ritual.
- Offer stamina training in gamelike conditions.
- Offer tips for supplementing strength training.

General Advice on Methods

Retraining

In improving techniques that have become automatic over long periods of time, the instructor should try—before she recommends the very difficult retraining—to change basic tactical attitudes through appropriate movement tasks. Therefore, before old movement sequences or grips can be corrected, one can convince oneself, for example, to play higher or more slowly. Only when such tasks do not lead to the goal, should pertinent corrections of movement sequences be used.

Correcting

Here, focusing on the main actions via appropriate activities is recommended (see suggestions for correcting movements, p. 34).

Scope in the main actions should be left up to the player, for the most part, and slight shortcomings should be accepted as much as possible. It is important to focus on appropriate rhythm and flow of movement. "Compelling" movement aids, ball machines, and videos can help the learning process.

Organization

Group instruction with three to four adults is a possible organizational format. It is even more important when types of play for developing competency and tactical reasoning should be central in teaching advanced adults. On the other hand, individual instruction is recommended for correcting specific individual problems.

Specific Methodological Problems and Activities

With adult advanced players in recreational tennis, there are often well-established mistakes and problems. This is a result of their history. As a rule, they have been playing for a long time, but have not always played tennis regularly; they have learned a lot themselves and many have been taught by different instructors. As already noted, a series of problems can be solved through a reasonable change of basic tactical attitudes. In this way, time-consuming, minimally motivating, and perhaps unsuccessful retraining can be avoided.

The following problems often surface with adult advanced players.

High Error Rate

Reasons for this are often to be found in a faulty image of the game, which is also promoted by an inappropriate orientation to world-class tennis. Excessive hitting speed, balls hit too closely over the net, and movements that are too "perfect" lead to many unnecessary mistakes.

Solutions
- Players are persuaded to set their own realistic limits; adults often need understandable reasons as motivation and a lot of patience to change.
- Use educational aids: Raise the net, play in the "T" area and half court, and intensify play with forward and backward spin.

Poor Positioning When Hitting the Ball

Reasons for this are insufficient reckoning of the ball and faulty (often "lazy") footwork.

Solutions
- Assign systematically varied (and prearranged) ball tossing (length, direction, height, speed, spin), along with tasks to watch the opponent's racket swing and the trajectory of the ball.
- Insist on continuous, purposeful movement of the feet, even while waiting for the ball.
- Emphasize foot and leg work, train with gymnastic warm-up.
- Always train the technique from the viewpoint of the movement.
- Practice hitting from difficult situations.

Poor Grip

Reasons for this lie in the player's educational history. In the case of poor grips, the position of the racket face, as a rule, is corrected by habituated rotation of the forearm.

Solutions
Retraining takes a long time or is even impossible because of the habituated movement. This should therefore be tried only:
- If the faulty grip makes new learning of techniques difficult (for example, if a backhand grip makes learning a topspin-forehand difficult) and
- If the student is very highly motivated to improve.

As an alternative it is better to:
- Avoid the existing grip and therefore to play more slowly in difficult situations and
- Use techniques that are compatible with your grip (for example, play a slice when the forehand grip is used on the backhand side).

Late Point of Impact

The reason for this can also be a faulty grip. Frequently, however, the reason is to be found in reinforcement of bad timing because of poor reckoning of the ball, in which compensating by using the wrist coupled with uneconomical expenditure of strength, always leads to an excessive number of errors.

Solutions

Try to improve the student's ball reckoning; on the other hand, it still helps to change the timing as follows:
- Hit under easier, prearranged conditions (establish the point of impact).
- Create a pressured situation, such as tossing balls particularly short; insist that the feet remain behind an auxiliary line; make sure that the racket swings out far past the point of impact.
- Change the rhythm between backswing and stroke; backswing during the initial flight phase of the ball— transition to forward swing when the ball hits the ground (mark the landing spot clearly).

Serving Problems

The sources of serving problems mostly result from inaccurate throwing of the ball, difficulties with coordination between throwing and hitting movement,

and a clearly expressed pause in the loop behind the back. They are rooted in the long history of adults and as a rule are very firmly established. Therefore, basic changes in the movement sequence are not recommended.

Solutions

Reduce hitting speeds in training and competition, also with first serves, because coordination problems arise for the most part with high movement speeds.
- Improve throwing accuracy.
- Simplify the situation temporarily (for example, serve from the "T").
- Allow a pause in the backswing movement, but shift it to the end of the reverse swing ("deliberate" pause before the swing into the bend, also for concentrating on throwing).

Weak Volleys

The reason frequently lies in learning the volley late and the resulting negative transfer of the ground strokes (too much backswing movement, no hitting directed forward or backwards).

Solutions

- Create a pressure situation: play the volley with the back to the wall or the "steering wheel volley" (grasp the racket head with both hands like a steering wheel and then play the ball as a volley, see Fig. 26).
- Use "overcorrection": play stopped volleys without backswing and hitting.
- Use the forward and back movement of the slice as an example, perhaps introduce via the slice.
- Play practice matches with "compulsory grips."

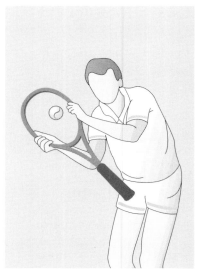

Fig. 26 For the "steering wheel volley," the racket head is held with both hands.

Playing Tennis Outside of Clubs

Until about 40 years ago, tennis was found exclusively in special tennis clubs and in departments of gymnastics and athletic clubs. In almost all midsize and large cities today, there are commercially operated tennis facilities that have their very own clientele. What brings people there, and what are the differences between these facilities and tennis clubs? First, there are latecomers to tennis who are looking for their tennis enjoyment at the commercial facilities. They have hardly any interest in competitive or team tennis. They want to book specific hours and not wait for a court to become available or for a partner. However, they are looking for personal success and gladly recognize the value of the tennis schools, without which commercial tennis facilities normally cannot manage.

The objective is, then, to become competent as quickly as possible so that you can soon make dates with other enthusiasts. Because there is almost always some arrangement for partners at the commercial facility, in contrast to the clubs, this goal can be realized quickly. For the most part, tennis schools offer well-defined courses which, at the lowest level, end with a first competency test after 10 hours of instruction (see "Elementary School," page 56).

The most important thing by far is having fun with movement and play. For this group, the good host is an important resource as a teacher for whom system and methodology are paramount. The specific methodological problems and solutions in this group are described in detail in the chapter entitled "Advanced Adults in Recreational Tennis" and need no further amplification.

The signs of the times indicate clearly, however, that, in the future, the position of the tennis club and commercial establishments will increasingly overlap because recreational sports are gaining ever greater popularity in the tennis club and thus give clubs a chance of surviving in the long term if they also offer the recreational player adequate opportunities and enticements. The commercial establishments could also create "club" structures within their facilities, thus appealing to the minority that likes team competition.

Tennis in Vacation Clubs and Camps, Tennis Weeks and Weekends

In recent years there has been a sharp increase in the number of those who have made their first forays into tennis at vacation clubs or were first confronted with tennis in travel-tennis schools in week-long or weekend tennis courses. There is a pronounced favorable climate for learning in such group courses, which are offered in a relaxed vacation atmosphere and in pleasant company of others interested in tennis. Furthermore, it is much better that the tennis instruction is condensed and success is faster and much more pronounced with 2–6 hours of tennis a day, compared with one lesson per week at home. Meanwhile, these advantages have also induced many tennis instructors to hold tennis camps and tennis weekends with their students in the sunny south, or at least in tennis facilities located outside of their clubs. The successes and recognition for tennis school are often outstanding and indicate new ways for the future.

Diverse programs with various drawing cards that are possible in multifunctional facilities work particularly well. They range from tennis and squash, badminton, golf, fitness, billiards, sauna, and solarium to culinary pleasures and social events such as dancing and other entertainment. These trends are unavoidable commercially and will likely play an important role for clubs, especially if they are to reverse the leveling off of membership, which is felt almost everywhere.

Today, it is possible to play sports—and especially tennis—in many ways. Thus, only in the rarest instances is it absolutely necessary to use narrowly focused sports facilities. It has to be fun and make a difference to people; otherwise, it will not work for much longer. This is true for clubs as well as for all enterprises and institutions having to do with tennis.

Tennis in Schools

According to student surveys, tennis is one of the most popular sports in the school sports curriculum. Unfortunately, there are a number of problems in its practical implementation. Are there qualified instructors (tennis instructors, sports instructors with tennis-specific training)? Where can school tennis be played (gym, paved area, school yard, club)? Is necessary equipment available (rackets, balls, children's tennis nets)? Is a classroom introduction to the game desired and possible, or is there a tendency to offer tennis as a separate sport for interest groups? In addition, are there problems to be dealt with: 1) authorization and liability if there is cooperation with a club, 2) setting goals, 3) structuring the lessons, 4) profitability, etc.

Tennis can be included in school sports in almost all schools if the school administration, faculty, parents, and students desire and support it.

In including tennis in the regular athletic curriculum, it is primarily a matter of introducing the basics of regulation tennis, which can be best developed further in a club, commercial tennis facility, or on the community tennis court. This introduction to tennis includes the objective that the students learn the sport of tennis in the context of school athletic instruction, especially in regard to playing sports in later life. This is especially important for viewing tennis as a life-long sport. Therefore, school tennis first deals with acquiring and improving

Fig. 27 A sample school tennis kit.

agility with rackets and balls as well as the direct experience of understanding the game. As one gets used to playing with racket and ball, playing cooperatively develops. Only with sufficient confidence, which allows a regular playing back and forth, can one move on to simple forms of playing against one another and competition, where the goal becomes making it difficult for the opponent to reach the ball.

Where the institutional, spatial, material, and personal requirements are satisfied—and the teaching plans of the individual districts require it to an increasing level—tennis can be taught as interest-group offerings, project weeks, noncredit courses, volunteer student sports organizations, talent groups shared between school and club, and finally, as part of a scholastic sports competition, such as

"Youth Training for the Olympics." For such situations, no particular pedagogical advice is necessary. The following tips mainly provide pedagogical advice for introducing tennis as a school sport.

Organizational Considerations

Number of Students

When introducing tennis as a team sport, the group should not be larger than 20–25 students, if at all possible. For a planned long-term training program over one or several school years, a group of 12–16 students is best when at least two tennis courts or a double- or triple-court gym is available.

Equipment (Balls, Rackets)

When there is no budget for buying beginners' balls and rackets, you can also use played-out tennis balls and old rackets (to be gripped closer to the head), which you can get from local tennis clubs. Equipment can also be procured through school authorities, sports authorities, parent–teacher associations, or sponsors. We can recommend a sample school tennis kit (see photo, Fig. 27, p. 64) with various children's rackets and balls, which can sometimes be borrowed from local tennis clubs or associations.

Best suited for school tennis are strung rackets with a regular racket head size, a limited weight (app. 10 oz.), and a total length about 24" long with grip sizes between 1 and 3. In addition to the well-known green balls approximately 3 $1/2$" across, we should mention the recently developed beginners' tennis balls. They are lighter and softer, and they travel more slowly and brake more sharply when they bounce. Because of their light weight, these balls are also less of a safety risk and thus help to avoid injuries or damage to property.

Courts and Nets

In all school gymnasiums and on outdoor playgrounds, in addition to the tennis court, there are court markings for other sports (basketball, badminton, handball, volleyball) that can be used as boundaries for tennis minicourts, or they can be made into tennis minicourts using tape or other markings. The courts or areas should be as small as possible at

first; they will expand with the increasing expertise of the students.

In the beginning, makeshift nets or rope, raised benches or a row of crates and even hurdles can serve as a substitute net. Gymnasium walls can be used effectively in tennis instruction, and various types of boundary markers (such as, tape, news-papers, or tires) are especially attractive for many tasks. Schoolyards and all larger flat surfaces in the area around the school offer good conditions for an introduction to tennis, if minicourts can be drawn and cord, rope, or nets can be suspended. Mobile tennis-practice units are ideal, and they can be put up and taken down quickly and easily.

Marking these minicourts incorporates the lines of the regular court and is supplemented with additional sidelines. However, new minicourt markings can be made in a very short time in gymnasiums and on playgrounds, using special line-drawing equipment.

People usually play crosswise on regular tennis courts, and thus, up to three minicourts can be utilized on each half of the court. The net should be approximately $2 1/2$–3 feet high. Movable children's nets in various configurations enrich school tennis, especially in the area of competition when there are similar requirements, such as court, net, and rules. At any rate, the size of the minicourts depends on the situation in the school. Dimensions of 30–35 feet length and 16–19 feet width are recommended.

Recommendations for Teaching and Learning in School Tennis

- First, make the best use of available space. The positioning markers such as lines, rows, alleys, blocks, and circles used in athletic instruction can be used, depending on the size of the group, and combined accordingly.
- Clear announcement of the exercises and a useful selection of exercises guarantee the necessary reliability in instruction.
- The instructor must also orient himself to the capabilities of the weakest students. The best students can also be used as "assistants" and thus, especially encouraged to be useful.
- At the beginning, enough time must be allotted for students to try out the new equipment.
- All exercises should be reviewed several times and also carried out as simple competitions.
- Partners should be rotated often so that both weaker and stronger students experience various play situations.
- From the beginning, all movement and practice assignments must be tried on the forehand and backhand sides, so that especially the backhand side will not be neglected.
- Ball placement always has precedence over speed. The trajectory of the played ball should be steeply curved; it should become flatter as ball placement improves.

- The requirements of balls, rackets, and court increase with the developing capabilities of the students.
- During the lesson, the instructor should participate, whenever the lesson allows it.
- All students should be entrusted with responsible assignments, such as distributing and collecting lent rackets, balls, auxiliary equipment, and the like.
- Circuit formats with various tasks at several successive stations are very well suited to an introduction to tennis in school; people can work intensively in little space.
- An introduction to tennis in the school deals primarily with forehand and backhand. However, volley and serve, as well as the simplest forms of the smash and lob can also be included.
- Simple tactical considerations and assignments should be built into the lesson from the beginning, especially when the students are already dealing with their first competitions on the minicourt.
- Documenting the lesson, which can be done with video, observes the experiences of the instruction for all participants.

Tennis with Advanced Students

Many schools also offer tennis for students who bring with them previous experiences from tennis clubs or commercial facilities. That is mainly the case when the school is participating in competitions such as "Youth Training for the Olympics." As in all similarly designed school competitions for other sports, such a differentiated sports group seldom reflects a genuine school sport subject, since it is supported for the most part by club players. However, in appropriate circumstances and with a good faculty, the foundation can be laid for a close cooperation between school and club, which ultimately benefits all participants. Thus, the school also shows its students that it fosters special extramural activities.

When lessons devoted to sports are allocated, and students have to choose between intro-duction to tennis and continuing their education, the responsible tennis faculty should make a strong case for introductory tennis, in order to give the greatest possible number of students the opportunity for this experience.

Tennis for Persons with Disabilities

Until now, books on tennis instruction have been directed to children, young people, and adults with either normal physical and mental qualities or, in terms of an even higher potential, exceptional talent. What has not been discussed, however, is whether or how people whose space—in the truest sense of the word—in learning and practicing athletic movements are limited because of physical and mental disabilities might learn to play tennis.

This includes the following groups of people:
- The physically disabled,
- People with disabilities involving internal organs (for example, heart-attack patients),
- The visually disabled,
- The hearing disabled,
- The mentally disabled,
- People with impairments due to physical ailments.

For all these groups, also, the positive is that playing sports can have a healthy effect. It lets the disabled student experience his own capability, leads to greater self-confidence, fosters social contacts, and brings hours of pleasure. It has not yet been recognized in many places that tennis can be very important for the disabled. Therefore, it is not a matter of considering tennis as being in competition with other sports.

Rather, the question should be raised, where there is interest and favorable circumstances that are necessary for playing tennis, which specific methodology in tennis instruction should be considered for the disabled. When dealing with the disabled, it is generally true that limitations of physical capacity, level of coordination, motor capability, and mental capacity must be reckoned with. Therefore disabled persons must be protected to a certain extent from excessive demands. In addition, the principle of opportunities for the disabled must be considered. That is, the functional capabilities of the disabled must be used to the limit on the one hand; on the other, the limitations caused by the disability have to be recognized. The methodology must be organized according to this principle (often meaning compromises). This means, for example, with sight-impaired persons that—insofar as the impairment is not too great— special fluorescing balls should be used. For the physically disabled who have, for example, lost an arm, this means that they have to learn to toss the ball from the face of the racket or to toss the ball with the racket hand when serving. It is a basic fact for the disabled that playing in a smaller area is particularly important when learning, and many continue to play on minicourts and with slow balls, even beyond the preliminary stage. Wheelchair tennis, which has grown dramatically in recent years, will be treated in the next section. Wheelchair tennis will clearly illustrate the principle of opportunities for the disabled.

Wheelchair Tennis

The principle of opportunities for the disabled primarily concerns the player's apparent points of view: The wheelchair player hits the ball from a sitting position and on the follow-through is directed by the capabilities (and limitations) of the chair. In addition, there are also essential differences among wheelchair players. These relate mainly to the extent of the disability, particularly to the function of the abdominal musculature. The less the abdominal musculature can be used, the less stable the upper body is and the more the player will have to be supported by the nonhitting hand when hitting. In such cases, it is recommended that the wheelchair player be secured to the back of the wheelchair seat with a belt, so that she can operate the chair more quickly and more skillfully and to attain better reliability and precision while hitting.

Just as footwork is very basic in tennis for "pedestrians," learning driving technique and ongoing training is important for appropriate use of the wheelchair. In wheelchair competitive tennis, the ball is allowed to bounce twice so the wheelchair player can reach it. In principle, the main action of hitting from the wheelchair is not different from general tennis. Certainly, because of her disability, the wheelchair player cannot carry out a series of auxiliary actions that are available to the nondisabled. For example, backswing movement is limited; weight transfer and using the body when hitting are hardly possible; with the backhand stroke, the left hand cannot assist with the backswing movement; and generally, the correct position for the point of impact is very difficult to achieve because there is no footwork. Proceeding from the principles of methods based on hitting the ball, it is recommended that when wheelchair players are introduced to tennis, the situation should be simplified in such a way that movement tasks are assigned from the beginning, providing the opportunity for early successful experiences. One such movement task consists of allowing the tossed ball to be stopped as a volley, where the wheelchair is located face-on or on a slight diagonal and close to the net. The player first grips the racket so that it is shorter. Smaller backswing and hitting movements determine the early concentration on the main action. After that, situations and tasks become increasingly more complex. The racket is gripped increasingly closer to the end; the distance to the net becomes greater; the student performs the tasks at a greater distance from the net; and the ball is returned only after it bounces. That is, after the volley, the player learns the ground stroke with forehand and backhand, and more and more auxiliary actions (changing grip, backswing movement, follow-through movement) are added. Such auxiliary actions should be geared to specific disabilities. Therefore, the following are recommended. Use the backhand grip for low forehand shots and the extreme forehand grip for high ones. The forehand grip is used, for the most part, to serve; if the backhand grip were used, the player would have to stretch so far that he would be in danger of losing his balance. Early on, the student should learn to make a one-eighth turn with the wheelchair before the stroke; after that, the ball is played in such a way that the student first has to move and then brake in order to be able to meet the ball. With forehand strokes, positioning the chair at an angle of approximately 45° to the desired trajectory of the ball is recommended. With backhand strokes, a 90° angle is best, which allows an even more pronounced face-on position with a slice. It is understandable that the various tasks are easier with foam balls or slowly moving beginners' balls. There is a difficult transition from playing to a toss by the tennis instructor or by the nondisabled partner to free play of wheelchair players among themselves. Therefore, the student should try to toss the ball for herself three or four times at first, before trying for a specific point. It is not possible, and not desired by wheelchair players, to set up a higher net so that the sense of play can be better transferred.

Independent of the various types of tasks and forms of training, the primary concern is that wheelchair players have fun with the game, that their self-esteem is raised, and that they have the opportunity to play regularly with nondisabled persons.

The Contact-Oriented Approach

The following section will discuss the contact-oriented method. It should be integrated into the technique-oriented concept presented on page 28. For instruction with beginners, it should be made clear which tasks belong to the individual levels. For instruction with advanced students, the contact-oriented method also gives practical tips, especially for correcting mistakes. Because the contact-oriented method relies on the concept of *functional movement analysis*, this concept will be treated first, so the relationship between the two is clear. In conjunction with this, the methodological steps for learning the most important stroke techniques will be described on the basis of the contact-oriented method.

The Functional Movement Analysis Approach

Tennis Course, Volume 1: Techniques and Tactics is based on the concept of functional movement analysis. It has replaced the earlier concept of <u>sequence analysis</u>. The three successive phases of sequence analysis are equally important. The phases are:

- Backswing movement (as a preparatory phase),
- Hitting movement (with the objective of meeting the ball),
- Follow-through movement (to finish the hitting movement).

The difficulty of this concept, which is oriented to a sequence of movements, is that the importance of the individual components of the movement were not weighted with regard to the movement sequence.

Questions regarding the importance of a particular form of the loop in the backswing phase, the purpose of extending the legs and shifting weight in the hitting phase, or the importance of follow-through in the direction of the shot is for meeting the ball optimally cannot be definitively answered. Even experts frequently do not agree on the importance of the technical elements and refer to the stroke techniques of currently top-ranked players. But even this comparison does not provide an answer. On the other hand, when demonstrating and correcting movements, it should be noted that particular components of the sequence, for example, placement of the racket face when meeting the ball, are considered important elements. Others, such as the height of the backswing movement and the position of the left arm, are considered less important elements. If one wishes to consider the importance of individual phases, one must do more than describe the sequence. For that, it is much more advantageous to choose an analytical approach that focuses on the function of the elements. Therefore, the tennis instructor must use an approach that puts the individual elements of the movement sequence in order, according to the central movement task. This concept is called the Goehner functional movement analysis.

The functional analysis approach can be explained well using the example of the stop volley. The objective of the stop volley is that the ball bounces just behind the net (if possible with reverse spin), so that the opponent can no longer reach the ball. This objective is attained through a short and flat racket movement forward and backward with limited speed during the hitting phase. This action is considered the main action. It fulfills the two functions necessary for the objective; that is, the forward-and-back movement of the racket is intended to create the reverse spin, and the slow movement of the racket and the movement of the wrist on meeting the ball causes the ball to stop.

Further actions, such as short backswing movement, bending the knee closest to the net, shifting the weight, bending the arm are auxiliary actions. They are effectively meant to prepare for and support the main action, but they are not exactly prescribed specifics.

These examples help answer the question, what should be considered as right and wrong when executing the movement? The main action necessary for completing a particular movement task is established. Deviation from this established movement is wrong and must be corrected during instruction. With respect to the auxiliary actions—especially within the backswing and follow-through phase and less within the hitting phase—a large operational space is sometimes allowed for the movement, with its respective advantages and disadvantages, that it is difficult to establish the boundaries.

Auxiliary actions should be considered wrong and should be corrected during instruction, if they do not support the main action effectively, or might influence it negatively or obstruct it. Therefore it is recommended that we speak not only of mistakes, but also of deficiencies because the transition boundary between deficiency and mistake is fluid. Deficiency means that the auxiliary action does not support the main action optimally. Deficiency becomes a mistake when the disadvantages of the auxiliary action outweigh the advantages.

Because the auxiliary actions use relatively large operational space, the individual expression of the movement can best be shown to advantage in them, particularly because the backswing and follow-through phase can be viewed as a time sequence and can make possible the greatest operational space. This particular individual expression of the movement is called movement style and is expressed principally in the spatial and temporal structure of the whole movement. Characteristics of this individual movement dynamic and form include range and rhythm of movement. Therefore, in dealing with correcting a deficit it depends on how significant the disadvantages of the auxiliary action are compared with the advantages and to what extent correction will negatively influence individual style.

Relationship of the Contact-Oriented Method to the Functional Movement Analysis Method

This relationship can be explained by discussing five themes:
- Significance of a methodological approach;
- Fundamentals of the contact-oriented method based on an understanding of functional movement;
- Instructional levels of contact-oriented methods;
- Difference between the contact-oriented method and earlier approaches;
- General methodological fundamentals, concepts, and activities that are also used in the contact-oriented approach.

Significance of a Methodological Approach

It should be emphasized that a methodological approach does not provide any guaranteed formula for teaching tennis techniques. However, it does offer fundamentals (principles) that can help the instructor to examine other instructional methods, to develop her own, and especially to handle problems that arise spontaneously during the lesson in such a way that even the individual qualities of the students can be taken into consideration.

It is essential to understand the principles behind the contact-oriented method, in order to be able to plan the lesson independently and to make movement corrections according to instructional methods.

Fundamentals of the Contact-Oriented Method Based on Understanding Functional Movement

- From the beginning, the main action is central. Tasks are assigned that can be carried out by executing the main action only (playing with minimum swing over short distances). Auxiliary actions follow only after the main action has been learned.
- Among auxiliary actions, those that are closely coordinated with the main action are taught first, followed by those that serve as preparation and support for previously learned auxiliary actions.
- Including auxiliary actions then follows from changes in the situation (for example, greater distance from the net requires more swing, and thus a pronounced backswing).
- Movement sequences are frequently characterized by functional overlapping. In the backswing phase of the basic forehand stroke, the following should be considered: bringing the racket back in an arc, rotating the upper body, lowering the center of gravity, and so on. Instructional activities should remove such overlapping initially. That is, using the backswing as an example, the arm is raised first from the hitting position and later from the ready position with upper-body turning.
- When constructing individual exercises, students often run into problems; what has been learned can become "unlearned." Remediation must be planned; that is, where there is repeated failure that is rooted in faulty execution of movement, a student can go back to previous levels. In order to avoid separating individual movement components from their functional connection, auxiliary actions should not be practiced in an isolated situation.
- Movement tasks are central. The instructor must determine if they are useful from a functional standpoint and must formulate them in such a way that it is clear to the students which tasks are to be completed.
- Students should carry out and recognize the functional significance of the instructional activities for themselves.

Instructional Levels of the Contact-Oriented Method

The individual types of strokes in tennis are taught on several different levels, according to systematically developed basic patterns. The time spent at each level can vary significantly and depends on the success of the student.

Most important for the student is setting the goal of learning to play tennis with and against various partners. It is not enough, and can only be an intermediate step, for a student to be happy playing with the tennis instructor and her ideal toss. Therefore, tossing the ball to the student appropriately for the different levels (stationary ball, throw, toss) becomes very important.

When teaching hitting techniques, there is first a preliminary step in which the student gets ready to play by learning what the instructional objective is, by warm-up and habituation exercises or working out with familiar stroke techniques.

This is followed by four instructional levels:

Level 1

- Learning the main action from the hitting position.
- Permitting small lead-in and backswing movements because they are natural. However, they may not influence the main action.
- Varying the main action through various handicaps, such as playing over obstacles, in different directions with various points of contact.
- Learning the proper grips and points of contact in relationship to the body (height, distance, etc.).
- Playing a stationary ball, or even a ball that has been thrown a very short distance.

Level 2

- Learning auxiliary actions that are closely coordinated with the main action.
- Learning the backswing, hitting, and follow-through movements from the hitting position.
- Returning an approaching, thrown ball, first from the hitting position and then into the hitting position following transition from the face-on position.
- Indicating clearly the shifting of weight when hitting.

- Learning backswing movement in all permissible variations, including straight-line.
- Hitting balls at a slow pace in the "T"-area that were tossed precisely by a partner or the tennis instructor.

Level 3

(The most important level on the road to competency)
- Making a fluid transition from the ready position to the hitting position (exception: serving).
- First, the instructor stands on the student's half of the court and provides the stationary and different types of tossed balls (exceptions: volley and smash).
- Training in perception and judging distance through announced balls tossed by the instructor and balls judged by the student himself.
- Training in footwork and movement coordination.
- Training in hitting rhythm and timing by adjusting movement to the trajectories of balls tossed in various ways.
- Intensifying tossing the ball by moving from the planned to the completely free, unfamiliar situation and through tossing over the net. When the instructor moves from tossing to throwing over the net depends on the capability of the student and the instructor's own expertise.

Unfortunately this third level is often very brief in tennis instruction, because the instructor usually compensates for the deficits of the student by calculating the effect of the ball—in movement coordination and in timing—by adjusting his tossing to the student. Therefore, there is usually a volley over the net, but unfortunately it is only with the instructor. The ball does not arrive so precisely and planned when playing with partners and friends; increasingly successful ball contacts are significantly reduced. The competency of the student is only insufficiently developed.

Level 4

- Learning complete movement from the ready position with ideal and variable tosses (exception: serve). The complexity of the requirements of the situation are fully grasped by increasing the difficulty of the tosses.
- Increasing the distance between the two players. This is best accomplished by having the student remain at her usual distance from the net while the instructor moves back to the baseline one step at a time. In this way, the student can always manage the increasing distances with a small stroke she has learned and has to lengthen this only when she moves back herself.
- Returning tossed balls quickly, also in various directions.
- Returning tossed balls to the target area with spin.
- Executing complex plays according to established tactical patterns.
- Executing complex plays with free choice of tactical solutions.

Difference Between the Contact-Oriented Method and Previous Approaches

Earlier methodological approaches mainly followed the concept of sequence analysis. This meant, for example, that to learn the basic forehand stroke one should first practice the backswing movement separately and then move to the hitting phase (loop). In contrast to this, with the contact-oriented approach, hitting (oriented to the last component of the hitting phase, particularly at the height of the point of contact) is the main action and the most important aspect right from the beginning because it is crucial for the success of the stroke and all other movements are geared toward this main action.

This does not mean that this destroys the totality of a movement. Rather, the situation is simplified in such a way that the technique for executing the movement task can be considered a holistic movement. Examples of such simplified and therefore holistically experienced main actions include simply letting the ball bounce at the net after it has been tossed when one is first learning the volley or returning a tossed ball with a short grip (without any particular emphasis on the backswing movement or other auxiliary actions).

The Contact-Oriented Approach

Partner throws the ball for a serve.

General Methods, Approaches, and Activities and Their Relationship to the Contact-Oriented Method

Of course, important general points of view, such as those presented in this curriculum, also work for the contact-oriented method:

- All the different types of learning can be considered. Although there is cognitive learning, in which the students can experience for themselves the significance of the educational activities, learning by success, learning by model, and learning as internal play are indispensable. The emphasis on the individual types of learning basically depends on the ages of the students, their individual circumstances, and the instruction itself.

- The course of the learning process in three phases (basic coordination, fine coordination, and stabilization of the fine coordination against disruptive influences), therefore, fits the contact-oriented method.

- As mentioned earlier, holistic images also are of primary importance in the contact-oriented method. Here, the inductive method is recommended for younger students, in conjunction with movement tasks, even if the learning progresses more slowly. However, demonstrations and movement instructions can also fulfill the same purpose.

- Basically, the contact-oriented method is allied more closely with the technique-oriented method and less with the play-oriented approach. However, the instructor should not favor only one of these concepts in his teaching.

Use of Methodological Sequences

The sequence in which the individual stroke techniques for the contact-oriented method is presented can be changed, of course, because they do not represent an obligatory sequence.

There are good reasons, of course, for learning the smash before the serve, the stop volley before the volley, the volley before the ground strokes, or the backhand slice before the backhand ground stroke.

The individual stroke techniques are presented on the following pages in a format where: (1) The <u>actions</u> the player must execute in order to be able

to complete the assigned task are described in the left-hand column; (2) <u>explanations</u> (descriptions, tips, methodological aids, graphics) pertaining to execution of the action are in the two right-hand columns; (3) the accompanying illustrations clarify individual explanations and do not present a complete picture of the methodological process. The individual actions are small steps that build on one another and, for teaching and learning hitting technique, do not have to be taught in the sequence presented.

Some actions can also be skipped if the situation allows.

The knowledge of methodological steps offers the tennis instructor the possibility to classify the skills level of the students so that she does not require too little or too much of them. If a student does not succeed at an assigned requirement, he must continue working at the point where he was last successful. He must proceed from that point in smaller steps in order to make progress. The individual success of the student always determines the methodological path he will take with the help of the instructor.

Tossing in order to learn the volley.

Ground Stroke—Forehand and Backhand

Actions	Explanations

Swing the racket back and forth with loosely extended arm to the point of contact.

Student stands in hitting position—sideways-on or slightly open for the forehand and sideways-on, behind the "T" (facing the net), for the backhand—and executes the main action with a ball guide, stationary ball, or gently tossed ball.

Play with the forehand and backhand grips, which can be checked using the stick method. The ball is met sideways-on in front of the hip with a firm grip and open racket face.

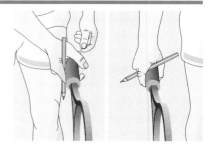

Fig. 28 With the forehand grip, the stick points downward (left).
Fig. 29 With the backhand grip, the stick points forward (right).

Swing the racket back and forth to the point of contact (variation of the main action)

The back-and-forth movement can be shallower or steeper. It is clearly visible when one plays over barriers of various heights or target markers (cords, ropes).

The instructor can guide the student's arm or work with her as in a mirror (timing). After meeting the ball, the racket moves in the direction of the departing ball.

Fig. 30 Instructor guides the student's arm.

Fig. 31 Instructor and student execute the movement mirrorwise.

Backswing, hitting and follow-through movement from the hitting position; shifting of weight

Student lifts hitting arm from below and pulls the racket back and upward in an arc, lets the racket descend in an arc with a fluid transition, and initiates the stroke movement toward the front and upward.

Student executes the upper and lower arcs (loops) by swinging around a racket held out sideways-on by the instructor. Offer variations of the backswing movement if the situation (student) requires them. Show clearly the shifting of weight by stepping from the back to the forward leg (backhand earlier, forehand later) or by two steps from the sideways-on hitting position shifted laterally into the same hitting position, with a right-left step combination with the forehand and a left-right with the backhand. Transition from the face-on position to the net into the hitting position, then backswing, hit, and follow through.

Fig. 32 Student executes the backswing and hitting movement around the instructor's racket.

Actions	Explanations
Backswing, hitting, and follow-through movement from the ready position; shifting of weight	Student stands in ready position a few feet behind the middle of the "T"; gently tossed balls should be hit over the "T". The backswing movement is introduced from the ready position by rotating the upper body with simultaneous turning step with the leg closest to the point of contact; the center of gravity is transferred by bending the knee downward. Execute a dry-run, following the instructor's example or together with the instructor. Simultaneously, the instructor begins to throw the ball and the student begins the backswing movement. Adjust the movement to the flight of the thrown ball. The racket follows the trajectory of the thrown ball; when the ball bounces, the racket is also low and behind. Train for correct timing of the hitting movement through spoken support by the instructor ("backswing and hit," "step to the right and swing," "turn your shoulder"). 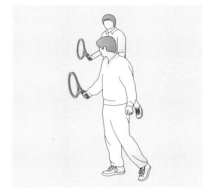 **Fig. 33** Student executes the movements along with the instructor.
Footwork to achieve the correct hitting position from various directions and different distances and hitting the ball	Student stands behind the "T". Instructor tosses the ball from different positions on the same half of the court as the student. First, the toss direction is announced; later, the student must calculate the trajectory herself. This is training for perception, distance judgment, and calculating the correct distance from the point of contact.	Train for footwork with corresponding step combinations and coordination of footwork and hitting technique. Toss the ball over the net, first with precision and announced and then variably, followed by volleying over the net.
Playing from the ready position to various points and from different court positions; increasing distances and meeting the ball at various point-of-contact heights	Student stands behind the "T". The distance between student and instructor is increased as the instructor first moves toward the baseline one step at a time, and then the student also moves back in the direction of the baseline. The ball is tossed with varying speed, height, and spin. The operational space for the movement to be played by the student illustrates his good tactical solutions of individual play situations and allows his	strengths and weaknesses to manifest themselves. Experiences like this help to develop tactical approaches based on the type of student and player. The instructor switches from ball tosser to opponent and, in gamelike forms of training, tests the sureness, precision, and effectiveness of his students' ground strokes, even strokes with different point-of-contact heights.

Service

Actions	Explanations	

Extending the bent hitting arm to the point of contact (main action)

Student stands behind the "T" (short distance from target point); the racket hangs behind his back from a bent hitting arm (upper arm extended to the shoulder axis, elbow angle of less than 90°, hitting hand at head level).

The ball is tossed by the student himself; if the ball cannot be controlled, it may be thrown by the instructor. The hitting arm is extended to the point of contact, and as initial movement for the main action the hitting arm is first bent somewhat more. The ball should be hit over the net in a pronounced arc to the opposing service line area. The grip must be such that the racket face at the point of contact is perpendicular to the take-off direction of the ball.

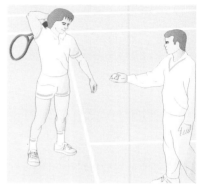

Fig. 34 Instructor tosses the ball to the student for a serve.

The position behind the "T" can be varied. The more to the side it is, the more the backhand grip is necessary. Turning the forearm, which is necessary for meeting the ball with the backhand grip, can be taught separately—meeting the ball with the edge of the racket and then swinging with the racket edge pointing toward the point of contact and hitting with the racket face (by rotating, the forearm just before the point of contact).

The ball is tossed by the student himself or by the instructor.

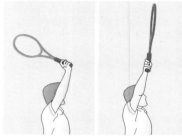

Fig. 35 Ball is met with the edge of the racket.

Fig. 36 Hitting arm is turned outward shortly before the point of contact (pronation).

Backswing, hitting, and follow-through movements; tossing the ball

Tip regarding the similarity of the service movement to a throwing movement: The movement of the hitting arm can also be practiced separately (without throwing the ball). When doing this, it is best if the left arm moves upward as the right arm begins the backswing movement. The length of the backswing movement (long swing to the rear or raising the racket to the side) is adjusted to the capabilities of the student.

Throwing the ball can be practiced separately in this way: the right arm should execute the back-and-forth movement (beginning of the backswing).

Fig. 37 Instructor and student practice throwing the ball with back-and-forth movement of the hitting arm mirrorwise.

Actions	Explanations

Provide aids for judging height and direction of the ball throw. Use mirror-image work with the instructor. For the hitting movement, the instructor can lead the student's arm; the focus is training coordination of the left and right arms.

The hitting position is increasingly moved backward from the "T" to behind the baseline; the ball should be hit securely into the opposite service line area. The stroke movement is done more and more quickly.

To achieve a relaxed hitting movement, the racket can be held at the grip by three fingers.

Fig. 38   Instructor leads the student's arm.

Backswing, hitting, and follow-through movements; tossing the ball; shifting of weight; extending the legs and body

When the ball finally leaves the left hand at head level, body weight must be on the left leg. Offer several different variations for the starting position: weight on the right, on the left, or on both legs; at the end of the backswing movement, the left leg is sharply bent and is extended for the beginning of the hitting movement. When the left leg is extended completely, the racket is still in the deepest point of the loop behind the back. After the contact, the right leg supports the body weight. As the leg is extended very dynamically, the player takes off from his left leg. When doing this, approximately 90% of all players support body weight on the left leg.

Serving to various target points, and from different positions

The service should be hit long and left and right into the service line area. The position behind the baseline can vary between the center mark and sidelines. Speed should gradually be increased.

Serving with Spin

Extending the bent hitting arm upward to the point of contact

The student stands behind the "T"; the racket head hangs behind the back from the bent hitting arm. The racket must be held with a backhand grip. The point of contact for the sliced service is above and to the right, in front of the body. To ascertain the location of the point of contact, a ball guide is used. The ball hangs from the ball guide at the desired point of contact. Extend the arm to the point of contact. The initial movement for the main action (bending the hitting arm) is introduced by bending the knee and bending the upper body backwards (especially for a twist service).

To attain the side spin during the sliced service, face the right net post during the hitting movement; to attain the forward spin during the twist service, swing the racket almost parallel to the net to the right, above. Serves are played with limited speed but with noticeable spin.

With the twist service, the trajectory of the ball should be particularly high over the net.

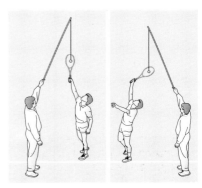

Fig. 39   Point of contact for the sliced service is located to the right and above, in front of the body (right).

Fig. 40   Point of contact for the twist service is located above, behind the head, somewhat lower than with the slice (left).

Actions	Explanations	
	Serving over a cord that has been stretched over the net at an appropriate height. The hitting position is gradually moved back from the "T" to behind the baseline.	
Backswing, hitting, and follow-through movement; tossing the ball; shifting of weight; extending the legs and body	With the twist service, the sideways-on hitting position is especially pronounced. It is also helpful here on the backswing to swing the hitting arm higher than with a straight serve and sliced serve (above shoulder level) because it is easier to achieve the necessary more pronounced arch and to get ready for the direction of the stroke. After the ball is hit, the right leg is extended to the side and backward in order to maintain balance. Special attention should be paid to support the hitting movement by eliminating the arch (twist) and rotating the upper body in the direction of the stroke (slice).	 **Fig. 41** Initial movement with back tilt of the upper body and bending of knee (left). **Fig. 42** After meeting the ball, the right leg is extended backward.
Serving to various target points, and from different positions	The twist service should be played mainly from the left on the opponent's backhand side; the trajectory should be relatively high. The sliced service should be played from	the right on the opponent's forehand side; the position behind the baseline varies between the center mark and the sideline.

Smash

Extending the bent hitting arm to the point of contact (main action)	Student stands close to the net with hitting arm bent (upper arm parallel to the ground and forearm raised vertically), racket tip points downward. Hint on grip: Instructor tosses the ball from a short distance away; the hitting arm is extended to the point of contact. As initial movement of the main action, the hitting arm is somewhat more sharply bent. The ball should be met with extended arm and played distinctly in front of the "T". **Fig. 43** Hitting position for smash, close to the net.	
Extending the bent hitting arm upward to various points of contact (variation of the main action)	The ball is tossed at various heights and should be hit with extended arm; the hitting movement becomes increasingly steeper forward and upward. The ball should be met at various heights and different distances from the body.	 **Fig. 44** The hitting arm is extended (well in front of the body) to the point of contact.

Actions	Explanations
Backswing, hitting, and follow-through movement from the hitting position; shifting of weight	Student stands in sideways-on hitting position near the net and holds the racket in front of his body. In the starting position, the racket can also rest on end on the edge of the net at the beginning in order to teach the different backswing movement as compared with the serve (bring the racket up high to the back and above in front of the right side of the body). Simultaneous raising of the left arm leads to a tipping of the shoulder, which is an important preparation for the hitting movement. During the hitting movement, the body weight is shifted from the right to the left leg.

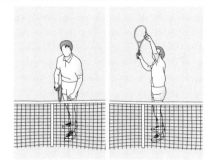

Fig. 45 Racket rests on the edge of the net.

Fig. 46 Racket tip and left arm indicating the intended point of contact.

Pay attention to the relationship between flow of movement and timing.

Hit to various targeted points (left and right) by adjusting the sideways-on hitting position relative to the target direction. Transition from the face-on position to the sideways-on hitting position; then backswing, hit, and follow through.

| **From the ready position, footwork to attain the optimum position under the expected point of contact with backswing, hitting, and follow-through movement; shift in weight** | Tossing and playing the ball are varied (left and right, shorter and longer). Student turns from the ready position to the hitting position and adjusts to the trajectory with appropriate footwork and by maintaining the sideways-on position. |

Fig. 47 Assuming the hitting position (left).

Fig. 48 Ball is caught with the arm extended vertically upward (right).

With small steps forward and backward (in the direction of the singles lines and adjusting steps toward and away from the net, student moves to the various court positions and smashes from there, also at different speeds and to various target points. To check the correct position under the point of contact, the ball can also be caught with the extended left hand.

| **Hitting from the ready position to various target points, and when the ball is tossed from a greater distance** | Student stands approximately 6 feet from the net in the ready position. Instructor varies the tosses in length, height, and direction and throws from increasingly greater distances. |

Fig. 49 Ball is smashed not directly, but after it bounces.

Student adjusts to the different trajectories of the ball through appropriate footwork (side steps, crossover steps, etc.), smashes to various target points and with varied speed.

When tossed very high, the ball is difficult to smash because it falls almost vertically and calculating the point of contact requires a lot of experience. In these exercises, the ball can be smashed only after it bounces on the ground.

On moving to the hitting position, the left arm and racket are raised in advance. Speed and direction of the smash stroke follow tactical requirements; later, allow student to decide type of play.

Jump Smash

Actions	Explanations

Jumping from right leg and extending the bent hitting arm to the point of contact (main action); landing on the left leg

Student stands approximately 3 feet from the net in sideways-on hitting position, extended left arm points to the intended point of contact; the hitting arm is bent, and racket tip points backward. The tossed ball should be hit in mid-jump.

The ball must be thrown in such a way that the student has to jump backward and upward to the intended point of contact because otherwise the "scissors-legs" cannot be taught. While landing on the left leg, the right leg points forward and to the right. The footwork can also be practiced without hitting movement or as a practice stroke movement without a ball.

Fig. 50 Student jumps upward to the rear (left).
Fig. 51 During the landing on the left leg, the right leg points forward (right).

Backswing, hitting, and follow-through movement from the hitting position

Student stands in the sideways-on hitting position close to the net and holds the racket in front of her body.

The backswing movement can be varied. It is easier for some students to support the take-off by executing the backswing movement with a lower back-and-forth movement (as with the serve); others make

out better with the backswing in front of the body. Transition from the face-on position to the net to the sideways-on hitting position and then backswing, jump, hit, follow-through, and land. The focus is on teaching the coordination of the jump and hitting movement.

From the ready position, footwork to achieve the appropriate hitting position and smashing from the jump

Instructor varies the tosses. For the backswing, these things happen simultaneously: place right leg behind, rotate the body to the right into the sideways-on position to the net, raise both arms. Teach the appropriate footwork for the desired hitting position. Student must adjust steps or move forward in the direction of the baseline.

Slam to various target points and adjust the hitting speed to the position of the point of impact (very far behind the point of contact requires a slow hitting movement).

Fig. 52 Preparation (backswing) for a smash from a jump.

Fig. 53 Footwork (left foot in front of the right foot: crossover in front) for the appropriate hitting position.

Volley—Forehand and Backhand

Actions	Explanations

Extending the bent hitting arm slightly back and forth to the point of contact (main action)

For the forehand volley, the student stands in a slightly open hitting position; for a backhand volley, she stands close to the net in the sideways-on hitting position. The instructor throws the ball from a short distance. Use forward grip for the forehand volley and the backhand grip for backhand volley. The ball should be met directly in front of the body and should be returned gently to the instructor. When extending the arm, the raised arm should be held as steady as possible. The racket face is somewhat open.

Fig. 54 Instructor throws the ball for a forehand volley.

Extending the bent hitting arm to the point of contact (variation of main action)

The student should get the feel of the relationship between the variation of the main action and the take-off height and distance of the ball, as well as the strength of the spin. The racket head can be brought to the point of contact more or less steeply back and forth or parallel with the ground. The position of the racket face at the point of contact can vary from perpendicular to wide open.

Backswing, hitting, and follow-through movements from the hitting position; shifting of weight

Student stands in the sideways-on hitting position approximately 6 feet from the net and holds the racket in front of the body (racket head at head level). Instructor throws the ball from various distances; the student adjusts to the backswing and hitting movement in timing and position to the trajectory and its target point. The hitting movement is supported by a weight shift downward toward the front.

To coordinate the shifting of weight and the hitting movement, the leg closest to the net is raised simultaneously with the backswing movement of the arm; when meeting the ball, it is again lowered while bending the knee in the direction of the net. To check the stroke direction, the follow-through is paused just after the point of contact; after the stroke, the racket is almost parallel to the net.

Fig. 55 The leg closest to the net is raised with the backswing movement (left).

Fig. 56 The leg closest to the net is lowered when meeting the ball (step).

Backswing, hitting, and follow-through movements from the ready position; shifting of weight

Student stands in ready position approximately 6 feet from the net. When the ball is thrown, it is played thus: turn and step with the leg closest to the point of contact, keep the other leg in the original position, rotate the upper body, and raise the forearm (hitting arm) to the rear and above. The hitting movement is supported by shifting one's weight (step in the direction of the point of contact).
Possible aids: Instructor offers verbal support for the timing sequence of the movement; instructor presents visual orientation for the

Actions	Explanations

| | direction of the hitting movement (for example, the edge of the net); instructor leads the student's arm; during the backswing in front of the body for a forehand volley, student holds the upper part of the hitting arm with the back of the left hand to guide the backswing movement. On the backswing for the backhand volley, the left hand pulls the racket close to the body.

A ball machine helps to provide precise play. |  |

Fig. 57   Using the left hand under the right upper arm to control the breadth of the backswing movement.

Footwork to achieve the correct hitting position from various directions and different distances as well as hitting the ball

Play the volley from the forward position after an attack shot or after a serve.

Play the volley from a move sideways, hitting the ball while jumping.

A ball machine helps to provide precise play

Playing from the ready position to various target points and from various court positions; meeting the ball at different point-of-contact heights

Throw the ball from various distances and directions and with variations in height and speed. The ball is met above or below net height. The ball is played to various target points corresponding to the hitting position and in keeping with the correct execution of the tactical task.

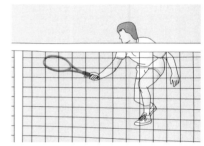

Fig. 58   Meeting the forehand volley below net height.

Lob—Forehand and Backhand

Swinging the racket steeply back and forth to point of contact with open racket face (main action)

Student stands in the hitting position behind the "T". The racket is lowered to the ground next to the rear leg. Instructor stands at the net and throws the balls gently to the student's forehand and backhand. Student plays high over the racket held vertically upward by the instructor; use of forehand and backhand grips on corresponding sides. Student stands behind the "T" and returns the balls gently tossed by the instructor.

As an orientation aid, a cord can be suspended at various points above the net; the higher the lob, the more the racket face has to be opened by turning the forearm.

Frequently switch between ground stroke and lob to get a feeling for the difference and development of the lob movement.

Actions	Explanations	
Backswing, hitting, and follow-through movement from the hitting position; shifting of weight	Student stands in the hitting position behind the "T". Return of the racket in a loop with fluid transition to the hitting movement forward and upward. The upper arc of the backswing movement can be more or less steep; with the lob, a pronounced lower arc in the loop with deep bending of the knee being important. Straight-line backswing backward and downward can be substituted as a variation if the student has problems getting under the subsequent point of contact with the arched backswing movement.	With slamming, there is a pronounced forward and upward extension of the knee and a pronounced stretch with long follow-through in the direction of the departing ball. In order to bring the student's center of gravity down, the instructor's throws must be short and shallow. Transition from the face-on position into the hitting position and then backswing, hit, and follow through.
Backswing, hitting, and follow-through movement from the ready position; shifting of weight	Student stands in the ready position in the center, behind the "T". Instructor throws the ball from a position near the net. The transition from the ready position to the hitting position is accompanied by rotating the upper body with a simultaneous turning step with the leg nearest the point of	contact and is completed by a subsequent step of the other foot. Dry movement following the instructor's example to get the feel of the typical lob-backswing movement by swinging the racket around a large, soft ball, such as a waterball.
Footwork to attain the correct hitting position from various directions and different distances; hitting the ball	From the "T", the student returns as lobs balls that have been played in different ways by the instructor. At first, the instructor can compensate for all the student's mistakes in judging distance and timing through compensatory play. If the hitting distance is too limited, the ball should be tossed farther away from the student and vice versa. If the hitting movement is too fast, the instructor tries to get more order in	the hitting movement through slow, gentle tossing. In all instances, vocal support by the instructor can have a retarding or accelerating effect on the student's movements. With variable tosses, the student herself tries to adjust her distance and timing to the situation.
Playing from the ready position to various target points and from various court positions; lobbing from matchlike playing situations	Play the ball from different distances and directions with variations in height, speed, and spin. Student plays the balls to various target points in keeping with his hitting position and appropriate for the proper result for the tactical task at hand. High lobs are played in pressing situations to the opponent's baseline in order to gain time for assuming the next good court position. If the opponent plays too short, a lob can also be played offensively, relatively shallow, so that the opponent can no longer run to the ball from the net position.	The lob can also be used as return against an opposing server storming the net. The instructor plays the role of the opponent with the student and runs through all play situations in which the lob can be used to advantage.

Topspin—Forehand and Backhand

Actions	Explanations

Swing the racket back and forth fast and steeply to the point of contact (main action)

Student stands in open (forehand) or sideways-on (backhand) hitting position behind the "T"; the instructor throws the ball with a high trajectory from a short distance. Use the forehand grip for a forehand topspin and the backhand grip for a backhand topspin.

During the back-and-forth movement, the racket face remains vertical. Catch a tennis ball between the racket face and the net; roll the ball over the net by moving the racket upward (becoming aware of the direction of the main action). At the beginning, the played balls should travel at least 6 feet above the height of the net (suspend a cord above the edge of the net).

Fig. 59   Ball is caught between the racket face and edge of net.

Backswing, hitting, and follow-through movement from the hitting position; shifting of weight

Student stands behind the "T" and hits the gently thrown balls in a downward trajectory, using a jump.

Play into designated areas in front of the opposite "T" and determine the bounce distance of the balls (effect of spin), that is, which combination provides the greatest distance between the first and second bounce of the ball.

Weight is shifted from the back to front leg on the backhand side on the backswing and on the forehand side when swinging through on the topspin strokes. Transition from the face-on position to the net into the hitting position and then backswing, hit, and follow through.

Backswing, hitting, and follow-through movement from the ready position; shifting of weight

Student stands in ready position behind the center of the "T" and contacts the gently thrown balls between knee and hip level.

Playing the ball: a turning step with the leg closer to the point of contact, rotating the upper body and raising the hitting arm; for the forehand topspin, many students find it easier to initiate the backswing movement by raising the elbow back and upward.

The backswing movement begins delayed, approximately with the bounce of the tossed ball. The hitting movement is initiated and supported by the sharp extension of the knee, which can lead to raising the leg up as the racket follows through.

Control of the final position after topspin strokes: open forehand position, sideways-on backhand position, racket above head level.

Footwork to attain the proper hitting position from various directions and different distances and hitting the ball

Playing the topspin strokes with motion along the "T" to the left and right, forward or backward.

Using topspin strokes with lower and higher points of contact; coaching distance judgment with variable tosses of the ball.

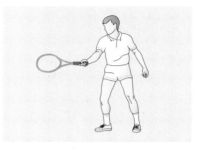

Fig. 60   Point of contact of topspin at hip level.

Fig. 61   Topspin point of contact at shoulder level.

Actions	Explanations
Playing to various target points and from various court positions; meeting the ball at different points of contact (high, low, forward, back)	Task: Using the surrounding court fence, determine which topspin strokes directly in front of the baseline have the highest contact point on the surrounding court fence (wall). Recognize the best amount of spin and pressure in topspin strokes.

The ball is played from appropriate distances and directions with variations in height, speed, and spin. The target areas involved are designated by tactical considerations.

Student plays topspin strokes at various distances from the net, also with appropriate footwork. All topspin strokes are played through for their possible use in offensive and defensive completion.

Exploring tactical variations with regard to the opponent's behavior, such as moving up to the net (topspin short crosscourt or topspin lob, etc.).

The student's strengths and weaknesses that become visible in this way will suggest tactical approaches she can use in competition.

The instructor takes on the role of the opponent and tests and monitors the effectiveness of his student's topspin strokes in competition and matchlike types of competitive play. |

Slice—Forehand and Backhand

Swinging the racket from back and above shallowly to the front and down to the point of contact (main action)

Student stands behind the "T" in the sideways-on hitting position; the instructor throws the ball from the net. Use forehand grip for forehand slice and backhand grip for backhand slice. The ball should be returned to the instructor in a gentle arc.

Before beginning the main action, the handle points toward the net for the forehand slice and toward the left-hand net post for the backhand slice.

Fig. 62 For the forehand slice, the handle points to the net or in the direction of the stroke at the beginning of the main action.

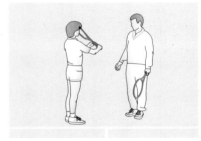

Fig. 63 For the backhand slice, the handle points to the left net post or decidedly leftward toward the stroke direction at the beginning of the main action.

Swinging the racket from back and above to the front down to points of contact at various heights and various distances from the body (variation of the main action)

Student should experience the relationship between a variation of the main action and resulting trajectories and distances as well as the strength of the spin. The main action is sometimes shallower and sometimes steeper back and forth. The position of the racket face at the point of contact varies from almost vertical to quite open. A low point of contact located far in front of the body requires a wide hitting position and is particularly good for learning the slice.

Fig. 64 Wide hitting position for a slice with a low point of contact.

Use of Methodological Sequences

Actions	Explanations
Backswing, hitting, and follow-through movement from the hitting position; shifting of weight	Student stands in the hitting position behind the "T" or farther from the net (auxiliary between "T" and baseline) and holds the racket in front of the body. Instructor throws from the net. Student adjusts her backswing and hitting movement to the approaching ball. Toss variations: the instructor throws the ball overhand so that the student can meet the ball in a rising arc. Support the movement by speaking; the hitting movement is supported by a marked shifting of weight forward and downward. Provide visual orientation for the direction of the hitting movement (marking on the ground) and the end of the follow-through movement (head of the ball tosser). Transition from the face-on position to the hitting position; then backswing, hit, and follow through.
Backswing, hitting, and follow-through movement from the ready position; shifting of weight	Student stands in the ready position behind the "T"; instructor throws from the net. On the backswing there is a rotation of the upper body, turning steps as the racket is simultaneously brought back and upward. Support for the control of the backswing distance on the backhand slice; the racket head touches the neck. To execute a good shifting of weight, use a wide hitting position and follow through far to the front. 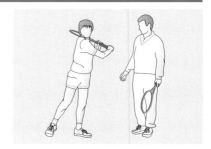 **Fig. 65** Upper body rotation and backswing for the backhand slice.
Footwork to attain the correct hitting position from various directions and different distances when hitting the ball	Student stands in the ready position behind the "T"; instructor tosses balls to different positions. Student moves to the appropriate position and hits the ball with a slice at the correct distance from the point of contact. Coach coordination of footwork and hitting movement. Hit the slice at various points of contact heights.
Playing from the ready position to various target points and from various court positions; meeting the ball at different points of contact	Tossing the ball from various distances with variation in height, length, sideways direction, and speed. Student plays the slice from various court positions and from greater distances. The ball should be met in both a rising and descending arc and should be played tactically correctly, appropriate to the situation (court position, incoming ball, position of opponent).

Stop—Forehand and Backhand

Actions	Explanations

Moving the racket from behind and up to downward to the front to the point of contact (main action)

Student stands approximately 9 feet from the net in the sideways-on hitting position. Instructor throws the ball from the net.

The ball can also be thrown overhand (see ball tossing on page 35) so that the student can meet it more easily in its rising arc.

The hitting movement is relatively short; the ball is met with an open racket face and should fall just behind the net with backward spin after a high trajectory.

The ball can be played down the line or crosscourt over the net; the crosscourt direction makes it easier for the student to play the ball just behind the net.

Fig. 66 The ball is thrown overhand.

Backswing, hitting, and follow-through movement from the hitting position; shifting of weight

Student stands approximately 12 feet from the net in the hitting position and holds the racket in front of his body. On the toss, the student executes the backswing movement in a shallow overhead arc. During the hitting movement (forehand stop), the left leg takes a step in the direction of the point of contact. Movement of the arms (first upward and then outward) is supported by the bent left knee).

The student should have acquired the feel of rotating the racket face around the ball.

To get a feel for the limited range of movement, the movement can be practiced while standing close to a fence. Student plays the stop just over a racket that a partner holds approximately 5 feet high and approximately 4 feet from the net; this indicates where the culmination point of the trajectory has to be with the stop so that the ball bounces just behind the net.

Fig. 67 Getting a feel for the limited range of movement by practicing the movement close to a fence.

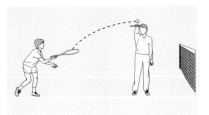

Fig. 68 The stop is executed just over a racket held by the partner, indicating to the

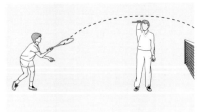

student that the culmination point of the trajectory is directly in front of the net.

Actions	Explanations	
Backswing, hitting, and follow-through movement from the ready position; shifting of weight	Student stands behind the "T" in the ready position. A closed racket face during the backswing makes it easier for the student to execute the hitting and follow-through movements. Instructor throws first from the net and then moves farther and farther back to the baseline. Student must adjust the swing of her movement to the faster approaching balls (swing becomes more limited).	Student stands behind the "T" and holds the racket with slightly open face in the expected point of contact. Instructor throws from the baseline. Student lets the ball bounce from the racket in an ascending arc and checks how far the ball travels in the direction of the net. It is easy to find out how much (or how little) movement (swing) of the racket is required at the point of contact to get the ball to travel just over the net.
Footwork to attain the correct hitting position from various directions and different distances when hitting the ball	Student stands behind the "T" in the ready position. Instructor first throws from the net and later from the baseline, using a variety of tosses (left, right, short, flat, high, and with spin).	Student tries to achieve the correct distance from the point of contact by running to it or backing off and to meet the ball in an ascending arc. The swing of the hitting movement must be adjusted to the distance from the target.

Half-Volley—Forehand and Backhand

| Swing the racket with extended arm parallel to the ground to the point of contact (main action) | Student stands at the "T" in the hitting position. The racket head is located just above the ground approximately 4 feet behind the point of contact for a half-volley. The point of contact is established just above the "T" using a ball guide. The racket is moved forward from the resting position (lower edge of the racket on the ground) to the point of contact. Use grips as with the forehand and backhand ground strokes.

Aids for correct timing: practice soccer drop-kicks with tennis balls. After success with drop-kicks, try playing a half-volley just with the hand or using a choked up tennis racket; bouncing the ball on the ground and hitting it with the racket should then follow as soon as possible.

The instructor can lead the movement (hitting hand). She throws the ball or has a student throw. To learn the rhythm (ball bounce, point of contact), the student places his racket at the point of impact. The ball is thrown indirectly toward the racket face. |

Fig. 69   Racket face is slightly open at the point of contact.

Fig. 70   Instructor throws the ball indirectly toward the racket face resting vertically on the ground. |
| Swing the racket forward and upward to the point of contact (variation of main action) | Half-volley with gentle face-on ball; throw with the ball bouncing at a designated spot ("T", line, etc.). | Play over the net in various directions (targets, obstacles, visors, etc.). Learn the relationship of hitting position and flight direction of the ball. |

Actions	Explanations
Backswing, hitting, and follow-through movement from the hitting position; shifting of weight	Student stands in the hitting position behind the "T"; instructor throws the balls in such a way that they can be met on the "T" approximately 3 feet from the center. The backswing is performed in a shortened flat upper arc. The main feature should be an acceleration of the flat hitting movement and meeting the ball soon after the bounce. There is always a weight shift onto the deeply bent leading leg because the ball should be met at the low center of gravity at the level of the leading leg. Transition from the face-on position to the net to the hitting position; then backswing, hit, and follow through.

Fig. 71 The hitting movement continues just above the ground to the point of contact.

Actions	Explanations	
Backswing, hitting, and follow-through movement from the ready position; shifting of weight	Student stands in the ready position approximately 3 feet behind the "T". When the ball is thrown, use a turning step with the leg closest to the point of contact, rotating the upper body and the hitting arm making a horizontal arc to the rear. Verbal support of the temporal movement sequence.	Visual orientation aids for the location of the point of contact and for the direction of the hitting movement (court lines and additional markings). The ball can be tossed in a high arc (slower) or flat (low bounce). The instructor should pay attention to which efforts best help the student.
Footwork to achieve the correct hitting position from different directions and various distances when hitting the ball	Student's starting position is approximately 3 feet behind the "T". Instructor throws slow and high into various areas of play in order to give the student	enough preparation for the half-volleys. When sufficient confidence has developed, the student decides which balls he will play as ground strokes and which as half-volleys.
Playing to various target points and from various court positions; playing the half-volley in matchlike situations	Initially, student stands in the ready position at first behind the "T" and later behind the baseline center. The instructor varies the height, speed, and spin of the tossed balls. Play the half-volley down the line and crosscourt to the opposing baseline and also	short crosscourt (with topspin) as a pass. Student must learn and understand that half-volleys can be used not just in emergency situations but also, purposely, as surprise shots for the offense (with short shots from the opponent) and as passes.

Skills Development: A Training Foundation

Individual sports can be differentiated not only because they express different skill sets but also because they differ by the expressions of skills. For example, the significant factors in rowing are not the same as in floor exercises, and the stamina demands for tennis, for example, are not the same as for table tennis. By analyzing each sport, it is possible to determine the importance and hierarchy of individual factors, which can in turn be used for identifying and developing talent, as well as for planning and scheduling training.

When analyzing tennis, the most interesting aspects are those necessary skills and their interconnections, which are important for best dealing with the movement task and for achieving the individual's best capabilities (Fig. 72).

Fig. 72 Overview of factors influencing athletic capability.

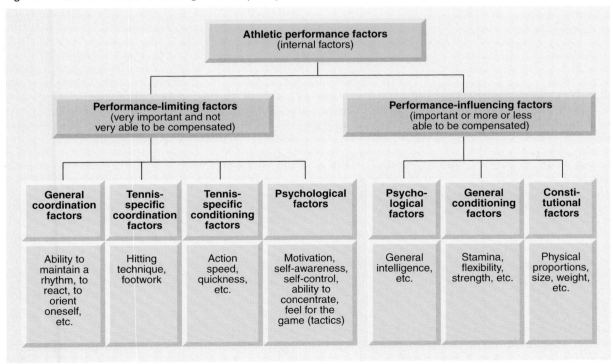

Constitutional (anthropometric and functional) factors such as body size, weight, proportion, leverage, and muscle mass play an increasingly important role in tennis. There are also coordination factors specific to tennis, such as stroke technique and footwork; conditioning factors such as strength, stamina, and speed; and psychological factors such as will, level of commitment, toughness, ability to concentrate, self-discipline, anticipation, and a sense of the game. Some of these factors are also closely linked to the concept of tactics. Besides these factors, which depend on the individual, other external factors (for example, influence of environment, such as family, friends, school, profession, trainer, training opportunities, and travel) are also important. All these factors combined determine—although to different extents—the athletic capacity of the player.

The following tennis-specific identification and categorization of individual factors is the result of a comprehensive analysis of the sport. Research focused on three areas:

- Functionally anatomical and bio-mechanical data, as well as data on conditioning and coordination via a general study of tennis techniques.
- Data on conditioning and coordination via a careful analysis of the competitive situation.
- Data dealing with movement technique and anthropometrics via the analysis of world-class players.

In the following, some motor-skills factors dealing with conditioning are presented as examples from

this research. The psychological principles are covered beginning on page 181 .

Physical and Biomechanical Analysis of Tennis Techniques

A particularly high level of coordination and dexterity is necessary for the following reasons:

- The stroke sequence interval to the point of contact is approximately 0.5–0.9 seconds, with some variation among different types of strokes.
- The contact interval of the ball on the racket strings is 0.003–0.005 seconds, with a maximum contact area of 5 in.
- The racket speed when hitting the ball varies between 0 and 75 mph.
- On baseline shots, the ball reaches speeds of up to 45 mph and on serves sometimes more than 75 mph.
- The number of ball rotations, a maximum of approximately 150 rotations per second, is very high.

Coordination can best be trained in children and young teenagers and, therefore, must be made a part of the training for young people. The intended high ball speed, primarily with serves and hard shots, requires the ability to achieve a high acceleration of the racket, which requires good coordination as well as action, speed, and agility. The high impact of the ball on the racket and the very short total contact

time for ball and racket put great stress in the forearm. Therefore, agility and enduring elasticity are necessary. Therefore, a high value must be placed on specialized and age-specific strength training in the training process.

The average 1- to 1.5-second flight times for the ball on baseline strokes and the average ball speeds indicate that there is enough time to prepare for the stroke and that the actual backswing movement, in relation to the stroke sequence time, can begin relatively late. The speed of the ball in a serve (more than 75 mph) and passes (up to 45 mph) require a good ability to anticipate as well as a very good reaction time and a great speed and agility. These findings lead to the conclusion that coordination that is linked to a given situation must be trained on a regular basis.

Analysis of the Competitive Situation

The pressure in a tennis match occurs at intervals:

- The relationship of average playing time (periods in which the ball is in play) to total duration of the match is approximately 1:2 to 1:5, depending on the court surface.
- A volley on clay courts lasts an average of 8 seconds; on grass and fast paved courts, it is much shorter, sometimes only 2–3 seconds; the subsequent pause lasts an average of approximately 20 seconds.

Generally, this allows enough time for recuperation, even between volleys. The average running distance of 1700 yards per match for two sets indicates a medium demand of stamina. The anaerobic condition during the volley prevails.

The longer straight sprint distance in a tennis match rarely exceeds 14 m. The average distance is 4 m. Thus, a tennis player needs a different type of speed from, for example, a 100- or 200-m sprinter.

Tennis-specific speed is characterized by:

- Starting power, agility, (explosion power, concentrated muscle work);
- Ability to accelerate, accelerating muscle power, agility (elasticity);
- Movement execution, speed of movement and action;
- Braking power before a change in direction (eccentric muscle work).

The most important type of speed is burst speed. It helps with short distances. Starting power can be partially compensated for by a good ability to anticipate and a superior reaction time; this often provides enough time to execute the stroke. Concerning the distribution of strokes used, match analyses (world-class men) for clay courts show on average:

Ground strokes   approximately 55%
Returns   approximately 15%
Service   approximately 23%
Volley   approximately 4%
Other strokes   approximately 3%

On hard courts, astro-turf, and especially grass, the percent distribution changes, and service, return and volley gain dominance. As an example for this, you can look at the various percent distributions for Boris Becker (Fig. 73).

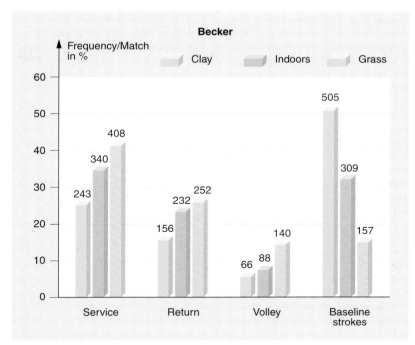

Fig. 73   Average frequency of the various stroke categories in relationship to surface material for Boris Becker. (The statistical mean value refers to the clay court results.)

Aspects of Physiological Potential

Effective Period of Stress

The effective (real) playing time in tennis competition is, on average, approximately 20–25% of the total playing time. The playing time per volley on clay courts averages 7–10 seconds, with a frequency peak between 5 and 7 seconds.

The faster and shallower the ball bounces, the shorter the volley. On grass courts and fast indoor surfaces, the average playing time per volley is approximately 30–50% lower than on clay courts. In individual cases—especially when particular types of players meet—extremes occur, as in 1991 in both final games in Wimbledon between Stich and Becker on the one hand and in Paris between Agassi and Courier on the other. In Wimbledon on grass, the effective playing time took 3:42 minutes per hour and a volley lasted 2.65 seconds on average. In Paris, on clay, the effective playing time was 14:56 minutes per hour and a volley lasted 10 seconds on average.

Because the volley lasts such a short time and because of the submaximal muscular demands with longer volleys, the anaerobic metabolism (via glycolysis) is rarely considered, so that the lactic acid content and increase in the muscles normally remains limited. The lactic acid level (lactate) in arterial blood is generally 2–3 mmol/l and increases briefly to 4 mmol/l only in exceptional situations.

The length of the individual brief pauses between the volleys (max. 25 seconds according to competition rules) is normally enough to completely rebuild the potential of energy-rich phosphates (adenosine triphosphate and creatin phosphate) in the muscles via aerobic metabolic processes. Because of the long total playing time, which can last more than 3 hours when playing two sets and for effective increase of the range of stress in tennis training, one needs a solid basic stamina. A high specific capacity for stamina has the additional advantage that in high-intensity stress phases (level and intensity of stimulus), lactate production (formation of lactic acid) remains limited, and in the volley phase there can be a rapid regeneration of energy-rich phosphates. This prevents a lactic acid build-up in the muscles, so that the optimum coordination capability and agility remains throughout the total competition period. This also holds true for training because quality and quantity greatly influence performance ability in competition.

Heart Rate

The average heart rate of tennis players of various ages and performance categories during competition is between 140 and 150 beats per minute. With women, the average pulse rate is approximately 5–10 beats per minute higher. The irregular fluctuations of heart rate document the continuously changing stimulus level, duration, and intensity. Corresponding to intermittent stress levels in tennis, heart rates that sometimes equal the individual maximum are reached (for example, 170–190 beats per minute for adults and more than 200 beats per minute for children). The increase in heart rate is partially the expression of an elevated physical demand. Immediately before a service or before a decisive phase (break point/set point), we see short-term increases in heart rate of 10–30 beats per minute.

Circulatory System

Average values of heart rate, blood pressure, blood lactate, and actual playing time point to a pressure intensity of approximately 45–60% of the maximum capacity of the circulatory system during a tennis competition. Strong baseline players, on average, have greater demands so that they reach more quickly the level of intensity desired for effective fitness training, which is the maximum circulatory capacity at approximately 60–75%.

An increase of the stimulus on the circulatory system results in achieving the optimal level of intensity for improving the stamina capacity. This also engenders excessive demands on stress whose extent is difficult to predict and control. This fluctuation, which is especially evident in tennis, between positive effects on health and productivity on the one hand, and the possibility of damage, particularly for the heart and vascular system on the other, is particularly difficult for older players with limited training and for all people with (to some extent and not yet diagnosed) metabolic and circulatory illnesses (for example, diabetes, high blood pressure, advanced arteriosclerosis). Elevation of systolic blood pressure to values above 250 mmHg under competitive conditions, as well as unavoidable shifts in electrolyte balance (for example, magnesium in serum below 0.70 mmol/l in longer-lasting competitions in substantial heat) can provoke serious, acute dangers to health, such as death from heart disease on the tennis court, especially for the groups of people mentioned earlier.

Energy Metabolism

The more intensive the demand of the individual volley, the more powerfully the carbohydrate metabolism is activated. The longer the stimulus lasts, and the more limited the stimulus level and intensity of the individual volleys and the entire competition, the more important the fat exchange becomes. The analysis of metabolic-intermediate products during a tennis competition indicates that during a tennis competition on clay courts, energy is supplied primarily via the breakdown of carbohydrates (approximately 50–75%), and only secondarily via the breakdown of fats (approximately 25–50%).

A decrease of the blood-sugar level in the course of a tennis

competition or tennis training of the usual duration (1–2 hours) probably occurs because the carbohydrate reserves (in the muscles and liver) were not appropriately maximized before the start of the competition or were depleted by the rigors of previous intensive training or competition. As a result, after intensive tennis training or during the course of a tournament, the glycogen reserves (stored forms of carbohydrates as starch in the liver and muscles) must be rebuilt rapidly and comprehensively via foods rich in carbohydrates. With the rapid succession of activities in training and competition, easily digestible carbohydrate-rich between-meal snacks can be recommended to maintain performance capability. Players who tend to have low sugar should take a potassium-rich carbohydrate supplement in connection with fluids, so that in the following doubles match there will be no undesirable drop-off in performance level.

Loss of Fluids and Electrolytes

Mainly because of perspiration secretion, tennis training and especially competitions (due to the elevated psychological demands) lead to increased fluid and electrolyte loss. Weight loss during a 90-minute tennis competition is on average 3–5 lbs. for men, although an average of $1/2$ liter of liquid are consumed; women lose approximately 50–70% of this amount.

In the course of a tennis competition, we find a highly

significant decrease of potassium and magnesium in the blood with a simultaneous increase of sodium and calcium and no essential change in plasma volume. As a result, a generous intake of water in combination with specific electrolytes and perhaps enriched with carbohydrates (5–20%) is particularly recommended. Because of the losses due to perspiration, the intake of magnesium and potassium should be monitored carefully, especially because the amount ingested in food (magnesium) is often too low, and also because of its importance in metabolism and for the function and regeneration of the muscles. Particular advice for absorbing such materials that determine performance from the salt-water balance will be covered more closely in the section entitled "Nutrition for the Tennis Player" (p. 243).

Psychological Requirements

Forms of behavior (and thus also performance) grow out of the interaction between the needs of the individual (the player) and her environment, that is, they rest on the interaction between the actual requirements (playing tennis) and the potential for the individual to be able to deal with these requirements. Therefore, psychological demands in tennis grow out of the structural needs that tennis presents. Such structural needs include, for example, the various interactions with one's opponent or even the rules.

Interactions

Interactions with one's opponent cannot be understood simply by their outcome; rather, they are determined mainly by the mutually influencing play intentions of both players (and also by their body language). In tennis, it is therefore important to be able to observe effectively the opponent's behavior and the strengths and weaknesses of his techniques and tactics, and also to interpret his condition and psyche reasonably (intelligently). It is also important to influence one's opponent through one's own tactics and body language (dominant behavior).

Rules of the Game

The parameters of play are framed by the constant demands of the rules of the game. The most important here are the scoring rules and the play breaks. In tennis, it is particularly interesting psychologically that each individual game in each set must be won by at least two points and that scoring begins again after each finished set, no matter how it ended. Particularly, the scoring unit "game" gives the sequence of a match a particular characteristic. Compare tennis with table tennis, where, for example, being behind 8:20 can hardly be caught up because the leading player only has to score one point. In tennis this can well be the case when behind 1:6 or 2:5. That heightens the psychological significance of the score and such questions as whether one should play more for risk or more for security and whether there is still hope despite being behind or skepticism in spite of being ahead, although looking at the end result, each point is, in principle, equally important. Therefore optimism (confidence) and self-confidence play a very important role in tennis. It is also of great psychological significance that, after each volley, there is a break (up to 25 or 30 seconds) and that, except after the first game in a set and after a tie breaker, the sides change after two games, which is linked to a maximum 90-second pause. Because each pause offers the possibility, on the one hand, of recovering from the previous stress and strain; on the other hand, each pause means that the competition has to be taken up anew so that each pause can lead to a new initial situation which the players have to deal with psychologically.

In tennis, therefore, there must be significant readiness to perform (motivation to perform), which has to be summoned up again and again; that is, the players must get motivated again after each pause and maintain this motivation during the volley. The greater the pressure during the entire match (for example, in a long and tiring match), the more the will has to be involved in order to be able to be ready with staying power and thus to avoid letting the readiness to perform wane. Because each volley ends with gaining or losing a point, and many volleys end dramatically, there are frequent stress situations in tennis. Therefore, the pauses are not simply preliminary to the next action; they also serve to work out stress at the same time (or ahead of time).

This means that tennis requires a great amount of stress tolerance, psychological stability, self-discipline, and ability to work out stress.

Variable External Demands

The parameters of play are also determined to some extent by variable demands such as bad weather, audience, and condition of the court; the players must always adjust themselves psychologically to them. Frequently, serious stress situations also arise.

Tennis Techniques

Finally, note that in tennis it is particularly difficult (because of the relatively fast flying ball, meeting the ball beyond the reach of the hand with the aid of a racket, and the size of the court) to always hit the ball in such a way that it precisely achieves the desired direction, height, distance, and spin.

The difficulty in meeting the ball is all the greater in a match. As the ball travels to the player faster, the more ambitious are the player's targets—which are linked to meeting the ball—and they become even more so as the player is physically and psychologically stressed. This difficulty and the interaction with the opponent brings with it great cognitive demands. Therefore, one should cultivate the ability to correctly perceive the ball, the opponent, and one's own position; to concentrate on meeting the ball; and to act tactically correctly (analysis of the game).

Analysis of World-Class Players

Word-class players can be divided into four types:

1. Serve and Volley Players

These players have the following characteristics:

- Very strong first serve, which can force return errors or make direct points.
- The first, and also the second, serve puts opponent under permanent pressure so that the server can play the majority of the first volleys in a relatively good position.
- High percentage of successful first volleys.
- Very good perception and anticipation significantly increases chances to intercept the opponent's passes at the net. Doing this puts the opponent under such pressure that she increases her error rate considerably.
- Strong smash from all positions.
- Very well-developed take-off power, coupled with impressive balance.

However, this group of world-class player (best represented in the past by Stefan Edberg), who serve and volley on all surfaces (even clay), is shrinking.

2. Full-Court Players

These players have the following characteristics:

- Ability to serve and volley and to play from the baseline, depending on the court surface.
- Sure and precise baseline shots and returns.
- Ability to play continuously from very near the baseline and to meet the ball regularly at the culmination point in front of it.
- Ability to attack balls played shorter by the opponent, that is, to make direct points (winners) from them or to play attack shots and to move forward to the net.
- Very good coordination abilities and excellent conditioning level.

This group of players is relatively strong and is among the most successful in world tennis. Names such as Becker, Ivanisevic, Krajicek, Sampras, Stich or Novotna, Sabatini, Sukova, and many more prove this. It is very interesting that almost all the players in this category play the backhand with one hand.

3. Baseline Players

These players have the following characteristics:

- Sure and aggressive baseline shots with forehand and backhand.
- Ability to control play from the baseline and to keep the opponent permanently under pressure.
- Ability to play close to the baseline or in front of it and to meet the ball as often as possible in the culmination point or in front of it (also as a half-volley).
- High level of precision even with greater ball speed.
- Very good angle play.
- Ability to hit aggressive, yet sure returns.
- Ability to hit very good passes.
- High speed and very good balance.

This group is growing, and the youngest players especially have a tendency to play this way. Players such as Graf, Hingis, Huber, Pierce, and Sanchez-Vicario among the women and Agassi, Chang, Courier, Kafelnikov, Medvedev among the men document this assertion. In contrast to the group of full-court players, this group is dominated, with few exceptions (for example, Graf), by those who play backhand with both hands.

4. Defensive Players

These players have the following characteristics:

- High topspin shots from the baseline with forehand and backhand.
- Playing position is considerably farther behind the baseline.
- Sure and extremely consistent play with baseline shots.
- Tendency to avoid offensive or attack shots.
- Well-developed running technique and stamina.
- A lot of patience and self-discipline.

Today, there are hardly any world-class players in this category (earlier, there were a few, for example, Borg and Vilas).

Surely there are players who, in the course of time, will move from one category to another or will be borderline cases, such as Bruguera. Different types of fast surfaces also force players to change their tactical operations accordingly. Therefore, it seems that in the future the full-court and the baseline players will dominate world-class tennis.

The current world ranking list as well as the development of the up-and-coming young generation seems to indicate that, with certain exceptions, the trend is moving toward full-court and baseline tennis players. Of the serve-and-volley players, almost all the successful ones are older, with the exception of Edberg. This is beside the fact that their number was already small. The defensive players have almost disappeared, at least in world-class competition.

One could say that the aggressive players are dominant; the players try to get the point through their own initiative and are far less willing to wait for their opponents to make a mistake.

In the future, play will probably be even faster and more aggressive so that running speed will have to be improved, which will lead to an even more athletic development of players. In addition, success when volleying depends more and more on the ability to master the most difficult situations. For this, one needs not only an excellent basic technique and a broad stroke repertoire but also the ability to use techniques that can now only be imagined. Therefore, the periods of practice in competitive tennis must be shortened, and the periods of competition-like training must be expanded. Training must increasingly fit the actual events of a match; individual match situations must be modeled on normal sparring. Thus, the value of special tactical training will also increase. The prerequisite for mastering difficult situations is impeccable physical control. This is determined mainly through strength and coordination abilities and skills. Balance, adaptability, footwork, and leg position when hitting are important factors and decisive for the success of the shot.

Analyses of world-class players have shown conclusively that there is a relationship between the return (perhaps the most important stroke in tennis today), pass, and footwork. Because these two strokes have to be used very frequently in difficult situations, footwork must be emphasized even more in training.

Because achieving success can be expected only with year-round high-level performance, the following are important:

- Developing technically into an all-round player who can play well on all kinds of court surfaces.
- Effective cyclical scheduling.

Specialists (clay, hard courts, indoor, fast surfaces, etc.) have problems maintaining good performance throughout the year because the court surfaces change almost constantly. Therefore, technique and style must be taught even to young players in such a way that they can later deal with all types of surfaces.

That requires not only a broad stroke repertoire but also the ability to hit balls hard as half-volleys when they are rising or at the culmination point in order to set the pace, play extreme angles, and take advantage of all possibilities to win points. Therefore, strokes with forward spin will continue to dominate, even if they have less spin but greater speed than a few years ago. The slice is especially good for changing the pace or gaining time, as a backhand attack shot or as an individual tactical choice; however, it will not play a dominant role in the foreseeable future.

Improving the volley itself among baseline players is unmistakable because a good volley continues to be the best possibility of winning points. There is no doubt that every good tennis player today must have an excellent serve. And the importance of a good return is also growing. The return is surely the most important stroke. More and more frequently, this is a decisive factor in a match, especially with players who have comparable serves. In order to master these techniques of contemporary tennis, coordination and compliance with biomechanical principles and rules are enormously important. Deficiencies in these areas cause limited ball speed and loss of precision and security.

Anthropometric prerequisites also play a more important role than previously. The first 15 of the ATP men's world ranking list currently averages approximately 6' 1" and in the women's, it is 5' 8". It happens that among the top 15 men, only one player is shorter than 5' 10" (Michael Chang). The average among the top 10 is over 6', and among the top five even a bit higher. Among the women, the average of the top five is 5' 9". This leads to the observation that the average height is increasing and that tall players dominate world-class competition. Related to this conclusion, talent scouts will be looking at the height of future players.

Also, more attention must be paid to cyclical scheduling, that is, effective planning of training, competition, and regeneration. It is impossible for competitive and world-class athletes to play at maximum capacity year-round. Therefore, it is important that in all categories and at all levels of play, there are specific focuses within the summer and winter seasons, in which players strive for their greatest individual potential.

Experience shows that one can achieve three annual peaks. Therefore, stages for development in tournaments must be planned to precede these peaks and thus serve as preparation. In addition, at least two periods must be set

aside each year for psychological and physical regeneration.

The growing number of injuries among top players today is the result of operating more or less without a plan for health concerns. There is too much improvisation in planning for the year, so that the player cannot achieve his potential performance level because of injury, illness, or overtraining.

Of course, tennis should not be considered solely from the viewpoint of a world-class sport. It is primarily a sport for all, a leisure activity. Tennis is an ideal sport for every age, so long as it is played sensibly and so long as the age-specific demands are respected. False pride, especially among the older seniors, can lead to health problems, as well as bad technique or diminished psychological condition. If the recreational player really wants to have fun with tennis, she should be careful that she is healthy enough for her level of engagement in the sport.

As a rule, tennis has periodic stress. The relationship of stress to pause is 1:2 and 1:4. The average of the stress period on clay courts is 8 seconds and on faster courts (astro-turf, hard courts, grass), 2.8 seconds. Fast starts and jumps require good take-off power in combination with the ability to anticipate, plus reaction speed. Covering short distances quickly requires a great deal of agility.

To execute the hitting and running techniques in constantly changing playing situations, the player needs optimal coordination and speed of action. Compared with other sports, basic speed and flexibility are not absolutely necessary in tennis. And stamina

does not have to be at the highest levels; however, it should be there in the form of enduring elasticity in the hitting arm and in leg musculature. In the area of motor skills, well-developed coordination as well as agility must be considered as limiting factors that cannot really be compensated for. In addition, fast reaction time and take-off power as well as speed of action are important requirements. All other factors are important, but they can be more or less compensated for.

Although aerobic stamina and flexibility in a tennis match do not necessarily limit performance, development in both areas is very important. Excellent aerobic stamina (basic stamina) is absolutely necessary for the quality of daily training lasting several hours. In addition, it guarantees an ability to regenerate quickly both during and after demanding training units. Very good muscle flexibility and wide swing of the limbs is also very important for tennis technique, speed, coordination, and prevention of injuries.

Considering factors affecting movement techniques, footwork must be taught and trained. And good technique is, of course, a basic requirement for excellent performance.

Skills Development: A Training Foundation

Excellent aerobic stamina, good muscle flexibility, speed, agility, and coordination are all necessary to compete on the world-class level in tennis.

Developing and Predicting Performance

In every training program, one tries to improve performance potential for competition (or at least to maintain it). The more the improvement of performance potential is viewed from the perspective of <u>long-term ability development</u>, the more important the question of talent becomes. In this context, we first consider <u>aptitude</u>, because such a thing is used to judge whether young tennis players are suited for tennis as a competitive sport. That is, whether they will later be able to achieve excellent performance. However, an aptitude is not a performance predictor (in the sense of a diagnosis of genuine capabilities) but rather a performance prognosis. That is, one tries to predict, based on examples, whether a 12 year old could belong to the junior hopefuls and in 6–8 years will find his way to the top.

It will help to link talent in three closely related problem areas and then treat them in three stages:

- Determining what talent is: This stage includes understanding the conceptual and theoretical identification of conditions and qualities that characterize a person as "tennis talent."

- Searching and selecting talent: The goal of a talent search is to find those people who exhibit the defined qualities, using research techniques and organizational measures. If such players are found, there is the question whether they should be channeled into specific athletic activities that offer encouragement and whether the "nontalented" should be excluded from this support.

- Fostering talent: This stage includes using all means possible to help the selected talent achieve the expected future high achievement.

Defining Talent

The first question focuses how the concept "talent" can more accurately be determined. This concept is frequently linked to the idea that some people are born with it and others have inherited it, relatively independent of training. However, this concept involves a central problem—hereditary factors and environmental influences, as developmental psychology shows, are effective in learning processes that are inextricably bound together.

Therefore, high achievement is possible only when hereditary factors and educational influences (for example, via the trainer) affect each other positively.

Therefore, the concept of talent must cover not only personal qualities but also those fostered by environment. Because determining talent involves a prognosis of achievement, it is advantageous to test very young tennis players in a specific developmental period, to see whether they exhibit future potential.

This leads to the following general definition of talent:

> A person who exhibits particular physical and psychological qualities that will most likely lead to future high achievement in favorable environmental conditions can be considered as athletic talent in a specific developmental period.

Developing and Predicting Performance

This general statement prompts closer elaboration of four parts of the definition in the form of questions.

? ■ In which developmental period should talent be sought and selected for support?

To answer, two important facts are considered:

First, the experience that the time lapse from the beginning of systematic skills training to attaining the highest competitive phase is approximately 8–10 years.

Second, in general movement theory, it is noted again and again that the prepuberty period represents a significant developmental period for acquiring motor skills.

If we assume from this that the most important tennis techniques should be learned at this age, then the talent search must begin in the eighth to tenth year.

? ■ Which physical and psychological qualities, which are viewed as internal factors, and environmental qualities, which are viewed as external factors, determine the development of skills in tennis?

In terms of internal factors, we should add here the physical abilities (speed, coordination, strength, flexibility, etc.), motor abilities (stroke technique, running technique, feel for the ball, etc.), cognitive abilities, (feel for the game, concentration, etc.), and motivational abilities (performance

motivation, psychological stability, etc.). Desirable external factors include, above all, the skills of the trainer, the assigned training requirements, the support of family and friends, and also the support through the club, the league, and even society.

? ■ How demanding should the prognosticating process be, and at what point should the capabilities be attained?

When asking about the criteria for prognosis, it is important to determine which performance level should be set as a goal. Is it the league level or that of the national or even international top competitors? Because it can easily be seen that, with increasing performance requirements, there are not only higher demands in terms of the individual factors that determine performance, but that among these factors increasingly less compensation is possible. As the performance level increases, it is a question not only of reaching a specific skills level but also at this level, which relatively few players reach, of considering the current breadth of national and international competition, many almost equally talented competitors are shut out. This also shows that, with the increasing performance level, the influence factors become more important; therefore, the performance prognosis in tennis is particularly difficult because there is not, as in track and field, for example, a specific measurable dimension (for example, approximately 22 feet in the broad jump) but rather a

contest among competitors, whose number and strength cannot be estimated at the time of the prognosis.

With the question concerning the level at which the skills used for prognosticating should be achieved, it is therefore wise to proceed first from a somewhat lower level (for example, considering international tennis from a world ranking-list position at 100 and considering national tennis from a median position on the German ranking list), and then consider this level as the basis for the latest selection process.

Experience shows that several years of training, and particularly of competition experience, are still necessary to reach and stabilize the skills phase within the framework of this selection process. If one takes male tennis players as an example, and assumes that systematic training should begin in prepuberty at the latest, that the best performance age is between 22 and 28, and that 3–4 years should be estimated for the last phase of the selection process, then there is a span of 8–10 years for the central phase of skills development. Thus, the achievement used for prognosticating should occur somewhere around 18–21. In other words, at this age, referring to our example, the position on world ranking lists at 100 or a median position on the German ranking list should be reached. The central phase of fostering talent continues to focus on this point.

? How can one determine the characteristics that should indicate talent at the time of the talent search?

According to these considerations, one can (mainly viewing internal factors influencing skills) test those characteristics an 8- to 10-year-old child should have in order to be designated as tennis talent. In this test, which can be performed in four steps, it should be noted that the factors determining skill are more or less important at different times during the development of the skills.

Step 1: For identifying talent in any sport, one should first imagine the ideal athlete at the time of the highest skills phase; that is, one tests the requirements profile in the sport and which top athletes represent this the best. One weighs all significant internal and external characteristics at the time of the top performance used for prognosticating. At the same time, one should test which factors can be compensated for. Thus, too little hitting arm strength can be compensated for by better coordination (more swing).

Step 2: Then one should ask oneself, whether these characteristics have to be expressed to a favorable degree at the time of the talent search and selection. This shows that, for example, strength should be less important before puberty, and can be trained well mainly in the teen years; therefore, no special attention should be drawn to this factor during the talent search.

Step 3: On the other hand, however, one also notes, for example, that the ability to learn motor skills is much more important as a prerequisite for learning in the phase of talent-fostering and provides more effective support in this phase than in the top competitive phase. Therefore, one should also always pay attention to how important individual factors are for developing skills in the talent-fostering phase. Thus, it can happen that one finds factors that are equally important for all phases of skills development and cannot be compensated for, such as performance motivation, that is, motivation for intensive training as well as for the highest level of participation in competition.

Step 4: Finally, one should test whether the development of these qualities can be predicted. The more clearly the development of a quality can be predicted, for example, body size determined by heredity or—more importantly for tennis—the relatively stable general skills that are acquired through early learning experiences and their further development such as being able to handle the ball proficiently (feel for the ball), the more important it is to include such a quality in the talent search.

So now, what are the implications for talent searching and fostering according to these theoretical considerations?

Talent Search

For the talent search, it can be concluded that the following personal factors are particularly important:

- Factors that are very important at the time of the high-performance phase,
- Factors that can hardly be compensated for during the high-performance phase,
- Factors that are very important for developing skills in the talent-fostering phase,
- Factors whose development can be accurately predicted.

Foremost among these characteristics are speed, agility, general coordination, motor skills, feel for the ball, desire to perform, and psychological stability.

Such factors can be tested in various ways. Although ability to learn, performance motivation, and psychological stability should be evaluated by observing behavior (because there are currently no adequate testing procedures), there are tests for motor skills at this age.

For fostering talent, it can be concluded that those variable qualities are to be optimized. Depending on the person, these qualities include strength, stamina, and tennis-specific coordination and tactical abilities, in addition to all factors related to training and competition planning.

Promoting Talent

The factors identified earlier, which can be influenced by training, may not be improved to such an extent that if one specializes prematurely in particular skills, the development of athletic skills is accelerated far too much. According to more recent findings in general tennis instruction, increase of this type that is too quick can be followed by a subsequent stagnation. In other words, under some circumstances, a higher ultimate skills level can result from gradually developing skills. It also depends on an appropriate development of skills.

Physical trainability and psychological ability to withstand stress should be measured in the course of development in children and young people in such a way that the physical and psychological developmental potential reaches its highest possible final level of athletic performance, while avoiding physical and psychological overtaxing.

In measuring physical trainability and psychological ability to withstand stress in terms of a long-term training program, which includes four areas—training in the basics, development training, skills training and top performance training—various main emphases must therefore be established concerning training, competition, and coaching (see Table 11).

Age	Developmental segment	Training segment	Setting goals
4–7	Pre-school	General development of athletic motor skills	– Acquiring the most varied elementary sports-motor skills (individual movements and combinations of movements)
Girls: 7/8–11/12 Boys: 7/8–12/13	School-age	Sport-specific but varied training in the basics	– Learning a varied tennis technique (from ground strokes to, e.g. stop-volley) – Acquiring various general athletic movement patterns – Creating conditioning foundations – Accumulating first competitive experiences
Girls: 11/12–12/13 Boys: 12/13–14/15	1st stage of puberty	Developmental training	– Systematic development of conditioning factors (including strength, stamina) – Stabilization and individual expression of techniques – Improvement of tactical abilities, depending on the player's situation – Improvement of psychological factors (attitude toward competition and training) – Gradual transition from youth to adult tournaments
Girls: 12/13–16/17 Boys: 14/15–18/19	2nd stage of puberty	Skills training	
Girls: app. from 16/17 Boys: app. from 18/19	Early adult		– Break through to world-class – Stabilizing physical and psychological performance factors – Adult tournaments – Striving for personal best

Table 11 Model for long-term training development in tennis.

Training in the Basics

It is an unchallenged fact that the prepuberty period is an important phase for acquiring motor skills. Children of this age have good leverage and a good power-to-weight ratio; they are adept and learn intuitively.

If the prepuberty period is a good age for learning motor skills, then this developmental phase should be used mainly for acquiring diverse and general (therefore, going beyond tennis) movement patterns. Such general movement patterns lead to a greater probability of a higher tennis-specific capability in later individual competitive situations

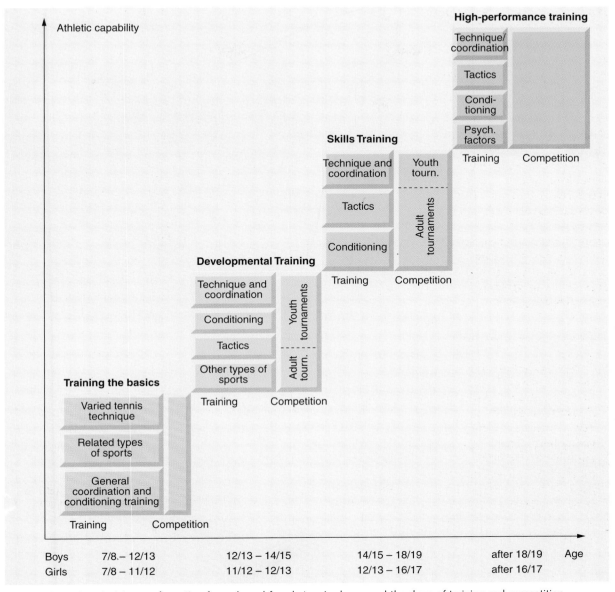

Fig. 74 Long-term training configuration for male and female tennis players and the share of training and competition.

because such competitive situations are always "new." Moreover, they remain so because of the vagaries of the opponent's playing style, the court surface, balls, weather conditions, and the like.

Recommendations for Training School-Age Children
For training the basics with school-age children, the following general recommendations help (and not only for tennis):

Stamina (see also the chapter entitled "Training Conditioning," p. 153).
Aerobic stamina can already be profitably trained before puberty because (except for intensive and one-sided stresses) with a healthy child there are no limitations with regard to ability to take stress.
A good aerobic capacity should be developed early on to prepare for the high stresses expected in the later training period. Basically, intensive anaerobic stresses should be avoided because they do not fit the requirement profile;

children have a more limited ability to deal with anaerobic stresses. Anaerobic stresses are not suitable for children and also require a good aerobic capacity, which is not yet developed because of their young training age.

Strength (see also the chapter entitled "Training Conditioning," p. 152)
Children should be directed through a strength-training program only for general strengthening because a general, total-body coaching of strength is the necessary prerequisite to avoid sports injuries and the basis for future training of maximum strength and agility.

Speed (see also the chapter entitled "Training Conditioning," p. 152)
When the performance ability of the central nervous system plays a central role in completing a task (as, for example, with reaction speed), then this can be recommended for preschoolers and school-age children because the central nervous system is already well developed and there are no limitations with regard to the ability to take stress. With the increasing importance of strength (particularly agility), the most effective training period shifts to older school-age children and teenagers.

Flexibility (see also the chapter entitled "Training Conditioning," p. 152)
Children are essentially more flexible than adults. Therefore intensive flexibility training (stretching) is not necessary until the end of the elementary school years. To prevent the orthopedic

Fig. 75   Hockey as a team sport used for training the basic skills.

problems that arise because of one-sided stresses, a general, flexibility program with active stretching exercises that simultaneously develop the musculature is recommended.

Coordination (see also the chapter entitled "Training Coordination," p. 117)
Coaching of coordination abilities is central to training in school-age children. For this, the movement pattern should be as varied as possible. At the beginning of the long-term training process, coaching general athletic movement patterns has a broad scope. Basic training focuses on a tennis-specific development of coordination abilities, in which the tennis instructor should be careful that this is as "broad" as possible (all stroke techniques and forms of footwork) and always connected with a general

coordination training program. What does general and varied basic training in tennis mean from a practical point of view? Improving coordination abilities is central. With that in mind, we can differentiate a sport-specific and a general coordination coaching.

- Sport-specific coordination coaching refers to learning a varied tennis technique (*Tennis Course, Volume 1*); that is, all movement patterns basic for future competitive technique should be practiced in their basic forms until prepuberty.
- General coordination coaching is oriented to the requirements in tennis, on the one hand. On the other hand, general coordination coaching occurs in the context of related sports so that later specialization in tennis relies on the fundamentals of broader movement experiences.

Besides tennis techniques, other skills have to be taught: eye/hand coordination, foot/point-of-impact coordination, the ability to anticipate, and dexterity in complex athletic situations that are similar to tennis. This includes basketball, soccer, and hockey, among the ball sports (see Fig. 76). But such games should not be considered merely as an entertaining exercise. Rather, it is the goal to systematically improve the appropriate motor skills (such as dribbling with the left and right hands). That is, to emphasize the quality of executing the movement. And two-sided (bilateral) development should also be a part of this.

Speed can be improved not only in game sports, but also in classical track-and-field training (practicing starts, coordination-running, etc.). For improving basic stamina, there is long-distance running, particularly cross-country runs lasting 40 to 50 minutes. Strength and flexibility can be improved as part of a general comprehensive sports gymnastics program. For improving footwork in tennis-specific coordination, running is useful, including such variations as hopping, skipping, sidesteps, and the like. There are countless possible combinations. In addition, we also recommend jumping rope. To the question, what are the practical consequences of such ideas, we offer the following suggestions for an average training week:

For 10 to 12 year olds, the scope of training runs from the lower limit of 6 hours per week to an upper limit of 12 hours per week. The following is an example of a 10-hour-per-week workout:

- 4 × 2 hours ("60-minute hours") of tennis training; 3 of these 8 hours should be devoted to conditioning.
- 2 hours general coordination and conditioning training.

This means that all together approximately 50% is devoted to general fundamentals (2 hours general coordination and conditioning training and 3 hours tennis training focusing on conditioning), and 50% to tennis technique in the narrower sense.

Fig. 76 Acquiring general coordination skills in complex athletic situations that extend beyond tennis but that are related.

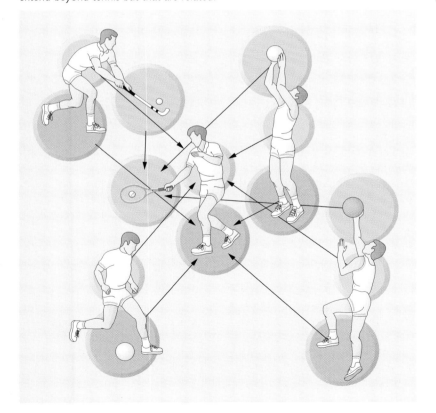

These recommendations are aimed at the higher goal of attaining future national and international recognition.

It is obvious that these recommendations cannot always be realized; therefore, it should be noted that in older age groups there is some possibility of catching up. However, the recommendations do show how, depending on the goal (for example, in a club that has midlevel expectations and offers less training), each possible training area can be apportioned. However, this should not give the impression that this view of basic training is universally accepted.

The central problems of carrying out basic training in tennis follow:

- Many trainers in the clubs and districts do not yet know about basic training.
- Mainly, parents should be enlightened. Because many parents can really not understand when the trainer offers, even requires, something else besides playing tennis.
- There are often difficulties when organizing general training outside of the tennis court. For the most part, indoor participation falls off in winter; then it is even more important that forms of general coordination and conditioning training be transferred to the tennis court.
- A particular problem is that basic training at first produces a more limited increase in skills in tennis; that means that others, who specialize very early, temporarily "move ahead." Patience and far-sightedness are necessary here.

Therefore, for children under 10, there are only regional exhibition tournaments. On the 11- and 12-year-old level, there are no international competitions.

The whole approach to basic training in prepuberty should be summarized by the word versatility, compared with specialization, so that competitions in this age group should not place emphasis on ranking.

Developmental Training

A few years ago, puberty was still viewed as "easytime." In the meantime, the realization that children and teenagers in this phase of development are very highly trainable has surfaced, primarily because of the results of sports medicine research. Therefore, conditioning training in the narrow sense, the optimization of physical factors that determine performance, especially strength and stamina, must characterize the period of developmental training as a further focus.

At the same time, actual specialization now begins. It aims for expression of technique in one's own style, as well as for systematic competition planning. Concerning the expression of individual style, it is appropriate in puberty and postpuberty to tie together various factors: the recently acquired strength components with the existing swing components, but also the physical development as well as the development of motivations and attitudes as a basis for building up the individual tactical playing situation. Even if puberty no longer represents an easy time,

it must still be observed that development in puberty and in postpuberty often proceeds more irregularly than continuously. Therefore, the phase of developmental training should be linked to the principle of continuous monitoring, in spite of occasional lapses in progress.

Skills Training

Skills training is based on the principle of stabilization of developmental factors. This gradual stabilization is characterized mainly by the fact that a balanced relationship should be sought among various determining factors in which the following three relationships should be particularly stressed:

- First, it is helpful to set up a balanced relationship of training and competition components by establishing a reasonable cyclical schedule. At least semiannual plans should be drawn up. They should include competitive high points, targeted training stress periods and regeneration phases.
- In training itself, balance means that technique, tactical, and conditioning training are of equal importance.
- Concerning competitions, a gradual transition from participating in youth tournaments to participating in adult tournaments is wise. At about 15, this relationship could slowly change in favor of adult tournaments. With youth championships, the player should learn to win against perceived and actually weaker competition through her own initiative and to prepare with

the idea of success fresh in her mind. With adult tournaments, players gather important information and learn to struggle through and defend against the stronger and often more pressured play of someone older.

Peak-Performance Training

In peak-performance training, the objective is to break through to the top, that is, to struggle through to the absolute top, among the very best players in terms of a final selection process. According to the <u>principle of gradual transition</u>, new focal points should be set:

- Training is increasingly viewed as preparation for competition in the narrow sense.
- Particular weight is placed on balance in the competitive situation. This means that a reasonable relationship should be sought between domestic and international, and between smaller and larger tournaments for the district leagues, and for clubs.
- Therefore, in this phase, cyclical scheduling is also especially important.
- Finally—and this is a result of establishing focal points—the coach wins rather than the trainer; therefore, being coached (either alone or in small groups) becomes increasingly important.

Fig. 77   Example of an exercise in world-class competitive training.

The road from child player to professional is a very long and thorny one. Those who take it bear a lot of responsibility. It is understood that along this road there are many open questions. And it should be understood as a possible result that a player can become overtaxed; that is, that many who set goals that are too high stumble, sometimes inevitably. In spite of this, <u>proving one's talent</u> in tennis is hardly a problem because there are so many competitive possibilities at various levels. In addition, the reward system for success, even at mid and lower skills levels, is expressed in such a way that the social network can be viewed as very restricted, so there are hardly any real dropouts. In spite of this restricted support network, the long-term development of training and competition from childhood to professional, covering approximately 15 years, can succeed only if the support system that sustains it is self-contained and is imbedded in the social and political system that surrounds this support system.

General Basics of Training

Structure and capacity of an organic system are determined by heredity as well as by quality and quantity of demands made on it by the environment—and mainly, by training. The whole training process depends on the ability of an organism to adapt to environmental and training stimuli. The adjustment processes required by training are monitored via a variety of measuring feelers, directed by regulating mechanisms. However, training also means stress, which leads to building energy reserves and sometimes the morphological structure of body organs. As a result, stress causes a decrease in capacity. This decrease can be stopped only if the organism has time to heal and regenerate. Therefore, systematic training not only concentrates on stress but also takes regeneration into account. Stress and regeneration form a unit and, as a result, are equally important.

At the capacity bounds, the athlete walks a very narrow tightrope. On the one hand, to maintain a high skills level, he must choose intense and comprehensive stresses. On the other hand, this causes the danger of overtaxing, which leads to overtraining and a decrease of skills when repeated several times. Training pedagogy has developed general principles, mainly from experience in individual sports such as track-and-field and swimming, that are systematically and wisely incorporated in keeping with the biologically based adaptive processes of the organism and that contribute to a further increase of skills.

Fig. 78 Phases of change of capacity after stress stimuli:
1, phase of decrease of athletic capability;
2, phase of renewed increase of athletic capability;
3, phase of supercompensation and elevated capability.

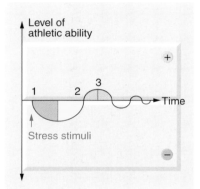

Although the aspects discussed continuously overlap and form fluid transitions, to maintain a systematic approach they can be divided into the following segments:
- Stress and adaptation
- Stress and regeneration
- Overtaxing and overtraining

Stress and Adaptation

From a biological perspective, physical stresses in training cause functional adaptations that can become evident according to the type and duration of the training stimuli in the areas of energy and morphology. Depending on the type, duration, and frequency of tennis training, the tennis player also experiences characteristic adaptation effects of her coordination and conditioning skills. For training children and adolescents, it is important to let coordination skills develop earlier and faster than constitutional skills.

Specific stresses and training stimuli are necessary in order to improve athletic capability. In the biological model, this proceeds schematically in the following sequence: stress → disruptive homeostasis (fluid-balanced state of cells and the organ systems) → adjustment → supercompensation (elevated functional level).

After the stress, there is a temporary decrease of athletic capability followed by a renewed increase above the beginning level (supercompensation). If there are no further training stresses, the capability gradually returns to the beginning level (see Fig. 78). As an example, a longer lasting demand on stamina leads to a build-up of glycogen reserves in the muscles. In the regeneration phase, the organism not only reacts with a replenishment of the glycogen reserve but also tries to increase its glycogen reserves beyond the original value (supercompensation).

This is a matter of a protective mechanism that, in the case of repeating a similar stress, should prevent a renewed depleting of the reserve. The whole approach to physical training relies on this reaction of the organism. With tennis players, it can be carried over to training for strength and speed.

In sports, supercompensation can be recognized quickly in beginners through a continuous increase in athletic capacity. With advanced players, the transfer process sometimes takes considerably longer, and only the accumulation of training effects that can be detected immediately allow a mostly sharp increase in skills, which is also characterized as delayed transformation (Fig. 79).

Advances in skills (higher level of adaptation) happen very quickly at the beginning of

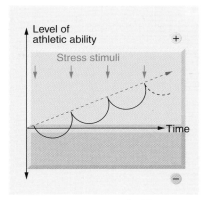

Fig. 79 Improvement of athletic capability through optimally timed training stimuli.

training and then become progressively slower and more difficult. The degree of change when homeostasis is disturbed is responsible for the following. As the training levels increase, the related stresses cause increasingly limited disturbances of the inner region of the cell (for example, biochemical balance), resulting in increasingly limited evidence of adaptation. The training level then alters the organism's response reaction to a given training stimulus. This is also true for one-sided training stresses that lead to a stagnation of the skills improvement after a short time. Only the addition of some new training stimuli (for example, for tennis players, training on unfamiliar surfaces and systematically including doubles competitions) enable further adaptation processes in the sense of an increase in skills.

Only excessive stimuli trigger a reaction in the body, and only several repetitions of excessive stimuli lead to training effects. The threshold value of the training stimulus follows only the

strength and extent of the stimulus, as well as the capacity of the person involved. For example, for an untrained person, a stimulus intensity of 40% of maximum strength can already represent an increase in capacity, whereas for a highly trained power athlete only stimuli upward of 80–90 percent of maximum strength are effective. In tennis, beginners and advanced players are already able to improve their tennis-specific coordination with a twice-a-week training program, while for the majority of international-class players a twice-a-day training program is the minimum required for improving capacity.

For optimizing stress in the individual training units, one needs deeper understanding of the individual stress components and their complex interactions. Generally, the following stress norms are used to characterize training:

- Stimulus intensity (as a more precise expression, we suggest stimulus level or stimulus strength, although the term stimulus intensity is used in training pedagogy): Level (strength) of the individual stimuli.
- Stimulus density: Temporal relationship of stress-and-regeneration phase.
- Stimulus duration: Duration of the effect of the individual stimulus or stimulus sequence.
- Stimulus extent: Total duration of the stimuli per training unit.

In tennis, training is characterized by the extent of the stimulus (total duration of the training stimuli) and stimulus intensity (sum of the stimulus strength and density as well as lengths of pauses), since the intensity of the individual stimulus is difficult to determine and represents complex training and playing forms a huge sum of various individual stimuli. In contrast, quantity and quality of speed training are determined to a considerable degree by stimulus strength, density, duration, and level, as well as the arrangement of pauses. If stimuli occur too quickly in succession (excessive stimulus density) or they last too long (excessive stimulus duration), or if the number of repetitions per training unit is set too high (excessive stimulus level), then this is related to the stimulus intensity (better stimulus strength). The specific effect of such training will thus deviate from the goal of a maximum speed development and will lead to an improvement of enduring speed.

Stress and Regeneration

The goal of stresses in training is the supercompensation of that organ structure responsible for capacity progress. The require-ment is that the regeneration is not destroyed too early by premature reuse, that is, by a stress that occurs too early. If, on the other hand, the regeneration is emphasized too strongly, the traces of the previous training unit are erased and the prerequisites for a capacity increase are lost. As a result, regeneration also plays a significant role in the effectiveness of training, second only to training content, intensity, and scope. The schematic of the three

variants of the alternation of stress and regeneration based on Jakowlew treats the ineffectiveness of training when the regeneration intervals are too large or too small (Fig. 80).

The regeneration period depends on the content, intensity, and scope of the training as well as on various external (for example, temperature and humidity) and internal (for example, individual skills level, age, and sex) factors. It differs

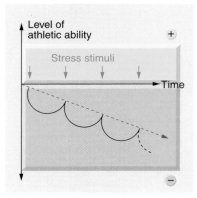

Fig. 80 Decrease of athletic capability due to stresses that follow one another too quickly.

further in various organ systems. Therefore, for example, regeneration happens very quickly after short stress periods (approximately 2–5 hours), even though the resynthesis rate for energy metabolism (for example, glycogen build-up) and especially regeneration of structural protein (for example, musculature or enzymes for energy metabolism) proceeds very slowly (taking more than 24 hours). For training, this means that a speed-oriented conditioning training or a very intense, short tennis training at the appropriate level allows a

second training session on the same day with no loss of efficiency. In contrast, an intensive, comprehensive tennis training or a long and hard competition on the same or even the following day should not be repeated in the same way.

Training pedagogy has demonstrated that it might not be wise to add each new training stress only when all the skills factors have been completely reestablished. Long regeneration intervals cannot be included in the training process because of time constraints. Besides, the scope of training necessary for top performance cannot be achieved. In skills training, therefore, training must start before the end of the regenerative processes. This is done either through a shift in accent of specific training stimuli or through accumulation of the same or altered stimuli (for example, according to the series principle).

This additional buildup of fatigue is a completely common variant of the stress sequence in top competitive level training. It leads to an even lower use of reserves (for example, energy potential) and promotes an even more comprehensive adjustment. At any rate, appropriately longer regeneration intervals must be included. To sum up, adhering to the following rules is important for tennis:

- For regeneration and supercompensation of capability, an optimal alternation of stress and recuperation should be sought.
- Because the time required for different organ systems to regenerate varies, there must be variations in training content and methods.

- Training even 2–3 times a day is possible according to the series principle, if the training stresses proceed in cycles.

If the training stimuli are too frequent or too early in the phase of incomplete regeneration, this can lead to overtraining and decline in athletic capability (see Fig. 80, p. 114).

Therefore, in sports, one tries to accelerate regeneration through supporting pedagogical activities (for example, individualization, variability in training, etc.), psychological (relaxation techniques, psychological well-being, etc.) as well as through physiotherapeutic means (vitamin enrichment, minerals and carbohydrates, massage, etc.). Basically, precise planning (including a training book) and regular research into the skills and health of the athlete offer good bases for the success of these measures. In this respect, there are still considerable deficits in tennis so that the capacity reserves are also not completely used up, even in top players.

Overloading and Overtraining

Overtraining can be defined generally as a reduction of capability in spite of unaltered training demands. The skills are often lost by various diagnoses of a subjective or objective nature. Generally, overtraining with predominantly sympathetic stress symptoms (Basedow type) is differentiated from that with parasympathetic stress symptoms (Addison type). With the Basedow

One student plays, the other takes a break.

type of overtraining condition (characterized by increased agitation), the athlete complains mostly of fatigue, internal unrest, sleep disorders, weight loss, and a tendency to perspire (perhaps with night sweats). With the less frequent Addison type of overtraining condition, a phlegmatic attitude and inhibited responses are more the rule.

In the laboratory, somewhat high levels of CPK (creatin-phospho-kinase), serum urea, and ammonia, as well as reduced levels of iron, magnesium, and potassium are detected. Moreover, a rise in the ratio of cortisol to testosterone as a measure of unbalanced protein-building and decomposition processes is considered as an objectifying indication.

In sports medicine diagnosis of skills, when the maximum capacity is reduced, accompanied by a simultaneous lower rate of maximum lactate formation, there is a further indication of an overtraining condition. In training, it happens that the athletes suffer decreases in ability, especially with secondary abilities such as speed and strength, and in the area of stamina.

The following points are often essential sources of overtraining and should therefore be avoided if at all possible:

- Unreasonably high training intensity and extent,
- High accumulation or density of technically difficult movement sequences in training and competition,
- Imbalance and monotony of training content and methods,
- Unbalanced nutrition,
- Close scheduling of competitions with insufficient regeneration intervals,
- Simultaneous infection (even of a minor type) as well as additional professional and/or personal stress,
- Setting unrealistic performance goals.

Because overtraining and the overtraining syndrome often result from an accumulation of physical and psychological stresses, the term overloading or *overloading syndrome* would be more appropriate.

According to Israel, the Basedow type of overtraining can be completely reversed with appropriate treatment, usually within 1–2 weeks. Besides eliminating all social and biological interference factors, therapeutic measures include substantial reduction of the (intensive) special training, transition to active recuperation, light massage, and, in some cases, a change of environment. Furthermore, adequate and substantial nutrition should be a focus. In serious cases, sleeping aids, sedatives, and psychotherapy (to calm and relax) must be considered.

Addison-type overtraining can usually be reversed within weeks, but in some cases, only after months. Here also, there is a reduction in the scope of training, sometimes linked to a change in environment. Physiotherapy and balneotherapy are important, and an intensification of the individual psychological counseling is promising.

Training Coordination

Tennis is a sport requiring a high level of coordination. Coordination skills are one of the most important factors that determine performance in tennis. Without good coordination skills, learning tennis techniques is demonstrably difficult. The totality of well-expressed coordination skills determines success in learning and refining movements.

The better the quality of coordination, the more directly, precisely, and effortlessly the movement goal will be achieved. If movement sequences become smoother and more economical, the level of fatigue decreases.

Definition and Classification

Physiologically, coordination is the interaction of the central nervous system (CNS) and the skeletal musculature with a defined movement sequence.

The quality of coordination is influenced by the speed of the movement and the information conveyed regarding defined movement. The main indicators for coordination are precision and economy of movement.

There is a distinction between intramuscular and intermuscular coordination.

Intramuscular coordination depends on the interaction of nerve fibers and muscle fibers within a muscle. A higher level of expression guarantees an optimal cooperation and timely, economic, and effective innervation of all necessary fibers of a muscle in a specific contraction.

Intermuscular coordination depends on the interaction of various muscles. It guarantees the optimal impulse transmission in the kinematic chain within a whole-body movement sequence.

Previously, the literature dealing with coordination skills focused on agility and dexterity. However, one cannot describe the total realm of coordination skills using these two concepts alone. Therefore, in the course of time, people have tried to make the components of coordination skills more precise and to codify them. (See Fig. 81.)

Most important, individual elements of coordination cannot be considered as independent components. There are a growing number of combinations and overlaps, and especially interrelationships that influence one another.

Coordination Skills

Within coordination training, we can choose specific focal points as needed. However, in principle one always has to coach coordination as a complex process for developing several parallel coordination skills.

Linking Skills

The first coordination skill, which is very closely linked to other components of coordination training, is the ability to link components. This is defined as the ability to effectively coordinate movements of parts of the body among themselves and in relation

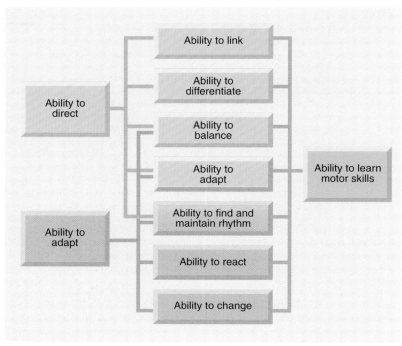

Fig. 81 Coordination abilities according to BLUME (1978). The definitions given come from the individual coordination abilities discussed by BLUME (1978).

to the whole body movement which is directed toward a particular targeted action. Therefore, for example, when executing a successful tennis stroke, it is necessary to have an optimal and precise linking of various partial-body movements of the lower and upper extremities, the trunk, and the head suited to the stroke and situation. In connection with this, we speak of a chain reaction of individual muscle components of this chain and, in a biomechanical sense, of a fine motor coordination of secondary impulses. This includes the correct sequence for using individual limbs as well as linking a whole series of varied types of movements within a movement sequence such as stretching (the legs), and rotation (of the hips and upper body), and bending.

In addition to a wide variety of movement sequences focusing on tennis techniques, tennis-specific training of this skill should include playing all types of ball sports, practicing throwing movements, and running, jumping, and other forms and combinations of movements, as well as combinations of these and other movements that can be incorporated into obstacle courses and the like.

Differentiation Skills

These recommendations also hold for the next form of coordination skills—differentiation. This concerns the ability to achieve a high level of fine-tuning individual movement phases and partial body movements, which are expressed with great precision and economy of movement. One such skill is necessary then, for example, when—depending on position, situation and target—a short, flat pass is to be hit crosscourt at a full run outside the sidelines or a hard crosscourt shot to the opponent's corner from the same situation and position.

Adjusting to the situation on the basis of diverse perceptions (visual, acoustic, kinesthetic) via various muscle tensions and relaxation is a prerequisite for situational technique management, which in practice is also called feel for the ball.

One can conclude from this that the quality of the differentiating skill depends strongly on the quality of the linking skills, that is, a fine-tuning of movement can be achieved only via a correct series of individual innervation impulses. Both skills combine for the most part with a third skill—balance.

Balance

Balance is the ability to keep the entire body in a state of equilibrium or to retain or reestablish the state during and after comprehensive shifts in body position.

Optimal balance means, therefore, maintaining balance during the stroke, or quickly regaining balance if it is lost after a shot while running, jumping, and the like. Differentiation, linking, and orientation skills are also essential.

In tennis, both static balance skills (using the backswing, hitting from a standing position) and dynamic ones (hitting while running or jumping, getting out of the way, etc.) are very important. Balance is controlled mainly via the position of the head with its vestibular apparatus and the upper body.

Perfect footwork, which one uses to correct and fit the position of the body's center of gravity in relationship to the ground, and lowering the center of gravity toward the ground are both extremely important.

Orientation Skills

Orientation skills should also be considered in close relationship to the three skills discussed previously. By orientation skills, we mean the ability to determine and change the position and movement of the body spatially and temporally, referring to a defined field of action and/or a moving object (ball, opponent, partner). Because the tennis player is almost always continuously moving during volleys and is always changing the position of the body on the court, space-oriented dynamic control of her own movement style is especially important. In addition, she must keep her eyes on the ball and her opponent (and in doubles, her partner and the second opponent).

Rhythm

A further coordination skill is the ability to grasp an acquired rhythm and to reproduce it as a motor activity, as well as produce an "internalized" rhythm that exists as an image that the player has of his own movement skills. In tennis, "internalized," temporal, spatial, and dynamic linking of the movement sequence, based on kinesthetic information, is foremost. This can be relatively stable, such as, for example, with the backswing or a stroke in a standardized position or situation; but it can also depend on the situation on the tennis court. Based on his perception of the particular situation, the player has to adapt his own individual hitting rhythm, that is, he must keep reconfiguring the situational hitting rhythm and act as the situation demands. This depends on his position on the court (far behind the baseline, in front if it, on the "T", etc.), on the type and speed of the approaching ball (fast, slow, high, flat, etc.), on the planned type of stroke (topspin, slice, etc.), on the intended ball speed (winner, attack shot), and on the direction and length (down the line to the baseline, short crosscourt, to the sideline, etc.). The ability to maintain an acquired rhythm also plays an important role during instruction.

Here, the instructor plays an important role in that he regulates the student's rhythm through demonstration or verbal advice during the student's running and hitting movements.

Reaction Skills

Reaction skills are a further component of managing coordination tasks.

Under reaction skills, we include the ability to perform effective, short motor actions quickly in response to a signal. In tennis, reaction skills are complex; that is, it is a question of the ability to react to a situation using a fast and effective initiation and execution of whole-body movement actions.

Based on the variety of signals, the tennis player has to make a definite, effective decision quickly and then complete the movement appropriately. For this, she needs a repertoire of alternative or varied possible solutions. The thought processes involved must take place intuitively and lightning-fast so that they can be used in effective movements under severe time pressure. Therefore, for example, she has to make an instantaneous decision whether a pass should be hit crosscourt or down the line, whether it should be a pass or a lob, whether a long volley or a stop volley is the correct solution; and the decision must be coupled with immediate execution.

Ability to Adapt to Changes

The quality of the reaction again depends on the quality of the coordination skills mentioned earlier as well as on the ability to readjust. By adaptability we mean the ability to adjust the program to new circumstances while performing the action, based on perceived or anticipated changes in the situation.

This ability is quite dependent on orientation and reaction skills. It plays an important role especially in tournament tennis because here the player is often confronted with a situation in which this skill is particularly important with oddly bouncing balls, with net balls, in urgent situations due to faulty anticipation (for example, if the opponent's first serve is expected on the forehand side and he serves to the backhand), with volley waves in doubles, on being "wiped out" on the wrong foot, and many more.

To master this situation successfully, speed and precision in perceiving the change in the situation are necessary, along with a storehouse of experiences from similar situations.

To sum up, we can say that all the coordination skills mentioned form a unit and that they are absolutely necessary for learning (and especially for mastering) the situational technique for use in a match.

In all sports literature, there are even more terms for coordination skills, such as eye-hand coordination skills, which should be assigned to linking ability. In addition, the concepts dexterity and timing include differentiation, linking, and orientation skills, whereas timing alone includes differentiation and linking skills.

Principles of Coordination Training

The more complicated a movement is, the greater is the importance of coordination. And good coordination is an effective protection against various sorts of athletic injuries (from falling, overexertion, etc.).

The basis of high-quality coordination efforts is a diverse repertoire of movements. The more this repertoire of movements is made automatic, the more the central nervous system is unburdened.

The goal of coordination training is thus establishing optimum motor-dynamic paradigms and adjusting to the ever-changing situation in competition. For coaching coordination skills, the following principles are important:

- A diverse athletic education with the goal of broadening the movement repertoire shortens the learning period and makes the training process of developing new movement skills and reinforcement of tennis techniques more effective.
- Intensified learning of tennis-specific techniques in both normal and difficult circumstances broadens the requirements of all techniques in every situation.

- Variable arrangement of the exercises increases the motivation of the learner and accelerates the adaptability skills.
- Tennis-specific coordination exercises on the tennis court complement the general coordination training.
- The phase between ages 8 and 12 must be used particularly for coordination training.
- Coordination training cannot be undervalued in any phase of development from beginner to top player.

Therefore it is important to emphasize general coordination coaching for children more than previously. It should be broadly structured, and practice should involve several kinds of sports, such as various ball sports, age-appropriate track-and-field disciplines (running, jumping, throwing), gymnastics, as well as skiing, surfing, or cycling. A further important consideration in coordination training is bilateral ability. This means that, in all coordination training, not only is the strong hand, foot, or side of the body regularly involved, but both arms, legs, and sides of the body are also. This helps promote general coordination skills to a certain extent, which is the basis for strengthening complicated, tennis-specific movement sequences in all possible difficult circumstances and positions.

Quality Indicators of Coordination Training

Coordination training must be structured systematically. The <u>first step</u> concerns the quality of coordination. It is not enough, for example, to play soccer, basketball, and hockey "just for fun," to finish various dexterity courses, or to do specific coordination exercises; it is more important to pay attention to the quality of the technical execution in the chosen programs. The higher the quality of the general coordination skills, the sooner positive results in learning and improving tennis techniques can be expected.

After individual coordination skills are learned, they must be improved in the <u>second step</u>, which stresses speed of movement in individual exercises. Reaching a high movement speed while maintaining precision is an important quality indicator of successful movements.

In the <u>third step</u>, simple or individual coordination processes should be linked with others, for example, shooting goals while bouncing a basketball, bouncing balls with rackets along with simultaneous slalom run with a soccer ball, or trampoline jumping while catching the ball and shooting baskets.

On the one hand, optimization of coordination skills can be achieved only through numerous repetitions of selected exercises. On the other hand, coordination training cannot be too extensive because of the danger of fatigue; it should be done as often as possible (ideally, almost daily).

Therefore, it is a good idea to complete each training session with short coordination exercises, approximately three series lasting approximately 3–5 minutes, and to include an additional coordination unit of approximately 20–30 minutes approximately twice a week.

In addition, the tennis instructor should also be careful not to offer too many and constantly changing exercises with no choice, to avoid changing them completely from session to session. He should also be careful that, for reasons of transferability, only so many types of exercises are practiced so that these can also be dealt with according to quality. Only then should he expand the repertoire. Basically, we can divide the general and tennis-specific coordination training as shown in Fig. 82.

Fig. 82   Forms of coordination training.

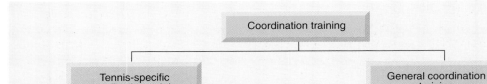

Training Examples

Before discussing the forms of training for the individual areas, it is necessary to stress some tips from training methodology.
With the exception of the large and small games, the following exercises should be done according to the repetition and short-interval methods. The duration of the stimulus varies between 20 and 60 seconds and four to six repetitions. The stimulus consists of approximately 3–12 series; the stimulus density should be structured in such a way that there is a complete regeneration with demanding exercises or those in which the stimulus duration is longer.
The speed of movement should be executed in a manner corresponding to the competition exercise.

Tennis-Specific Coordination Training

Special Exercises on the Tennis Court with Racket and Ball

Example 1

Catching and Throwing the Ball
- Both players stand behind lines (one behind the baseline and the other in front of the "T", facing each other). Then throw the ball, which is lying on the racket, to each other and try to catch it with the racket without letting it bounce on the racket (Fig. 83).
- After the catch, the racket with the ball is brought around the body and the ball is then thrown to the partner.
- After the catch, the racket is brought to the back and through the legs; the ball is then thrown to the partner from between the legs.

Example 2

Double Contact
Two players stand opposite each other at the net and toss the ball to each other over the net as a volley.
- On the first contact, the ball is played high short, and on the second contact tossed to the partner.
- The ball is played high in such a way that it has to be returned to the partner from a difficult position (left of the body, between the legs, while turning the body, behind the back, with the other side of the racket, etc.).
- The ball is purposely met in a difficult position (left at the body, between the legs, behind the body, with the other side of the racket, etc.) and returned from another difficult position.
- All three of these exercises are also performed with the clumsy, "wrong" hand.

Fig. 83 Catching the ball for tactile sense.

Fig. 84 Returning the ball as half-volley between the legs.

- The ball is played high with one hand, the racket changes hands, and the ball is returned with this hand.
- All forms of the exercises can also be played as a competition (11 or 21 points) in a service area. When the ball touches the ground or the net or an out is counted, the player is given a minus point.

Example 3

Half-Volley or Volley

The player stands on the "T" and tries to touch the ball tossed by the trainer and then always return it as a half-volley (or volley).

- The trainer tosses the ball regularly to the player's forehand and backhand side. The player then tries to return the ball as a half-volley or volley.
- The ball is now tossed irregularly and alternately shorter, longer, more to the side, and the like. The player must now adjust quickly to each situation.
- The ball is thrown as in the previous exercise, but it may be returned only with a forehand half-volley or only with a backhand half-volley (or volley).
- The ball may now be returned only as a half-volley between the legs: the arm with the racket approaches the ball behind the body (Fig. 84).
- The ball may now be met only to the left of the body (for right-handers) or a volley with the forehand side of the racket, while the racket moves behind the body during this stroke.
- These strokes can be altered in an established sequence (for example, right at the body, between the legs, left at the body).
- All these exercises can also be done with the "wrong" hand.

Fig. 85 Returning the ball while lying on one's back; the player holds a racket in each hand.

Example 4

Volley While Lying on One's Back

The player lies behind the net and tries to return balls played to her.

- The player holds a racket in each hand. The trainer tosses balls to her regularly and always close enough to reach. The player must try to return each ball (Fig. 85).
- The player now uses only one racket.

Example 5

Running Behind a Lob and Returning It

- The player stands in front of the "T". The trainer plays a lob above him. He tries to return it just before the second ground contact using a back-and-forth movement with the forehand side of the racket on the right side of the body with his back to the net.
- The ball should now be returned over the net between the legs.

Example 6

Passing the Racket

Two to six players stand behind the baseline. There is only one racket for the group. The trainer tosses balls (long, short, left, right, etc.). The players must take turns trying to return the ball. To do this, the racket is constantly passed along to the next player. The player who does not return the ball is out. At the end, there is a winner.

Exercises for Hitting Technique in Specific Situations

Example 1

Hitting at a Full Run
The player stands immediately behind the baseline. The trainer tosses him the balls regularly or variously in such a way that the player can return them directly at a full run.

- The player stands immediately behind the sideline. The ball is tossed to the open corner; the player must sprint 18–24 feet and return the ball.
- After the first stroke from the same location, a second ball is tossed to the other baseline half. The player must stop after the first shot, start again, run back, and return the second ball at a full run.
- The player stands at the center of the baseline. Five to ten consecutive balls are quickly tossed in different directions. The player must try to return all the balls.

Example 2

Machine Gun
The player stands behind the net. The trainer tosses 8–12 balls randomly in very rapid succession to various reaches and heights. The player must try to return all balls.

Example 3

Volley and Smash
The player stands behind the net. The trainer tosses a ball for a volley, or one to the other side of the body for a smash, alternately and quickly.

- The player must alternately play a low forehand volley and a backhand smash.
- The player must alternately play a low backhand volley and a forehand smash.

General Coordination Training

Partner Games

Example 1

Wall Ball
Concept: The ball is thrown against the wall; the opponent must catch the ball and immediately throw it back to the wall.

Equipment: Gymnastics ball or even a tennis ball.

Playing field: 18' wide (with four players, approx. 26' wide), 26' long (with experienced players, 30' long), with a dividing line that runs parallel to the wall 9' from it (with experienced players, 4^1/$_2$') Wall height: at least 10^1/$_2$'.

Players: 1-on-1, 2-on-2.

Length of Play: Three 10-point sets; appropriate pause after each set; to a win of 3 sets.

Rules: Task takes place in a corner formed by the dividing line and the sideline. The ball must bounce back from the wall into the court behind the dividing line. It may bounce on the ground only once before the opponent catches it. It must be returned immediately (1 second) from the point of the catch.

Variations
Position: Player stands approximately 5 feet from a wall (even a tennis wall), facing it.

Task: Touching or catching balls thrown against the wall by a trainer or partner or bouncing off the wall:
- First, only with the hands.
- Then with the legs (pay attention to the quality of the throw).
- Basic task with various balls (softball, etc.).
- Variations in ball speed.
- Balls are played indirectly (for example, ground/wall or wall/ground or wall/wall) at right angles.
- Tennis balls in two colors are used; balls of one color may be touched only with the hands; those of the other color, only with the feet.

Example 2

Bounce Tennis (See Fig. 86, p. 125)
Concept: Two players; ball is bounced in each pass into the circle in such a way that the opponent does not reach the ball.

Equipment: Gymnastics ball, hollow ball, or even a tennis ball.

Playing field: Circle of tires 3 feet in diameter.

Players: 1-on-1.

Length of play: to a win of 21 points.

Rules: The ball must hit something on each bounce within the circle. It may bounce only once and may be touched only once by the player. Balls that are thrown, or bounce above reach, or are bounced directly toward the players are unaccceptable.

Fig. 86   Bouncing the ball in a tire.

Small Games with the Ball

Example 1

Baton or Beer Coaster Hockey
Concept: Indoors. A tennis ball is driven into the opponent's goal using short batons or regular cardboard beer coasters.

Equipment: Tennis ball, relay-race batons, or beer coasters.

Playing field: Depends on size of gym; floor mats, poles, or boxes can be used as goals.

Players: Three to six on each side.

Length of Play: As agreed upon; two halves with a change of sides.

Rules: The ball may not be pushed except by hitting it with the baton or coaster. Only the goalie wears shoes. If there are no boundary lines, game may be played against the wall.

Example 2

Hitting the Ball with a Ball
Concept: Propel a medicine ball (soccer ball) across a marked court over the opponent's line.

Equipment: Medicine ball, gymnastics balls, depending on the number of players.

Players: 10-on-10 (depending on the number of participants).

Playing field: Square, for example, 30 × 30' or smaller; medicine ball is placed at the center. The teams each occupy diagonally opposing corners formed by the sidelines.

Rules: One may not walk on the court or the boundary lines. The medicine ball may be rolled only by hitting it with a thrown gymnastics ball. A goal is scored when the medicine ball crosses or touches an opponent's sideline. All balls should not be played at the same time; some players should have the task of retrieving missed shots.

Example 3

Soccer-Tennis
Concept: Using the foot, head, or chest, propel a ball over a line or a net into the opponent's court.

Equipment: Soccer ball or handball.

Playing field: Depending on the number of players. 35–50 feet long, 15–30' wide, divided at the center by a rope $2^1/_2$–3' high.

Players: 4-on-4. Also 1-on-1, 2-on-2, and so on.

Rules: Ball can be played with feet, chest, or head; with each pass, it may touch the floor once; it can be played three times in one's own court. Exception when playing 1-on-1: Only one contact in one's own court. Playing the ball in flight with head, foot, thigh, or chest counts as a second hit or as a pass. Fault: Touching the ball with the hand or arm, touching the rope, letting the ball touch the ground out of bounds.

Example 4

Volleyball Variation
Concept: The ball is hit by bouncing it over a low rope into the opponent's court.

Equipment: Volleyball, handball, or soccer ball.

Players: 4-on-4; also 2-on-2, 3-on-3, and so on.

Length of Play: 2 periods each 10 minutes long; also playing to 21 points with a change of court at 10 points.

Rules: The ball must be hit with a closed fist. It must bounce once on each toss. In the receiver's court, it can be tapped up to three times, where each player may touch the ball once. The ball is served from the rear boundary line standing on both feet outside the court (if desired, the ball may also be played with an open hand).

Example 5

Ball over the Rope
Concept: The ball thrown by the opponent over the rope may not touch the ground in the receiver's court and vice versa.

Equipment: Medicine ball, volley ball, soccer ball, and the like.

Playing field: 25 × 50', or depending on space limitations; center line is suspended 7 or 8 feet high.

Players: 5-on-5, 4-on-4, 6-on-6, and so on.

Rules: The thrown ball may not touch the ground or rope. It may be thrown three times by different players in their own court. Up to 21 fault points are played.

Example 6

Sideline Soccer
Concept: Soccer game with three groups of players: goalies, forwards, backs.

Equipment: Soccer ball or handball.

Playing field: 20 × 40 m, larger or smaller depending on the space configuration and number of players. Goals include the entire rear boundary lines.

Players: 8–30 (outdoors, on each side).

Length of Play: Two periods each 20 minutes long.

Rules: Six (2, 4) players in each group guard their goal line (playing with feet and hands). A goal is scored when the ball crosses the line at arm's reach. Six (2, 4) backs play the sidelines (both groups mixed). They play only outside of the court.

They shoot and throw the ball (they may use hands) to their forwards or pass it to one another. The remaining players are forwards. They may use only feet. Only forwards can score goals.

Example 7

Rolling the Medicine Ball
Concept: Propel a medicine ball by rolling it into the opposing goal.

Equipment: Medicine ball. Playing field: 6' × 30 feet, or depending on space configuration. Goals are the rear boundary lines along the entire length.

Players: Three to six on each side.

Length of play: As desired.

Rules: The ball may only be rolled or tossed no higher than hip level. Players may run up to three steps with the ball, but must roll it while doing so. The player with the ball can be engaged only when the ball is moving (if she holds it too long, the referee throws it). Goals can be scored only with a rolling—not a thrown—ball. Footwork is not allowed. Play starts at center court by draw or after a lost goal.

Small Games Without a Ball

Example 1

Day and Night
The groups sit opposite one another at the center line. There can be two players per group, or even up to six or eight. When someone calls "Day," the team designated "Day" tries to catch the "Night" team, which tries to run to the safety at the edge of the court and vice versa. This can also be played from a standing position, or lying on one's back or stomach, or other variations.

Example 2

Break Away

Two teams form two circles, one inside the other, that rotate by each other in opposite directions. At a signal, the members of the inner circle break out to the edge of the court (wall); the outer circle tries to stop them. It can also proceed the opposite way, with the inner circle catching the outer one.

Large Court Games

Soccer, hockey, basketball, volleyball, handball, and, in winter, ice hockey are especially recommended as large court games. These sports should be played according to regular competition rules. And one should be careful that technical quality and ball handling are given precedence. In other words, one should not just "play"; specific coaching of various aspects of ball handling (techniques of the individual sports) should be the focus.

Types of Exercise: Individual Exercises with Equipment

Example 1

Slalom Run

With the ball at his foot, the player runs through a slalom course of at least six gates (poles). He can run back and forth and his performance can be timed.

Variations

Like the basic exercise,
- With only the right foot,
- With only the left foot,
- With both feet,
- Running forward,

Fig. 87 Slalom run while bouncing a tennis ball and a basket- or volleyball.

- Running backward,
- But simultaneously bouncing a basketball with right, left, or both hands,
- But simultaneously bouncing a tennis ball with a tennis racket (Fig. 87),
- But instead of kicking a soccer ball, negotiate the slalom run with a hockey stick and ball.

Example 2

Mat Course

In the gym, mats (at least six) are placed alternately (left and right). The player is supposed to negotiate the mats to the left with a forward roll, and those to the right, with a backward roll. He will be timed during this zigzag run in one or both directions (forward and back). The same exercise can be varied by bouncing a basketball. It must be bounced very strongly on the roll,

so that it bounces high. During the roll, it may touch the floor only once.

Example 3

Obstacle Course

The player must quickly jump and run over obstacles (triangle of poles, auto tires) which are not too high.

Variations

- Various directions are required (for example, only backward).
- All obstacles are raised.
- Only one or two obstacles are raised.
- The player can advance on only one leg.
- The player must also use her hands to fend off balls that are thrown to her.

Example 4

Marker Course
The players run across the markers, for example, a rope.

Variations
- Running quickly with one floor contact between two ropes.
- Running quickly with two floor contacts between two ropes.
- Running quickly while alternating one or two floor contacts between two ropes.
- Running forward and backward while combining various floor contacts.

Example 5

Mixed Course
A course can be constructed as one chooses, of various types of obstacles and tasks. Poles, boxes, mats, medicine balls, and the like can be stacked against one another to make a many-sided coordination challenge for the whole body.

Running should be combined with various jumps, throws, types of climbing, rolling, and the like.

To make it more difficult, a ball can be balanced, a stick can be balanced on the finger, a tennis ball can be bounced with the racket, and so on.

Example 6

Medicine Ball Golf
Nine circles (1$^{1}/_{2}$' diameter) are designated as "holes." A zigzag path is formed by obstacles (equipment, mats, benches, string, etc.). The medicine ball is brought into play from the start position with the foot. The ball should always end up in the designated circles. Every kick with the foot counts. Whoever needs the fewest kicks is the winner.

Fig. 88   Keeping the ball in the air.

Example 7

Keeping the Ball in the Air
(Fig. 88)
The player keeps balls in the air by briefly touching them with various parts of the body.

Variations
- At first, use only feet (legs).
- Then, use the hands (arms/shoulders).
- Repeat for the "strong" and "weak" sides.
- Combine movements according to an established pattern, for example, moving the ball from below to above (from the legs over the arms), and so on.
- Use various balls (for example, soccer ball, handball, volleyball, tennis ball, rugby ball, balloon).
- Combine basic tasks using various balls in succession (for example, tennis ball, softball, rugby ball).

Example 8

Jumping on a Minitrampoline
The player jumps on a small or minitrampoline while simultaneously practicing throwing movements.

Variations
- Basketball throw.
- Handball pitch.
- Jumping variations, such as a half turn.
- Practice throwing from the nondominant side also.

Example 9

Roller Skating
The player learns the basics of roller skating, such as pushing off to the side, pushing off to the front, stopping, changing direction, crossing over, negotiating curves, and traveling backward.

Variations
- Travel around barriers and negotiate gates.
- Balance small objects while moving (for example, balls).

Individual Practice Without Equipment

Example 1

Rotating the Carousel
The player sits in the hammock and tries (either crouched or with outstretched legs) to turn himself sideways without losing his balance. The rotation is achieved by putting his hands out.

Example 2

Stomach and Back Seesaw
The player lies either on her stomach or on her back and tries to seesaw with legs stretched out and not using her hands.

Example 3

Hammock Roll

From the hammock, the player tries to roll from the side to the stomach position without using his hands and then to return to the seat.

Partner Exercises

Example 1

Stepping on Feet

Two partners stand opposite each other with hands behind their backs. Idea: Who can step on the partner's feet? Count to 10, if desired.

Example 2

Sole War

Two partners sit opposite each other in the hammock; the soles of the feet are turned up slightly, so that they can touch each other on the soles. They now try to get the partner out of the hammock by pushing (soles against soles) and tricking the partner. Count to 10, if desired.

Example 3

One-Legged War

Two partners stand opposite each other on one leg, hands behind their backs. Each tries to unbalance the other by pushing with the chest or shoulder so that she will have to put both feet on the ground. Count to 10, if desired.

Example 4

Knocking Over the Indian Club

Two partners hold each other with both hands. The Indian club is between them. By pushing and shoving, each tries to make the partner knock over the club. Count to 10, if desired.

A high level of coordination ability is required.

Training Techniques

The Importance of Technique

The status of technique varies considerably in individual sports. There are types of sports in which technique is relatively easy to learn and to master but certain conditional or physical elements dominate. In tennis, technique is one of the most important factors because only through technique can conditioning, tactical, and psychological skills be employed in the game. Accordingly, teaching and training tennis techniques must be granted a special status in the comprehensive development of a tennis player.

It should be particularly emphasized that qualitative and quantitative development of technique, as well as its learning pace is very strongly dependent on the developmental level of general coordination skills and on the conditional skills and abilities of each individual. This implies that deficiencies in the area of general coordination and in the areas of strength, stamina, speed, and their combination must inevitably have a negative impact on technique training.

Thus, one should not view teaching and training techniques as independent. Instead, they should be seen as an integral part of a comprehensive training program.

Types of Technique

Tennis technique is the achievement of the desired ideal movement, which is defined as the optimal movement for an individual athlete based on anatomical, biomechanical, and physical laws and principles. There are two categories of technique:
- Midlevel or even elementary execution of movement, the so-called basic form of technique, which is taught to beginners.
- Movement ability of top players, which originates in the basic form, but has been integrated into the player's individual style.

Technique is not essentially different for beginners or less-talented players versus top players. However, there are specific qualitative differences.

Depending on talent, effort, motivation, and goal setting, individual players reach various levels, and along with accomplishing goals, a differentiated expression of techniques with a corresponding ability. However, even most top players do not master all techniques perfectly.

Development of Tennis Techniques

Teaching tennis techniques is a progressive, continuous process that should adjust over time to the latest developments in methods and teaching.

The goals of learning, practicing, and training technique are:
- Acquiring stable basic patterns for techniques and automatic, long-lasting, and habituated technical abilities;
- Being able to use these technical abilities in all possible unforeseen, difficult, and unusual situations and positions;
- Maintaining optimal functionality under all conditions typical of a match.

Based on this, teaching technique can be divided into two levels.

First level: Learning techniques.
Second level: Training techniques.

It is important to emphasize both of these levels and to differentiate between them because they differ in practice and content as well as in scope and in the intensity of execution. In practice, however, the transition from level to level is not sharply divided, but rather fluid.

Learning Techniques

Acquiring the basic form (basic coordination) and the initial elements of refined form (fine coordination) falls under the first part of this level. The content of this phase includes: reacquisition, expansion of coordination skills, and acquisition of a broad repertoire of movements and experiences to achieve a refined tennis-specific coordination.

In the second phase of this level, refined form (fine coordination) is mastered, and the top form (best coordination) is achieved. Individual use of the particular stroke techniques, which can be employed in all possible situations and positions are formed and strengthened. These are practiced under simplified competitive conditions.

Principles for Learning Techniques
One should practice in such a way that the skills relating to tennis technique to be learned can be repeated regularly and with enough repetitions without distractions:

- Under good, stable conditions,
- With consideration of physiological processes, especially concerning energy needs and the relationship of work and rest,
- While maintaining regularity of coordination techniques.

Training Techniques

For training techniques, including familiar techniques in matchlike situations is most important. Technique should serve to resolve all imaginable problems. The goal of this level is perfecting fine coordination and achieving an optimal practical applicability of technical skills under changing— and in particular, under aggravated—conditions.

In the final phase of this level, tennis technique reaches a functional perfection, which exhausts individual possibilities to a great extent. Individual limits are finally reached. In other words, the content of this level consists of types of competition-oriented training under matchlike conditions and stresses.

Principles for Training Techniques
The technical skills are to be drilled in training

- Under changing conditions,
- In difficult situations and positions,
- With variations in movement,
- Under real and aggravated competitive conditions,
- With temporary allowance of some physiological overburdening.

General Advice for Learning and Training Techniques

An athletic movement is a dynamic, directed process that, among other things, depends on the level of coordination and conditioning skills of the player. In addition, in tennis acyclical movement sequences are also a factor.

In tennis, the movement sequence of executing a stroke is simple and uncomplicated in principle (with the exception of serving). The movement sequence

as such is not difficult, but the interaction with two pieces of equipment (the racket and ball) is very demanding on the total-body coordination abilities. It also happens that the one piece of equipment (the ball) must be controlled by the other (the racket). Therefore, it is an important task to manage the most comprehensive (movement) image for the student and to teach and illustrate for him diverse sensory and kinesthetic experiences while he is performing them. That means that, step by step, the student should be confronted with the theoretical knowledge corresponding to his current level of technique so that he can execute the movements knowledgeably. This applies especially to the basic-form phase.

Later, in the refined-form phase, attention is drawn increasingly to the most important details, that is, that the physical "reregistration" is good because it has no "disturbances"; the movement sequence thus becomes more and more automatic.

A movement sequence in tennis is considered to be automatic, then, when it progresses practically "by itself," to such an extent that the player can focus completely on tactics; this happens in the phase of acquiring the most refined form. Movement is then controlled and regulated without the player being conscious of it.

Individual Qualifications

Calendar Age

It is basically true that the younger the student is, the more varied the training must be. This is true in general and applies to tennis training as well. During the very favorable age for learning and skillfulness, roughly between 8 and 12, talented children learn the whole stroke repertory very fast. Therefore, the curriculum should be broad and not limited to the basic types of strokes. Above all, the playful element should be dominant, especially initially.

Training Age

The general capacity in the motor and cognitive areas increases with the training age.

Biological Age

In tennis training, the trainer must allow for individual variations in developmental stage around the average. This is especially important in group instructions, when putting together individual groups.

Individual Performance and Capacity for Stress

These two factors can change very quickly, depending on circumstances; that is, in tennis training one must consider the general and specific development in the intended program and must continuously adjust the content to the current skills status.

Training and Health Status

In addition to the various levels of muscle strength, stamina, speed, and technique, tennis requires consideration of motivation, current attitude, mood, and current health situation.

Overall Capacity for Stress and Regeneration

External influences such as school, profession, exams, family, and travel play an important role. With few exceptions, one should not engage in technical training when tired or exhausted.

Psychological Individuality

Every student has a different capacity and thus reacts differently to assigned training stimuli, content, and intensity.

Gender-Specific Differences

Especially during and after puberty, training requirements must be different for males and females. However, in prepuberty there is no essential difference in the ability to tolerate stress and the ability to learn.

Introduction to the Practice of Training

In tennis, as in all other types of sports, not only practical content, but other factors must also be considered to formulate a sensible training program: stress intensity, length of a single exercise, structuring of breaks, sequence of individual exercises in relationship to their content, and much more, are very important in contemporary tennis training.

Optimum success and a steep increase in skills are possible in tennis training only through a systematic approach and planning. A series of exercises with no choice and no goal can even have a negative effect on skills acquisition, and it at least causes a slowing-down and even stagnation of development.

The trainer should be careful that all types of strokes and techniques are practiced regularly and systematically. Several types of exercises can be used for practicing a stroke, depending on motivation or practical considerations. Monotony in training must be avoided.

Apportioning Stress

Length of Individual Exercises

Individual exercises have only one function, if done over a specific time span with the appropriate intensity. Individual technique exercise should last 20 minutes, as a rule, to achieve an optimal number of repetitions and the relationship of stress and regeneration. Shorter stimuli cause a decreased success for the student, or even none at all. On the other hand, exercises with high demands on coordination qualities—and these are almost all types of training tennis technique—may not exceed a level of fatigue at which the refined motor coordination can be impacted.

Training must be stopped as soon as there is any impact on the fine coordination or ability to concentrate. The allowable stress periods can be increased even in the refined motor area via a specific improvement of the general conditional status. Based on experience, then, an exercise without an opponent (the trainer tosses and the ball is hit only once by the student) lasts approximately 15–30 minutes. An exercise with opponents (trainer puts the ball into play and the students play two or more strokes) lasts approximately 20–30 minutes.

Specific coordination exercises, quickness, or speed, or take-off power exercises as part of the technique training last approximately 1–5 minutes per exercise with two to five series of 6–10 strokes per series and appropriate breaks between the individual series. In this way, one can best manage the scope as well as the intensity of the training, as needed.

Intensity of Individual Exercises

The intensity of exercise, that is, the number of strokes per series and/or the speed and use of force when executing the stroke, must be geared to the skills level of the player. The intensity also depends on whether the goal of learning or training technique is a matter of purely technical training or training techniques including conditioning elements.

Basically, for learning technique, the series consist of approximately 5–15 strokes per player per series. This should be followed by a break of approximately 15–25 seconds. In this way, there is no significant lactate formation and buildup. (This should remain below 2 mmol/l.) It should be pushed to the anaerobic condition region in order to achieve maximum coordination, learning speed, and intensity.

With technique training, the series should vary, as in a match. Therefore, short series of 2 to around 10 or 15 strokes should predominate; and longer series of 15–25 strokes or more per series should be interspersed. The total number of repetitions of a stroke and/or exercise should be between approximately 150 (learning technique: basic form, fine form) and 200 (training technique: best form, stabilization).

This number of repetitions is necessary in order to achieve a sufficient and thorough stimulus effect. One does not reach this through a lower number; and with a higher number of repetitions (more than 200), the central nervous system (which influences the quality of coordination and the ability to concentrate) becomes fatigued. This also happens if one continuously repeats long series of 30–70 strokes or more.

As already mentioned, such an exercise lasts approximately 20–30 minutes. This should be followed by a 2–5 minute recuperation break before the next training unit.

In group work also, stroke exercises should be arranged in series with individual strokes for each player. With a specific number of repetitions (5–15 strokes) in a series, the player can actually process suggestions or corrections more effectively.

As a rule, stroke speed should always be the fastest possible for the skill level and situation.

The measure of quality for this is the success quotient. At the beginning of training one assesses the weaknesses in the player's execution of movements; later on, the misdirection of the ball is assessed. The success quotient in this type of assessment criteria should be at least 60% for difficult exercises and 70–80% for easier ones. If the given goal measure is below 50%, the stroke speed for achieving optimal success in learning or training is probably too high; the player is overchallenged. If the accuracy is 90–100%, the player is generally underchallenged; the tasks are too easy, and the stimulus intensity and quality are too low.

Tips on Methods for Training Technique

In order to realize an optimal series of exercises over 20 minutes (more in the case of higher stroke frequency and in the correct series length without long breaks and interruptions), it is necessary to have a sufficient number of tennis balls available. It is a good idea to have a shopping cart with approximately 100–200 balls. Individual series of exercises within a training unit should be structured according to the following methodical principles:
- from easy to difficult,
- from slow to fast tempo,
- sequence of contents: technique, coordination speed, ability to react, quickness.

These areas must be trained uninterrupted and represent a point of completion for aerobic stamina. They are followed by exercises whose objective is improving anaerobic stamina.

The correct organization of a training unit is very important. Types of exercises for tennis-specific coordination and for quickness or explosive power (starting power, take-off power) must be relatively short (six to ten repetitions per series and two to three series with 1–2 minutes break in between) and must be done when rested. Therefore, it is recommended these exercises be scheduled between the individual technical parts of a training unit, after the break mentioned previously, before beginning the next exercise with a coordination or quickness exercise, and/or before beginning the whole unit with this training. In this way, within each training unit of $1\frac{1}{2}$–2 hours, one can train coordination and quickness approximately three times without endangering the organism because of fatigue.

Any type of tennis-specific stamina training on the tennis court must be scheduled at the end of the unit. Here are some important tips for training:
- Each training unit should begin with a sufficient warm-up: running, limbering-up exercises, stretching exercises, playing ball (10–30 minutes).
- On the tennis court itself, hit balls for at least 10 minutes, with the balls at first being hit slow and high in order to prepare the musculature and the organism for tennis and to promote rhythm and feel for the ball. Before match training, the length of hitting practice should be 15–20 minutes.
- After each training session, ease off or hit in a relaxed manner 10–15 minutes at a slow pace (pulse approximately 110–140 beats/minute), in order to initiate and accelerate the regenerative processes. In order to lead the players to the correct body-weight transfer and body movement in the direction of the stroke, the recommendation is to set up markers that force the player into a forward movement in the direction of the stroke both during and after it because they must touch these or run around them. With volley or smash training, the recommendation is to touch the net with the racket after completing the stroke in order to obtain the same effect.
- With the majority of group exercises without opponents, students should get out of the way by moving forward and in front of the group after finishing the stroke, before they get back in line. This prevents a premature backward movement during the stroke as well as a tie-up of students waiting to hit—as is the case with the usual lining up toward the rear.
- With a larger group (six to eight players), the recommendation with many exercises is that, after finishing the stroke, the player picks up several balls and puts them back in the cart. In this way, there is no crowding and no boredom among those waiting.
- If the player hits the ball into the net too often, the following helps: Each player must immediately pick up the ball that she has played into the net and put it into the cart or basket. In this way, she misses at least one round. Her concentration and precision will then increase dramatically.

Training Examples

One could fill a book with practical forms of training alone, because almost every trainer has created his own favorite forms or has modified exercises over time. Not all possible exercise forms can be described here, and in this context we recommend Born/Schoenborn (1990).

The exercises presented here represent a sample of a number of variations and combinations. Mainly, it is a matter of providing some examples to elucidate the principles that have been introduced. Many exercises can also be adapted for training one or two players. The trainer can function as tosser of the first ball or as sparring partner. As already mentioned, a shopping cart with 200–300 balls is necessary in order to control the range and intensity.

In addition, a perfect toss by the trainer is the prerequisite for success of any exercise. Not just speed, height, length, and direction of the tossed ball, but also the correct time interval between the tossed balls and the age and ability level of the player must be considered in planning the exercise.

Basically, the player should not be put under pressure by too-high, too-long, too-fast, or sloppy tosses when learning techniques. On the contrary, executing the stroke should be made easier in this phase, where learning quickly is encouraged. Foremost in technique training, then, is the purposeful modeling of difficult situations in order to set up conditions similar to a match.

With simpler types of exercises, ball-throwing machines can be used. The individual exercises proceed effectively only when the student understands the principle. Therefore, a precise verbal description of each exercise—or if possible a demonstration by the trainer or slowly going through the exercises at the beginning of the training session—should include an explanation of the rationale for the exercise.

The following exercises are grouped in two levels of difficulty. The first level always aims for the objectives of basic formation, refined formation, and stabilization of the individual stroke techniques. Examples 1–11 belong to this level of difficulty. In the second level, the conditions when executing the stroke in a manner typical of a game are altered; that is, contact height, hitting position and the degree of difficulty are increased. From Example 12 on, the exercises belong to the second level.

For optimal stimulus level, the following stress norms can be recommended for most types of exercises:

- Length of exercise: 15–25 minutes.
- Strokes per series: 7–20.
- Series pause: 15–30 seconds.

For all other types of exercises, see the tips given in the examples under the "Execution" section.

Diagrams of the exercise examples described below can be found on pages 141–144.

Exercise 1

Baseline Stroke

Objective: Basic formation, refined formation and stabilization of baseline strokes.

Execution: Students learn baseline strokes from the beginning through movement. They must move at least 3–6 feet to the stroke. After completing seven to ten strokes, they must move forward and sideways—a proper movement to the center with correct weight transfer.

Exercise 2

Volley

Objective: Basic formation, refined formation and stabilization of volley.

Execution: Students play the volley in the forward movement. After the stroke, they must move farther forward and touch the net before playing the next ball. In touching the net, they are indirectly prepared to hit in the forward movement.

Exercise 3

Smash

Objective: Basic formation, refined formation and stabilization of the smash.

Execution: Two players smash, two wait. After each smash, the players must touch the net. In this way, they are forced to play each smash while moving backward. The pairs switch after each series.

Exercise 4

Lob

Objective: Basic formation, refined formation and stabilization of the lob.

Execution: The lob should be practiced right from the beginning from the corner. The lob must go so high over the trainer's head that she cannot reach the ball even if she stretches her arms to the limit. While doing this, the baseline should be envisioned as the goal.

Exercise 5

Half-Volley

Objective: Basic formation, refined formation and stabilization of the half-volley.

Execution: The half-volley should be practiced from center court. The player must always run forward to the ball.

Exercise 6

Passing Shot

Objective: Basic formation, refined formation and stabilization of the topspin-passing shot.

Execution: Topspin is the best pass stroke. It should be practiced from the beginning from the sideline, because later it is most often used there.

Exercise 7

Attack Shot

Objective: Basic formation, refined formation and stabilization of the slice-attack ball.

Execution: The slice should be practiced from center court. First, the ideal weight transfer is achieved; and second, depending on the situation, the slice is practiced as an attack ball.

Exercise 8

Stop

Objective: Basic formation, refined formation and stabilization.

Execution: Like the slice, the stop is practiced at center court in a realistic situation. In this way, it also forces the player into the forward movement and is played as an alternative to the slice.

Exercise 9

Stop Volley

Objective: Basic formation, refined formation and stabilization.

Execution: The stop volley must also be practiced in the forward movement, near the sideline. As in volley training, the player should touch the net after the stroke, before he gets back in line.

Exercise 10

Service

Objective: Basic formation, refined formation and stabilization.

Execution: The service is practiced from the right and the left. First, the length and then the side-on placement are taught with respect to appropriate reliability.

Exercise 11

Return

Objective: Basic formation, refined formation and stabilization.

Execution: Because in the beginning phase the players cannot serve, the trainer herself must. Standing behind the service line to serve is best. One can control the pace very well from there.

Training Techniques

Exercise 12

Baseline Stroke
Objective: Strokes far behind the baseline.

Execution: The trainer plays long and high balls. The player must first fade to the rear, and then hit the ball in the forward movement before the group runs by and get into line again.

Exercise 13

Baseline Stroke
Objective: Strokes with a high point of impact.

Execution: The trainer tosses somewhat short but very high balls. The player must hit the ball at or above shoulder level in the forward movement.

Exercise 14

Baseline Stroke
Objective: Strokes for fast balls.

Execution: The trainer tosses very fast balls. In spite of this, the player must hit the balls in the forward movement of the body.

Exercise 15

Baseline Stroke
Objective: Overtaking a "winner" with forehand.

Execution: The trainer tosses four or five balls in a row from the forehand into the backhand corner. The player must overtake the balls and always play them only forehand, meaning that he must play them very fast as "winners." He can play the final ball down the line, when he has played the previous ones into the backhand corner.

Exercise 16

Passing Shot
Objective: Passing shot from outside the court.

Execution: The trainer tosses the ball in such a way that the player must meet it far outside the boundary line. From this unfavorable angle she must try to hit down the line as well as crosscourt.

Exercise 17

Passing Shot
Objective: Passing shot as a response to flat balls.

Execution: The trainer plays very flat balls near the baseline. The player must counter these and play them from a low point of impact as topspin- and as slice-passing shot.

Exercise 18

Passing Shot
Objective: Passing shot with a high point of impact.

Execution: The trainer plays high and long balls just in front of the baseline. The player has to hit these at shoulder level as topspin- or slice-passing shots.

Exercise 19

Passing Shot
Objective: Passing shot from midcourt.

Execution: The trainer plays balls flat and short into center court. The player must play them as topspin short crosscourt in both directions.

Exercise 20

Volley
Objective: Volley from the sideline.

Execution: The trainer plays balls hugging the sideline. The player must hit them either down the line or crosscourt while jumping. After meeting the ball, she should touch the net.

Exercise 21

Volley
Objective: Volley with a low point of impact.

Execution: The trainer tosses balls very flat and short. The player must hit them in a forward jump.

Exercise 22

Half-Volley
Objective: Half-volley next to or behind the body.

Execution: The trainer tosses balls in such a way that they bounce sideways behind or next to the player's body. The player must hit these as half-volleys.

Exercise 23

Attack Shot
Objective: Attack shot with a low point of impact.

Execution: The trainer plays the balls flat behind the "T". The player must hit them while running forward as a slice or topspin. After contact, he must advance even further.

Exercise 24

Attack Shot
Objective: Attack shot with a high point of impact.

Execution: The trainer plays balls high, approximately 6' in front of the baseline. The player must hit them at shoulder level while running forward as a slice or drive (forehand), and then continue running.

Exercise 25

Attack Shot
Objective: Attack shot from the sideline.

Execution: The trainer plays balls decidedly to the sideline. The player must play them as attack balls and then run forward diagonally to the center.

Exercise 26

Smash
Objective: Smash from a jump.

Execution: The trainer plays balls so high above the player that she can reach them only with the highest jump. Afterward, she must touch the net before the next ball is put into play.

Exercise 27

Smash
Objective: Smash after lobs above the left side of the body.

Execution: The trainer plays the ball above the player's left shoulder. The player must turn his whole body almost toward the net, move to the left, and smash from there.

Exercise 28

Smash
Objective: Backhand smash on the left half of the court.

Execution: The trainer plays balls above the player's left shoulder. The player must hit them as backhand smashes down the line (or crosscourt).

Exercise 29

Smash
Objective: Smash after the jump of the lob.

Execution: The trainer plays balls over the player who is standing at the net. The player must run back, overtake the ball, and then smash after a jump.

Exercise 30

Lob
Objective: Lob while running back and then turning.

Execution: The trainer plays balls over the player who is standing at the net. The player must run back and return the balls as lobs.

Exercise 31

Passing Shot
Objective: Passing shot with forehand, while running back, over the left shoulder.

Execution: The trainer plays balls over the player who is standing at the net. The player must run back and return the ball over the left shoulder with his back turned to the net.

Exercise 32

Passing Shot
Objective: Passing shot while running back.

Execution: The trainer plays balls over the player who is standing at the net. The player must run back, overtake the ball, let it fall low on her right side, and return it as a passing shot.

Exercise 33

Training Defensive Techniques
Objective: Reliability, patience, concentration, precision, rhythm, avoiding mistakes.

Execution: Two players execute each stroke in the same way. They play crosscourt/crosscourt or down-the-line/down-the-line and try to make minimal mistakes.

Variation: The trainer assigns a hitting technique in addition to the directions (for example, player A backhand-slice and Player B forehand-topspin).

Exercise 34

Training Defensive Techniques
Objective: Reliability, patience, concentration, precision, rhythm, avoiding mistakes through height and length of the strokes.

Execution: Two players hit forehand and backhand from baseline to baseline. They try to play each ball between the "T" and the baseline.

Variation: A rope or construction tape is suspended approximately 3' high. Each stroke should be played over the rope.

Training Techniques

Exercise 35

Training Defensive Techniques
Objective: Reliability, patience, concentration, precision, rhythm, avoiding mistakes in spite of hitting under time pressure.

Execution: One player hits alternately down the line and crosscourt from the forehand corner. The partner runs to the baseline and returns alternately forehand and backhand into the forehand corner of the opponent.

Variation: Ball tosser in the backhand corner.

Exercise 36

Training Defensive Techniques
Objective: Reliability, patience, concentration, avoiding mistakes in spite of intensive running precision, rhythm.

Execution: One player always plays crosscourt, and the other player always plays down the line.

Variation: Three players play 2-on-1, one player runs and plays crosscourt and her partner tosses the balls to her down the line.

Exercise 37

Training Offensive Techniques from the Baseline
Objective: Intensive offensive play, risk-taking, fast and aggressive play, playing balls early.

Execution: Two players hit balls from baseline to baseline. They stand in the forecourt and should play the balls early.

Variation: The trainer tosses balls from the net.

Exercise 38

Training the Down-the-Line Attack Technique
Objective: Practicing the attack ball down the line in the forward movement, passing shots.

Execution: The player attacks a ball played into center court down the line. His opponent plays the ball down the line. Finally, both try to win the point.

Variation: Down-the-line attack with the backhand; down-the-line attack with the forehand.

Exercise 39

Training the Crosscourt Attack Technique
Objective: Practicing the attack ball crosscourt in the forward movement, passing shots.

Execution: The player attacks a ball played into center court crosscourt. Her opponent plays the ball crosscourt. Finally, both try to score the point.

Variation: Crosscourt attack with the forehand, crosscourt attack with the backhand.

Exercise 40

Volley, 2-on-1
Objective: Volley in rapid succession.

Execution: One player plays volleys in various directions against two opponents. The trainer puts the ball into play or joins in.

Variation: Individual players in the middle, individual players in the left service court, individual players in the right service court.

Exercise 41

Volley—Lob
Objective: Volley and volley-lob.

Execution: Two players hit volleys to each other. The point is made after one volley-lob.

Exercise 42

Playing Out the Volley
Objective: To prepare for the volley under competitive conditions, ability to react, anticipation, doubles.

Execution: Two players hit volleys to each other from the service court. After the second hit, they try to outplay the opponent. The winner of the volley duel continues playing against the next opponent.

Variation: Crosscourt/crosscourt volley duel; down-the-line/down-the-line on a half of the court.

Exercise 43

Volley Rhythm
Objective: Find volley rhythm.

Execution: Two doubles pairs stand opposite each another in the service courts. Only volleys are allowed; one pair is always supposed to play down the line, and the other always plays crosscourt.

Variation: Playing out a set as in a competition (scoring as in table tennis).

Exercise 44

Serves to the Intended Target Area
Objective: To be able to play serves into an intended target area.

Execution: Two players serve simultaneously. They try to serve into marked target areas using prescribed stroke techniques, for example, slice-serve from the right to the outside and twist-service from the left to the outside.

Variation: Two players return simultaneously.

Exercise 45

Twist-Service
Objective: To practice twist-serves that bounce high and obliquely.

Execution: The players always hit twist-serves. They try to give the ball so much spin that it goes through a gate that has been set up at an appropriate distance.

Variation: Instead of the gate, a string or construction tape is suspended above the net.

Exercise 46

Serve and Net Attack
Objective: To place the serve, achieve a good net position, volley, return.

Execution: The server hits from the right into the center and follows the serve to the net. His

opponent returns through the center. The server tries to place the volley and moves closer to the net. The one who is returning tries to hit a pass to the net player.

Variation: First serves into the left service court, second serves to the opponent's body.

Exercise 47

Return
Objective: Reaction, anticipation.

Execution: One player serves. Another player practices returns. The return-player tries to play the returns very early and decreases the distance from the service line.

Exercise 48

Return
Objective: To shorten reaction and anticipation time, short backswing movement, go to meet the ball.

Execution: The trainer or a player serves. He stands immediately behind the service line. The student plays returns.

Variation: Returns from the left and right sides.

Exercise 49

Return of the Second Serve
Objective: To practice aggressive and risky returns, overtaking the backhand.

Execution: One player plays second serves to the opponent's backhand side. The return player overtakes the backhand and hits aggressive returns with the forehand.

Variation: Returns from the left and right sides.

Exercise 50

Return for Attack
Objective: To use the opponent's weak serves for immediate attack.

Execution: One player or the trainer plays second serves. The return player immediately goes from the return to the attack. The preferred technique for this is the slice, which is played long and relatively flat. After the return, the point is played out.

Variation: Returns from the left and right sides, slip in a return-stop as a surprise.

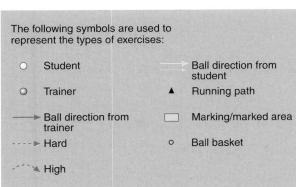

The following symbols are used to represent the types of exercises:

○	Student	⟶	Ball direction from student
○	Trainer	▲	Running path
⟶	Ball direction from trainer	▢	Marking/marked area
- - ▶	Hard	∘	Ball basket
⟍	High		

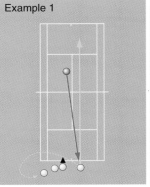

Example 1

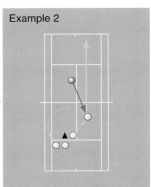

Example 2

Training Techniques

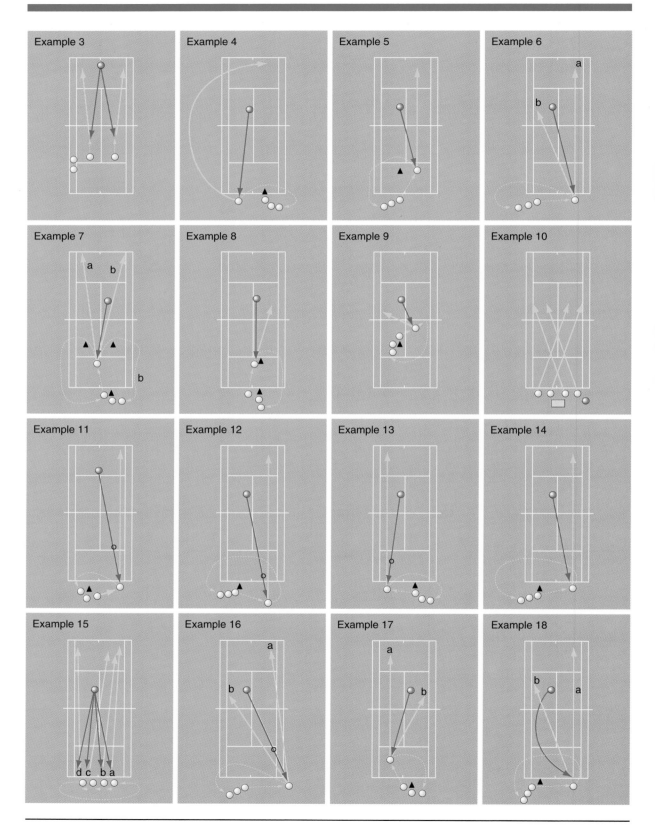

Example 3

Example 4

Example 5

Example 6

Example 7

Example 8

Example 9

Example 10

Example 11

Example 12

Example 13

Example 14

Example 15

Example 16

Example 17

Example 18

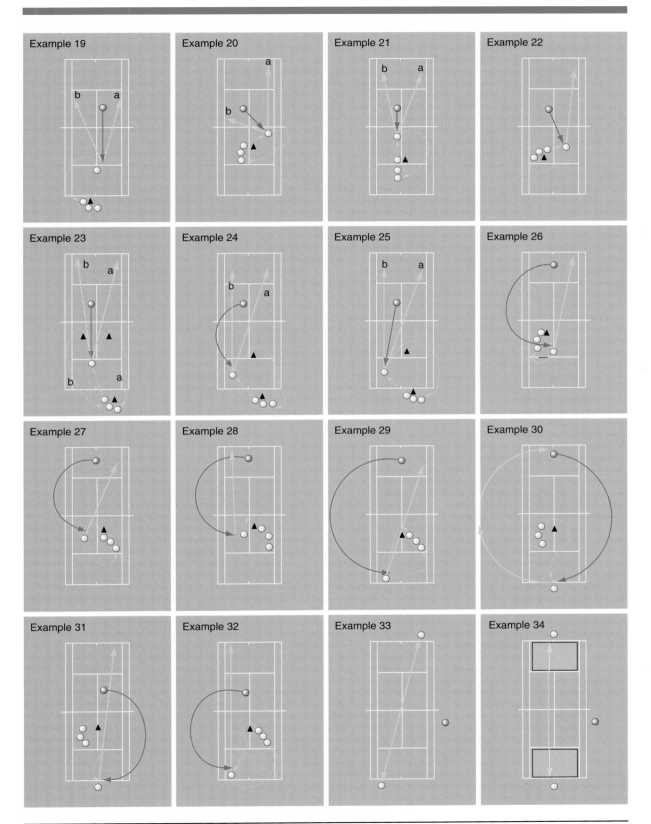

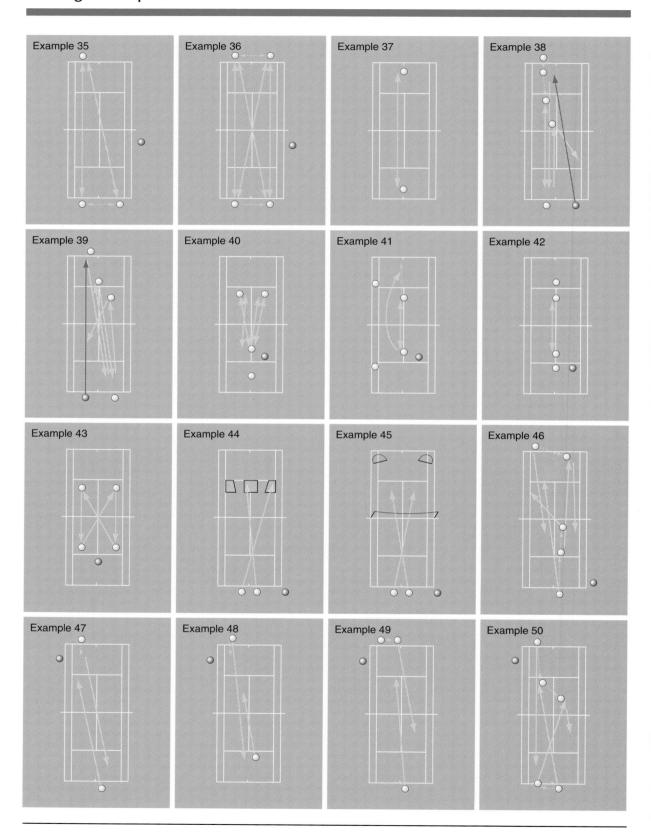

Example 35

Example 36

Example 37

Example 38

Example 39

Example 40

Example 41

Example 42

Example 43

Example 44

Example 45

Example 46

Example 47

Example 48

Example 49

Example 50

Training Tactics

Based on the four elementary tactical goals in competition, that is:

- Avoiding mistakes,
- Leading/forcing the opponent to make mistakes,
- Giving the opponent no opportunity to score direct points,
- Preparing and scoring direct points oneself,

tactical training should focus on technical, coordination, and mental abilities while taking into consideration the actual (the opponent is known) and presumed (the opponent is not known) abilities of the adversary, and should train in such a way that these tactical goals can be met.

In connection with this, four processes are of the highest importance:

1. One must observe what is happening.
   - What kind of stroke did the opponent execute (long/short, high/flat, crosscourt/down-the-line, straight/slice)?
   - Where is she? Where is she going? What is one's own position?

2. One must judge what one sees.
   - What possibilities are there?
   - What is the theoretically best solution?
   - Can the solution be applied, given one's own abilities and those of the opponent?

3. One must decide on a course of action (sometimes based on several possibilities).
   - How can one make the best of the situation, given the present circumstances such as sun, wind, and court surface?

4. One must act:
   - The necessary technical, conditioning, and mental abilities must be rigorously employed, depending on the decision.

The first three processes are dealt with in the head: perception, judgment, decision. Only these three steps are concerned with actual tactics. They lead into the fourth process, action, which is just as important as carrying out the tactical decision.

Tactics must be learned and trained just as specifically as the technical movement sequences, before they can best be applied in competition under difficult conditions. Therefore, there is a differentiation between

- Learning tactics and
- Training tactics.

Learning Tactics

Analogous to the individual techniques, which we can consider as basic patterns for completing movement tasks, learning tactics means to learn and utilize basic patterns. Basic tactical patterns are typical and effective solutions for individual game situations. Therefore, when we speak of learning tactics, we mean practicing certain tactical features of play that arise from the playing situation, so they can be carried out consistently. They are practiced without considering the opponent's behavior. Thus, it is not a matter of playing *against* each other but rather *with* each other.

Three points should be noted here:

1. For every exercise, the learner can freely choose, whether the situation facing him justifies initiating a tactical action (basic pattern). For example, after he has perceived and judged the situation, he must decide whether the opponent's somewhat shorter ball actually calls for a net attack or not (yet), because it appears that it is still too long.

2. If he attacks, as he decides in this example, he must decide whether it will be down the line or crosscourt; that is, the place where the approaching ball bounces "forces" the player to decide "correctly," like the theoretically best solution known to him in an analogous situation.

3. After deciding in favor of the attack, he must rigorously carry out the chosen tactical pattern.

Prerequisite for correct tactical learning is the exact knowledge of the theoretical sequence of the appropriate action. In this example, the player must know why he is running to a specific destination, where and when he should jump into the best hitting or turning position, and how he should react after the first volley.

From the viewpoint of method, tactical patterns considered should become increasingly more difficult, especially because of the decisions to be made. At any rate, the tactical plan in "learning tactics" is, for the most part, prescribed. The opponent's behavior plays no role in the perception, judgment, and decision processes.

Sample Exercises

- Players A and B toss from baseline to baseline. B is supposed to attack on short balls from A with a backhand. A may only pass (no lob). The attack shot is supposed to be long, so that A gets into difficulty and B can take a good net position. The direction of the attack shot (crosscourt or down-the-line) depends solely on the bounce of the ball (three-zone theory), independent of the opponent's weakness or strength. In learning tactics, one must first learn a basic pattern that is good for tactics, carry it out, and stabilize it. B hits the incoming volley crosscourt, regardless of whether it is a forehand or backhand volley. Thus she also decides—independent of her position and the point of impact—whether she should play the volley down the line, as a winner or as a stop volley. B must therefore note whether the ball is relatively short, that is, if it bounces in the "T" area, and whether—because of the trajectory, speed, and rotation—it should be played gently or hard, as an attack shot. She also must decide whether it should be hit crosscourt (from midcourt) or down the line (from near the singles sideline) (three-zone theory). After that, she must judge and determine as an alternative, whether she should attack or hold off, in order to proceed according to the tactical pattern.

- Player B attacks down the line or crosscourt, corresponding to the three-zone theory; but she now hits the volley down the line or crosscourt. In this case, B must deal with two alternative decisions, one after the other: first, if she should attack, and, second, how and where she should volley. Whether she attacks down the line or crosscourt is prescribed by the tactical pattern.

- Player B acts on the short ball from A; now she not only should attack down the line or crosscourt, but also can play a stop ball as an alternative, which she follows to the net.

Learning tactics, therefore, means putting basic patterns into practice, so that later it will be easy to embed the various possibilities, such as playing a slice-attack crosscourt or down the line or a stop ball and volley crosscourt or down the line, into a competitive situation.

Training Tactics

By training tactics we mean using the learned tactical patterns under difficult conditions in matchlike situations; that is, to have to decide among various possibilities (basic patterns), while simultaneously considering the opponent's behavior. Therefore, this is concerned with playing *competitively*.

Examples

- Players A and B are operating at the baseline. A is supposed to note each appropriate opportunity to come to the net with an attack ball. B can pass down the line or crosscourt quickly or gently, or play a lob. Therefore, B must note that A is attacking, where her attack ball bounces, and where A positions herself. Then B must judge which stroke it is, based on his technical skills, but also on his and A's positions and on A's strengths and weaknesses. Then he must decide what the best alternative is, and, finally, execute the appropriate passing shot or lob.

- Player B has the task of putting A under such pressure that her strokes become shorter; as a result, B can attack with a backhand-slice. Now he can freely decide to attack crosscourt or down the line, corresponding to the tactical basic pattern and to play the volley crosscourt or down the line, short or long. In addition, the direction of the attack ball and volley now depend heavily on the behavior (the position) and the skills of the opponent, that is, whether B can pass better forehand or backhand and whether he prefers crosscourt or down the line.

The previously described forms of learning and training tactics refer to the individual, recurring volley. Because in a match these volleys must be embedded in an overarching concept of match strategy, training tactics is also referred to as practicing particular strategies in the form of match training.

Examples
In the following examples, scores are measured in points, as in table tennis.
- Player A attacks only with the second serve, which she chooses in terms of spin, speed, and direction, and runs to the net. The point is played out. Player A serves until one of the two players has scored the agreed number of points. Technical objective for A: to immediately attack the opponent whose return and passing shot are weak.
- Player A has only one serve. Player B should attack this serve in any way possible, that is, he should attack A's weak side with the return, whose

spin and speed he chooses. The point is played out. The tactical objective for B is to use his own volley and smash strength.
- Players A and B play at the baseline. The ball is put into play underhand. The point should be made only from the baseline out (no stop). In this game, it is a matter of the tactical dimension of reliability and controlled risk, placement and change in rhythm in the context of baseline play.

Tactical training can also include a variation that Player A has specific tactical tasks, for example, to play only crosscourt or to alternate spin and speed. Player B must recognize this and react accordingly.

In learning tactics and training tactics, the processes of perception, judgment, and decision are foremost. Technique is necessary in order to be able to achieve the tactical objectives via action. If the technique is used poorly, technical advice and correction can be provided even while learning and training tactics. However, these should not form the focus of instruction and training.

Individual Prerequisites
The perception, judgment, and decision processes require physical qualities such as patience and concentration, courage and risk-tolerance, and discipline in practical playing situations, especially when the opponent's strengths and weaknesses are to be considered. However, players have these qualities in individually different ways. Therefore, in the following, these individual qualities should be discussed.

Although these prerequisites represent relatively dependable personality markers, they can still be influenced by effective and continuous training. This is particularly true for practicing with young people. In the following, some technique exercises for training specific qualities are included. Correction and tips should be limited exclusively to the corresponding tactical objectives of the individual examples.

Patience and Concentration
It is often desirable to keep the ball secure during play or to regularly repeat a specific stroke that is awkward for the opponent. For this, extreme concentration and especially patience are necessary. Impatient play disturbs the hitting rhythm and leads to careless mistakes.

Examples

- Hit balls for approximately 20 minutes (10 × 1.5 minutes, that is approximately 25–30 strokes; 25-second break each time) in regular, quiet rhythm, without essentially changing the hitting pace and rhythm. Tactical objective: Avoiding mistakes.
- Play the same stroke (for example, forehand-topspin or backhand-slice) for approximately 10 minutes in sequences of 15–25 strokes followed by a break of approximately 20 seconds. Tactical objective: To wait.
- Play as many balls as possible into the area bordered by the baseline and the service line. Tactical objective: Stroke length.
- Divide the service court into two or three lengthwise areas. Play the serve into one of these lengthwise areas. Here, the type of serve (that is, twist, straight, or slice) can be chosen. Serves that land in other areas are considered mistakes.

This type of exercise leads to particular concentration and gives the player the reliability that is a prerequisite for using the desired serve tactically in a match.

- As a match, four or six players play on two or three courts, individually, with a change in partners. After each 20-minute period (regardless of the status of the game), partners change, so that each player has played against three different partners after 3 × 20 minutes.

The difficulty is that, for one thing, the partners must repeatedly acclimate themselves to a new opponent, which requires a high level of concentration, and for another, they cannot be encouraged by a possible lead.

Courage and Risk-Readiness

Courage and risk-tolerance must maintain a reasonable relationship to the error rate that they necessitate. To avoid unnecessary careless mistakes, if there is any doubt, the same safe ball should be returned until the chance for an attack shot arises. This could be after the first ball contact, or maybe only after the 20th.

Examples

- Long balls are hit. The player attacks every short ball that bounces generally in the area of the "T". The points are played out.
- Player A hits only safe second serves. With the return, Player B should exert pressure, that is, the return should be hit back as a hard risk shot or as an attack shot, which the player who returns follows to the net.
- To practice the second serve under pressure (match condition), the player can have only one serve for the entire match. Only second serves that are executed aggressively lead to success. The points are played out.

Discipline

Discipline, that is self-discipline, is probably the most important basic requirement for serious tactical play, especially when there is internal tension (nervousness) and external pressure, due not only to one's opponent. This affects the execution of a single stroke or of a play (basic pattern) or the precise application of a tactical plan (match strategy).

Examples

- Both players are at the baseline. At a specific signal stroke (for example, short, shoulder-level ball to midcourt on the forehand side), agreed-on plays are practiced, for example, alternating stop balls and "winners." It is important at first to follow the prearranged sequence exactly (discipline), so that even the "tosser" (short, shoulder-level ball into midcourt) can fit into the basic pattern. After a specified time, play should be variable. The points are played out.
- Both players are at the baseline. Player A plays every ball, for example, to B's backhand, in which he may choose the type of stroke and speed, and can decide whether he should move to the net or just operate from the back court. The points are played out.

Training Serves

If the tactical plan requires a specific serve into a specific corner, this stroke should be trained systematically at first, for approximately 20 minutes (technique training). Then, there are whole plays (learning tactics), depending on the training program.

Examples

- Sliced-service to the right to the forehand side and move to the net (move away); return and volley direction can be chosen. The points are played out.
- Twist-service from the left to the backhand; return and volley direction can be chosen. The points are played out.
- Serve as desired, move forward. Return shot to the forehand-volley side or backhand-volley side, or, depending on how close the server is to the net, use a lob. Alternatively, the volley can be executed long or short (volley-stop). The points are played out.

These training examples can also be performed by several players simultaneously. One player returns, the others take turns serving. When all have served, the next player assumes the return position. In this way, points can be awarded, and after a specific number of rounds, a winner can be declared.

Training Returns

Sometimes the strategic plan calls for a specific return stroke, that is, with specific direction, speed, or stroke type (for example, slice or topspin).

Examples

- Player A serves to forehand or backhand, as desired. Player B tries to play each return into the opponent's court, according to the tactical plan (concerning stroke direction, length, speed, spin). The task could be, for example, to respond with a high topspin to the baseline or a stop in order to keep the opponent, who is moving forward and backward with difficulty, in motion.
- Player A follows her serve to the net. Player B practices the flat crosscourt or down-the-line return, as desired, as well as a return shot to the opponent's feet. The point is played out.
- Player A serves safe second serves. These balls are returned by Player B either offensively as "winners" to the server's corner (this allows the backhand to be overtaken) or more slowly to the baseline as preparation strokes, which are followed to the net. The point is played out.
  Basically, one should practice that which the tactical plan requires for a forthcoming match. This return training should last 15 minutes.

Baseline Play

Only training makes it clear how one operates most effectively against one's closest opponent. A partner should take on the role of the future opponent. In this way, the various alternatives can be played out purposefully and systematically according to the tactical plan.

Training Safe Baseline Play

Examples

- Practicing baseline play should last at least 15–20 minutes per unit. Partners play balls to each other as they choose, paying particular attention to stroke direction and type. Tactical objective for Player A: Avoid mistakes. Tactical objective for Player B: Provoke mistakes by constantly changing rhythm.
- Player A opens her game completely. Player B tries to return the ball for example, mainly with a backhand. Tactical objective: Play only to a corner (opponent's weakness).
- Player A plays only crosscourt, Player B chooses his stroke direction. Tactical objective: Through monotonous but safe play, force Player B to use technically difficult strokes that cause changes in direction, that is, to force the opponent to make mistakes.

In the last two examples, one player is significantly more pressured than the other. And it is very difficult for the pressured player to avoid making mistakes. Therefore, he must operate "tactically," that is, he must adjust to the stroke pace of the task; for example, he should occasionally return the ball higher (in order to gain time).

Training Offensive Baseline Play

Examples

- Player A plays as she chooses; Player B tries to exert pressure from the back court In addition, he can hit all the balls judged too short by A into a corner using a forehand or backhand (trying winners). The points are played out.
- Player A plays as she chooses; Player B operates as in the preceding example. In addition, he can also return the balls as preparation strokes, which he follows to the net. The points are played out.
- Player A plays as she chooses; Player B plays as in the preceding example. In addition, he can also return the balls judged too short as stops. The points are played out.
- The partners play a set. Player A should play the ball safely into the forecourt. On the other hand, Player B should risk something if during the volley the opportunity arises to exert pressure from the back court (or also overtake a backhand) and/or move to the net.

Playing at the Net

Service—Play at the Net

Initially, a player should follow only a slower serve to the net. This brings her closer to the net, with a good angle, and, as a result, can cover the court best. Service and return direction can be prescribed.

Examples

- A serves crosscourt from the right, runs forward, takes up the appropriate rotating position.
- B returns as desired. A hits the first volley down the line as a preparation stroke; B returns this volley as a passing shot. A moves closer to the net, in order to end the play with an offensive, down-the-line volley or a stop volley. B can still try to reach this ball and pass to A.
- Service from the left, return as a passing shot or lob; volley (at "T" height) down the line, or a smash. The points are played out.
- Service to the center, return as desired; volley if desired; passing shot if desired. The points are played out.
- Service to the body, return with forehand or backhand (passing shot or lob), volley as desired; pass or lob. The points are played out.

Generally, the strategic plan dictates the intended destination of the service as well as which return the opponent should use.

All these examples can be used in competition. And the table tennis 21-point scoring system has proved appropriate.

With this type of training, it is important that the stroke pace fits the practice routine or is altered to fit it. Therefore, one should not try at first to hit aces or to make direct return points. The server who is moving forward must be given the opportunity to complete the play. Of course, to make the practice more difficult and thus more like the situation in a match, the constraints can be varied each time.

Because a lot of time passes while one player returns to the starting position after the volley or smash, for this type of training for service-volley or preparation stroke and volley, a third or fourth player, who could be ready for the next play, would be ideal.

Attack Shot—Play at the Net

- Two players hit balls to each other. One notes the situation facing him, in order to move to the net with an attack shot. He volleys or smashes, while his partner/opponent passes or lobs. The direction of the attack shot results from the three-zone theory, and the objective of the passing shot or lob can be prescribed at first, but then later left open.

To sum up, we can say that many complex forms of training are suitable for training techniques, tactics, and conditioning as well as psychological aspects of playing tennis. Therefore trainers and players should always let each other know which training aspect they are focusing on at a given time.

Each type of training, with tactics as the core, should follow the often-articulated pattern:
1. Size up the situation,
2. Judge the situation,
3. Come to a decision,
4. Act on the decision.
Therefore, advice and correction should be based on these processes throughout the period of learning and training tactics.

Training Conditioning

In today's world-class tennis, real success is no longer possible without exceptional conditioning. In <u>tennis competition</u>, running and addressing the ball are improved by good conditioning prerequisites (for example, by running speed and running stamina), and the effect of individual strokes is also increased (for example, stroke speed and flexibility). In tennis training, the extent and/or intensity of stress should be increased only on the basis of a good level of conditioning.

Tennis literature recognizes various theories for conditioning (for example, physical state, motor types of motor demands, or motor-conditioning properties). Some authors also differentiate between conditioning skills (strength, speed, and stamina) and coordination skills (coordination and flexibility). In the following, we give the concept "conditioning" preference because it is widely used in sports and is familiar to tennis players.

For our discussion, we separate conditioning into the following four factors (Fig. 89):
- Stamina,
- Strength,
- Speed,
- Flexibility.

Fig. 89   Basic conditioning program.

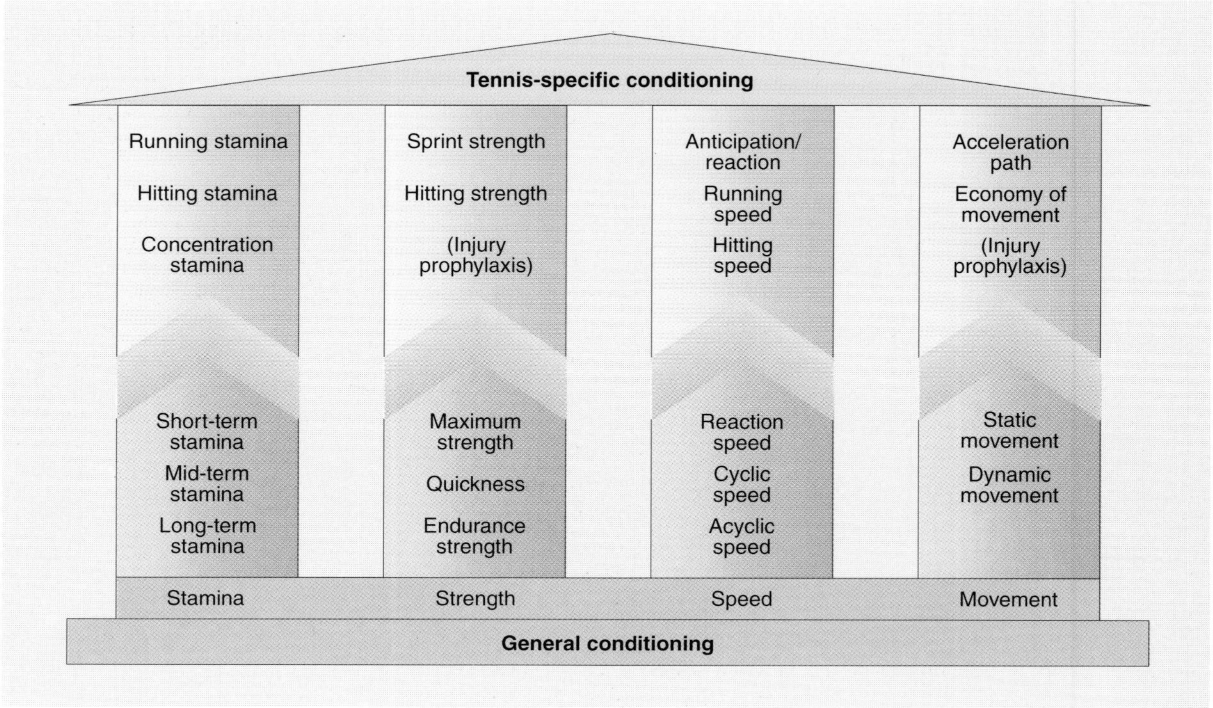

Stamina	Strength	Speed	Movement
Running stamina	Sprint strength	Anticipation/reaction	Acceleration path
Hitting stamina	Hitting strength	Running speed	Economy of movement
Concentration stamina	(Injury prophylaxis)	Hitting speed	(Injury prophylaxis)
Short-term stamina	Maximum strength	Reaction speed	Static movement
Mid-term stamina	Quickness	Cyclic speed	Dynamic movement
Long-term stamina	Endurance strength	Acyclic speed	

Tennis-specific conditioning

General conditioning

There are close interdependencies among these factors that can influence one another, sometimes positively (for example, strength and speed) or sometimes negatively (strength and stamina or strength and flexibility). Different aspects of strength need to be considered. On the one hand, the increase in strength required by training and the higher expenditure of strength can negatively influence stamina or change an already established stroke technique; on the other hand, deficiencies in strength can influence the development of speed (running and hitting speed), thereby limiting performance strength. Because of these considerations, the subchapter entitled "Strength" is geared mainly to the development of speed. In addition, a poorly developed musculature is often considered as the essential reason for the ever-increasing number of young professional players and internationally known top players who give up the game because of injuries.

In keeping with the desires of many tennis enthusiasts, we have created a home training program, which specifically aims to stabilize and strengthen overall body movement as well as resolve muscular imbalance. This program aims to create better protection against tennis injuries. Because this additional tennis training program should demand the least possible training time, and because workout equipment costs a lot in both time and money, one must be able to complete all the strength exercises at the workplace or at home (home training program). The reasons mentioned previously lead to the following categories:

- Stamina,
- Strength,
- Speed,
- Flexibility,
- Home training program.

Stamina

Definition and Importance

Stamina is generally described as the ability to resist fatigue with regard to an (athletic) stress. For tennis players, stamina includes resistance to physical and psychological fatigue in tennis competitions as well as tolerating stress and the ability to regenerate in training.

Tennis-specific stamina is therefore a complex ability that allows economy of movement and speed as well as the ability to concentrate and strength of will to work together based on the optimal energetic requirements in the working muscles.

In competition, the tennis payer should be able to run explosively without fatigue, even in the third (fifth) set (maintaining start speed) to the correct position (maintaining coordination), and should be able to play the ball with the greatest possible energy (maintaining hitting speed) in connection with coordination to the correct place (maintaining mental alertness).

The prerequisite for this is a good physical and mental regenerative ability vis-à-vis continuously recurring elasticity pressures so that each prescribed pace can be completed within the total playing time with no loss of physical and mental ability (especially speed, coordination, and concentration).

In training, the tennis player should be able to endure extensive and intensive stresses and recuperate as quickly as possible. Thus, tennis players need a high tolerance for stress as well as the ability to recuperate quickly.

The most important basis for this is well-developed, tennis-specific stamina built on a high level of basic stamina. Otherwise, there is always the danger of overtraining and the threat of a breakdown in capability.

The importance of stamina for increased capability on the tennis court can be verified through results of studies of tennis players.

Measuring and Monitoring Skills

An accurate assessment of tennis-specific stamina is possible only with a stress that is qualitatively and quantitatively similar to the stress occurring during competition. The advantage of appropriate monitoring processes lies in the most accurate possible assessment of tennis-specific stamina. In this regard, management of individual training should be initiated at the same time.

To measure the basic stamina of tennis players, a treadmill in the laboratory is the best method currently. It provides an accurate diagnosis of capacity that is related to motivation and simultaneously produces training tips that can be utilized precisely, depending on the training period (for example, basic stamina, speed stamina, recuperation). Here, it is possible to make an objective comparison of stamina between players of the same performance category (on average), and also a precise monitoring of specific training or competition events.

It also includes a review of initiatives of one's own, which are very important in skills training for young people as well as in rebuilding training (for example, following injuries). For reasons of motivation and to save time, these research methods are best done as a field test (for example, 400-m run) in small groups (for example, four to eight players at a time) with significantly higher participation levels by the players.

However, it is not sufficient to use this test alone to measure basic stamina because the running stresses are not uniform and continuous in tennis. On the other hand, they alternate acyclical movement sequences with continuous, concentric, and eccentric demands at irregular intervals. In addition, the energy expenditure differs with given tennis-specific stress, relating to the varied tennis-tactical game situation (for example, Sampras and Courier, Becker and Chang, or Graf and Sanchez-Vicario).

Results for basic stamina must therefore be combined with the professional judgment of the experienced trainer or supplemented by a standardized, tennis-specific stamina test. This is possible at present only through a ball machine test on the tennis court that gradually increases the demand.

For the tennis trainer who works primarily with students with lower skills levels, the total expenditure for the procedure cited will be too high. However, simpler tests, such as the Cooper or Conconi tests, are error-prone with regard to accurate measure of aerobic capacity. Thus, the recommendations resulting from these tests inevitably allow only rough estimates for training levels.

The tennis trainer obtains more reliable values for the current tennis-specific stamina of her players by using a simplified ball machine test (or by tossing balls from the ball cart) under standardized conditions.

For example, forehand and backhand strokes are played alternately to the baseline and increased in a 2-minute sequence to 18, 21, 24, and 27 balls per minute. For the experienced tennis instructor, at 24 balls per minute at the salient differences in running economy, hitting technique and successful shots can become apparent. At this point, relatively reliable estimates concerning the individual level of the tennis-specific stamina can be obtained.

Stamina Training Goals

Stamina training for tennis players pursues the following goals, in order of importance:
- Increasing the ability to resist fatigue in the tennis-specific working muscles (stamina, speed, and concentration) and in the mental-psychological area (concentration and will) for competition and training. To accomplish this, the training must be geared to tennis-specific stamina.
- Improving tolerance for stress and the ability to recuperate in training and competition. For this, a program that combines the training of basic stamina and of tennis-specific stamina is particularly effective.
- Increasing the level of general fitness for competition and training as well as improving general well-being. This simultaneously serves as a guard against health damage such as arteriosclerosis and obesity that, for the most part, can be traced back to lack of exercise and/or poor nutrition. This goal is mainly for middle-aged and older players who are particularly interested in health and fitness. A training program focusing on basic stamina is especially helpful for this.

Methods in Stamina Training and Practical Tips

Optimal stamina training requires detailed knowledge of the requirement profile of tennis-specific stamina and the physiological effect of the training methods and content. For the most part, stamina training methods can be divided into four main categories:

- Duration method,
- Interval method,
- Repetition method,
- Competition method.

Duration Method

In the duration method, improvement of the aerobic metabolic process is most important. The duration method *with constant speed* is used principally to develop basic stamina. For this, a defined distance is covered in a determined amount of time (for example, 60 minutes for a 12-km run) or a prescribed time with a particular heart rate (for example, a 40-minute run at 140–150 beats per minute). With the duration method *with variable speed*, aerobic and anaerobic metabolism and a brief switch-over to high stress intensity are trained, which expands the spectrum of organ functions related to stamina. The "steeplechase" is especially recommended for the tennis teacher; here, changes in pace are included, corresponding to natural topographical features (for example, meadows, hills, sand, and forest paths). It is supposed to be geared to the requirements profile in tennis and takes into consideration prescribed training goals (for example, regeneration running) and the player's current state of health. The various duration methods develop basic stamina and form the basis for introducing tennis-specific stamina.

Interval Method

The goal of interval training is chiefly in increasing speed-stamina because they are required in the short- (for example, 400/800-m run) and medium-time stamina disciplines (for example, 1500/3000-m run). Characteristic of the interval training method is the principle of the rewarding break, which—depending on the training goal, the distance, and the individual training level—contains the regenerative phases (for example, trotting breaks) of 30–180 seconds and leads to a decrease in heart rate to 100–120 beats per minute.

As a rule, this training method is less important for tennis players because it does not meet the tennis-specific requirements for stamina and speed. Additionally, it can impede the following training task because of high overacidification of the working muscles and can cause symptoms of overtraining. In individual cases, this form of interval training should be used to teach particular qualities having to do with the will (for example, enduring high overacidification increases staying power).

Repetition Method

The repetition method intends to repeat competition-specific partial requirements of stamina several times within a training unit. Here, following a complete regeneration or recuperation, a selected race (or special volley sequence) is run through (or played) using the stress level that is typical of a competition, or with the maximum speed, to the definitive capacity limit.

In the area of running training for tennis players, this method is only of secondary importance because this type of running stamina is not necessary in a tennis competition. However, in tennis training, this form of stress offers an interesting variation for improving tennis-specific stamina, especially toward the end of the preparation period and in the competition period (for example, 1–2 weeks before the season peak).

Competition Method

The competition method serves to develop competition-specific stamina, to build experience in techniques and tactics, and to monitor the toughness necessary for competition and the current skills level. The competition method is the most complex of the methods because it teaches all the special skills necessary for competitive tennis simultaneously. It follows that, for this method, the training must take place on the tennis court. Competitions (sometimes under conditions that have been made difficult, such as shortened breaks, are used as training content. They cause a higher level of exhaustion of various reserves and should lead to increased supercompensation via a subsequently lengthened recuperation phase. The competition method is used exclusively as preparation immediately before the season peaks.

Principles for Training Children and Young People

Stamina training for children and young people aims at developing a good, basic stamina and improving aerobic capacity. Thus, stamina training should emphasize range but never intensity. It should be noted here that stamina training has many diversions built in, interestingly, and has children in mind. Teaching aerobic stamina can begin with the early school ages (for example, first grade in elementary school), and it appears that girls up to 12–13 years of age and boys up to 13–14 years of age can be trained this way most effectively.

The principal training method for children and young people is the duration method. Conversely, the repetition and interval methods are not suitable because of the extent and density of stress, which require a demand of anaerobic metabolism. Because of the uniformity of the extended activity training and the danger of a transformation of fast (white) into slow but enduring (red) muscle fibers, one has to provide for continuous change via a complex and varied selection of training content and methods.

Managing Stamina Training

To manage stamina training, a mutual fine-tuning of the following components (stress norms) is necessary:
- Intensity of stress,
- Duration of stress,
- Frequency of stress.

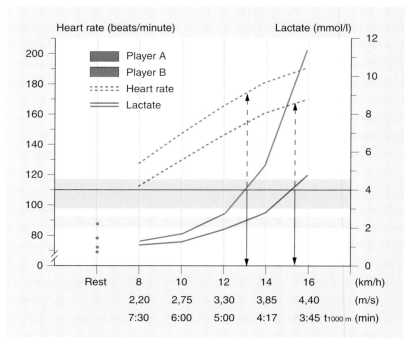

Fig. 90 Establishing the control rates, heart rate, and running speed for extensive and intensive stamina training using two international world-class competitors as examples.

The concept stress intensity used in general instruction on training and playing sports is inexact because it does not determine the intensity of the stress (stimulus strength) in an isolated manner but frequently presents a mixture or sum of various stress norms.

The intensity of the stress in stamina training is usually divided into extensive and intensive stress. With extensive stress, training is primarily in the purely aerobic realm, which is regulated most precisely by the lactic acid level in the blood (blood lactate). Special lactate-measuring devices have become commercially available for everyone. Tennis players who generally have low-to-midlevel stamina training levels find themselves in the aerobic area, when their blood-lactate concentration is below

approximately 3 mmol/l (Fig. 90). For running training, in a normal situation, this corresponds to a heart rate of 130–150 beats per minute or six to eight running steps (breath-step-rate) to one breathing cycle (breathing in and out). In practice, this means that a conversation is always possible during running training without a problem.

With children and young people the heart rate is approximately 10 or 20 beats higher; and with women, a higher heart rate (approximately 5–10 beats) is frequently allowed.

The standard value for the stress intensity (stimulus strength) that is easiest to determine is the heart rate. The individual pulse rate during training for basic stamina training should be about two thirds of the stress rate for recreational athletes and about three fourths for competitive athletes, who must be measured at the resting rate. The stress rate is calculated by subtracting the resting heart rate (measurement immediately before getting up) from the maximum heart rate (220 minus age).

Example:
30-year-old competitive player
(resting heart beat 65)
(beginning runner)
220 − 30 = 190   (maximum rate)
190 − 65 = 125   (stress rate)
125 × $^2/_3$ = 83
83 + 65 = 148   (training rate)

Extensive endurance training allows greater ranges of training (for example, 40–60 minutes, but also 90 minutes) than intensive endurance training so that particular adjustments in fat metabolism can be made through the burning of fat, while simultaneously protecting carbohydrate reserves. This form of training is also used as a regenerative measure in which running speed decreases even more and the duration of the run is simultaneously shortened.

Intensive endurance training is done in the context of aerobic–anaerobic transition to the anaerobic threshold, which, in the case of tournament tennis players (as a rule, intensely trained for stamina), is characterized by a blood-lactate level of approximately 3 mmol/l to a maximum of 4.5 mmol/l. (Tennis players who are specially trained for stamina run with lower lactic acid levels, for example, 3–3.5 mmol/l.) During extended activity training (cycling or downhill skiing) for a normal case, this

means a heart rate of 150–170 beats per minute or a breath-step-rate of 4–6 (inhale and exhale). As a result, most would have to stop a casual conversation because it would be extremely difficult. Even with young people, the heart rate can be approximately 5–10 beats higher. Intensive endurance training sessions usually last 20–40 minutes and can be continued at the most for 40–60 minutes (maximum lactate steady state). A training session of this type should not be conducted more frequently than twice per week; otherwise, the time for replenishing the glycogen reserve is too short and an overtraining syndrome threatens. The maximum oxygen absorption capacity is taken care of effectively via the intensive stamina training. For developing basic stamina, intensive extended activity training is the method of choice for tennis players. Basically, similar training effects for basic stamina can also be achieved in other sports if the largest possible muscle groups are used and there are dynamic movement sequences. Additionally, running, cycling, downhill skiing, and rowing are very valuable for tennis players.

For the purpose of better development of the whole body and especially because of motivation, a variation in types of sports is recommended, as long as there is opportunity and corresponding desire or curiosity. The frequency of stress in developing endurance capability should be at least two to three times per week. With daily stamina training (for example, at a training camp or in the preparation for the clay-court

season) faster progress can be made. One must be very careful that, with this high emphasis on stamina training, other somewhat more important skills components are not overlooked (for example, technique) or negatively influenced (for example, speed).

The elementary basis for a lasting development of tennis-specific stamina is a mid to high level of basic stamina. This also is important for other conditional factors such as speed and strength. Therefore, systematic building of stamina training begins with a running training program to increase basic stamina; with a fluid transition, this becomes a semispecific stamina training program (running training is oriented toward the conditions of tennis-specific competition), in order to finally train special tennis-specific stamina in a third phase on the tennis court.

A stamina training with the structure outlined here (basic stamina, semispecific running stamina, as well as tennis-specific stamina) should be carried out continuously for at least 4 weeks, and preferably 6–8 weeks in the preparation period (before competition).

To achieve a significant improvement of stamina, in this time frame, stamina training should be repeated daily or at least every 2–3 days.

For competitive tennis players, this kind of stamina training period typically runs from mid-February to mid-April so that, just at the beginning of the outdoor season, effective preparations for the tennis-specific technique and match training have been completed. In certain cases, extending stamina training through the whole winter half-year (for example, two or three times per week) can also be desirable. In line with this, the following winter half-year should be primarily devoted to speed training, including training for muscle building and strength.

Because professional tennis players are severely limited by their schedules and, as a rule, have a sound stamina foundation, their stamina training must last 2–4 weeks. Such a mid-length cycle, focusing on stamina, is repeated one or two times, depending on the schedule, performance level, individual play situations and the planned training goal.

Training Examples

Basic Stamina and Semispecific Running Stamina

Example 1

Jog at a fast pace for 40–60 minutes. Beginners start with 4 × 5, 3 × 10, or 2 × 20 minutes.

Example 2

Cross-country training for 30–60 minutes at a fast pace with brief changes of pace (for example, short sprints and up-hill, jumping, slalom, and mountain runs), depending on the topography or personal capability.

Example 3

Jog at a fast speed (60–90 minutes) including a systematic training to improve speed and quickness. As an example, immediately after finishing, 2 × 6 10– to 20-m climbing runs, 3 × 5 20-m sprints or 4 × 2 15– to 25-m zigzag runs are done according to the repetitions method.

Example 4

Immediately after a long jog of at least 30 minutes, a speed training session (for example, sprints, short sprints, zigzag runs in a competitive situation) or a tennis-specific speed training session in coordination with tasks promoting techniques and tactics (for example, passing shot from a pressured situation return after running back in response to a good lob).

Example 5

Soccer tennis (1:1, 2:2) with a softball, prellball, tennis ball (1:1) on half of a tennis court with alternating partners.
[Note: Prellball is a game similar to volleyball, with the ball hit over a net after a bounce.]

Tennis-Specific Stamina

Example 1

Stamina training with a ball-tossing machine: Forehand/backhand topspin crosscourt or backhand slice cross-forehand "shot" down the line continually alternating. Two players regularly switch after three to six strokes.

Example 2

Playing safe balls at the baseline:
- One player always plays the ball crosscourt; the other, plays it down the line. The assignment is alternated according to a designated rhythm.
- Both players play close, three times crosscourt and once down the line; after each shot, the centerline must be crossed over with one foot.

Each exercise is done with 4, 6, or 12 balls, so that the length of play with good players is at least 10–15 minutes.

Example 3

Play 2-on-1: The single player plays the ball crosscourt; the double players play the ball down the line. The positions are alternated after 5–15 minutes of playing time. This exercise can also be done with two players as a triangle game. With that, the runner always plays to the forehand (backhand) corner, while the one who is tossing remains standing on the forehand (backhand) side and hits the ball alternately into the forehand and backhand corner.

Example 4

Combined stamina and speed training:
- Two series with 5 × 2 passing ball shots while under running pressure,
- Six series with 2 × 3 smashes while running backward after touching the net.

This series approach allows sufficient range of training. The player is rested before the series begins again (repetition method).

Example 5

Tennis competition without serves scored like table tennis (set is finished after 11 or 21 points).Volleys by tossing underhand to the rear backhand or forehand side as prescribed (when playing on a half court, no volley can be played).

Example 6

Singles with short break (for three): With each point, two servers on one side alternate, while the receiver plays without a break. The server who is taking a break collects balls for the next volley.

Example 7

Training competition with increasing running work: One of two players may use only forehand (backhand) on the entire court. The other player plays the normal court with forehand and backhand. Players change sides after 10 points. At the start of play, the ball is played underhand for six plays.

Strength

Definition and Importance

From a practical point of view, strength in sports is the voluntary ability of the neuromuscular system to overcome resistance, to counteract it, and to halt it.

Strength appears in sports primarily in the forms of maximum strength, speed, and endurance strength. Maximum strength is the greatest possible strength that an athlete can exert voluntarily against a resistance with static or dynamic contractions (for example, weightlifting). Speed is the ability of the athlete to exert the highest possible pushing effort against a resistance in a given time (for example, a sprint start or service). Reactive effort is differentiated as that muscle performance that, within a cycle of lengthening and shortening (for example, high jump), displays an increased quickness. Endurance strength determines the ability to resist fatigue from long or continually repeating stress (for example, rowing).

Basically, muscle power is very important in all movements in tennis, when speed is required and greater resistances must be overcome. Above all, strength plays a dominant role in every explosive start for the ball. However, it can also be effective as a performance-determining factor in various tennis techniques such as service (arm and body strength), backhand smash, forehand shot, and fast backhand stroke with topspin.

These examples show that the tennis player needs an outstanding quickness, which is related, for the most part, to coordination (for example, backhand smash), speed (for example, service, forehand shot) and maximum strength (for example, abrupt stop and highest acceleration on reversing direction for the ball). The close relationship of the quickness with other factors means that, in contrast to speed, a strength deficit in tennis

players can be compensated for, because of above-average expression of other conditional and coordination abilities. At any rate, poorly developed strength (for example, leg strength or body strength) can limit the individual's best performance in tennis if this deficit is striking, or if there are no appropriate opportunities for compensation (tennis technique, speed, flexibility).

Most recently, orthopedic specialists and physiotherapists have reported that poor development of strength and elasticity in important muscle groups (for example, knee extensors or back extensors), as well as a significant muscular imbalance (particularly in the shoulders, lumbar spine, and thighs) are fundamental factors in chronic overuse, acute injuries, and irreversible sports injuries.

This leads to the following discussion of (tennis-specific) speed. To guard against typical tennis injuries, the most important muscular prerequisites should be developed in a home program; this topic is presented in a special chapter (see p. 173).

Goals of (Speed) Strength Training

Depending on the training period and training profile of the sport, two main goals can be identified for (speed) strength training:

- Increasing the muscle cross section (muscle-development training),
- Improving neuronal control through muscle work (intra- and intermuscular coordination).

Increasing the cross section (area) of the muscle fibers comes about by increasing the sarcomeres, and thus by increasing the number of myofibrils within the individual muscle fibers. Because a relatively long duration of the stimulus is necessary for the development of contractile proteins (via protein synthesis, training requires high repetition counts (10–15) and limited amounts of stimulus (50–80% of the maximum strength). This is generally referred to as the repetitive submaximal stress method and can be further differentiated according to load-level and contraction speed (body-building method, standard method).

By intramuscular coordination (IC) we mean the synchronous activation of the highest possible number of muscle fibers (recruitment) and the coordination of all participating muscles, agonists and antagonists, in a goal-directed movement. A desirable prerequisite for an efficient IC training is the largest possible muscle cross section. Thus, all athletes, who require a high level of the quickness based on an individually expressed maximum strength, will improve

intramuscular coordination in a second step following muscle development. Only the combination of muscle development and IC-training produces maximum strength. IC training requires stress intensities above 80% of the maximum strength.

These high intensities permit only limited numbers of repetitions (max. 6): method of short, high-maximum strength exercises. This training improves the ability to mobilize large innervation activities quickly and to process them so that a rapid and more comprehensive recruitment of muscle fibers (and motor units) are achieved. The high intensities frequently lead to mistakes in movement execution, so IC training is unsuitable for the beginner, for the most part (for example, using free weights or complicated technique sequences), and it needs professional oversight.

Optimization of intermuscular coordination makes possible an improved coordination of excitatory and inhibitory effort, as in cyclical movements, of tension and relaxation (for example, high step rate when sprinting) and in complex acyclic movements, a better coordination of submovements (for example, service).

The reactive stress method is helpful within the framework of a special jumping training program; the method is characterized by a fast lengthening and contraction cycle of the muscle. Here, one aims for an improved recruitment and repetition in order to optimize intramuscular neuronal control and also, to some extent, intermuscular neuronal control. For maximum recruitment of

motor units, one often employs his own tumbling body. All low jumping, multiple jumps, or hurdles belong to this category (plyometric training, eccentric training, hitting methods).

With all reactive forms of training, it should be taken into account that very high peak strength values (more than 100%) occur on landing, which over a long period can lead to damage of the passive movement apparatus in unprepared athletes. Previous sufficient muscle development is, then, a necessary prerequisite for carrying out this training. To increase repetition rate, the maximum avalanche rate of the motor neurons is elevated (for example, with a sprint). In this case, use of additional loading is proscribed; however, the usual situation is that, more often, the requirements are simpler (for example, sprinting uphill, tossing with light weights).

General Principles of Strength Training

Due to the extraordinary importance of hitting and running coordination for the player's total capabilities, the problem of coordination transfer after a strength-training session is especially important in tennis. This is particularly true with muscle development training of the upper extremities, because the coordination complexity of each stroke technique makes extraordinary demands. What makes the solution of this set of problems even more difficult is that different, individual strength deficits can be, in large measure, compensated for because of the limited weight of the mass to be accelerated (racket) under average development of other conditional and coordination abilities. Considering the set of problems cited, the following principles for strength training in tennis would be valid:

- Comprehensive strength training (including muscle development) in tennis is most necessary for the lower extremities and becomes more important in the case of poor running ability (for example, basically, in women's tennis), with special types of players (attack players), and with frequent play on hard surfaces.
- Muscle development and IC training on the body-building machine for the upper extremities are recommended only when there are obvious deficits. In most cases, training of special speed is sufficient, so that the first two training phases can be skipped.
- Strength training of the tennis player should focus primarily on improving the neuronal control during muscle work (special speed/intra-intermuscular coordination).
- Special jumping training of the upper extremities consists primarily in practicing for competition itself, and it aims for an improved repetition rate and recruitment. Varied exercises (imitating hitting exercises against a stretch band, with light or heavy rackets) can lead to an improvement of coordination in some cases with appropriately sensitive players.
- Strength training for tennis players should be done outside of the main competition period (for example, September/

October), and at least over a time span of 6 weeks.
- Strength training should always be closely interwoven with a corresponding coordination or recoordination technique training on the tennis court. This can be done right along with the strength training session and/or in a following unit.

Training Examples for Sprint Strength

Phase 1

Training objective: Muscle development/maximum strength.

Exercises: Leg presses (possibly leg curls, lifting the calf) on the body-building machine.

Method: Repeated, submaximal stress.

Duration: First to third week.

Stimulus extent: Two training units per week with at least three series of 10–15 repetitions each.

Intensity of stimulus: 50–75 percent of maximum strength.

Density of stimulus: Pauses approximately 1–3 minutes

Phase 2

Training objective: Intramuscular coordination/maximum strength.

Exercises: See Phase 1.

Method: Repeated high to maximum stress.

Duration: Fourth to sixth week.

Extent of stimulus: Two training units per week with three to six series with 1–6 repetitions each.

Intensity of stimulus: 80–100 percent of maximum strength.

Density of stimulus: Pauses approximately 2–5 minutes.

Phase 3

Training objective: Improving quickness.

Types of Exercises:
- Skipping slightly uphill, for 10 meters.
- Sideways jumping with small weights or disk weights (5–10 kg) fixed in front of the chest as extra weight.
- Uphill running for 20 m against measured resistance; partner slows down the subject with a stretch band.
- Knee-high running or long jumping on the soft floor mat.
- Short sprints for 10–20 m in soft sand on the beach or wearing a weight vest.
- Reactive strength training via a jumping course (for example, one-legged jump over small boxes and then two-legged long jumps).
- Maximum starts and backups or jumps to the ball on the tennis court (possibly with weight vest).

Particular Exercises:
- Short sprints for a maximum of 20–40 m, uphill or on the level with traction rope.
- Knee-high running for 5 seconds with maximal step rate.

- Side-steps with low center of gravity and maximum rate for 5–8 seconds.
- Maximum acceleration and optimal speed while running to the ball on the tennis court (for example, running 10–12 m along the baseline, finishing with a passing shot or running forward from the baseline and then returning for the following lob).

Training Example for Hitting Strength

Phase 1

Training objective: Muscle development/maximum strength.

Types of Exercises: Tricep presses on the body-building machine, imitated serves on the cable pull machine.

Method: Repeated submaximal stress.

Duration: First to third week.

Extent of stimulus: Two training units per week with at least three series with 10–15 repetitions each.

Intensity of stimulus: 60–80 percent of maximum strength.

Density of stimulus: pauses approximately 1–3 minutes.

Phase 2

Training objective: Intramuscular coordination/maximum strength.

Exercises: See Phase 1.

Method: Repeated high to maximal stress.

Duration: Fourth to sixth week.

Extent of stimulus: Two training units per week with three to six series with 1–6 repetitions each.

Intensity of stimulus: 80–100 percent of maximum strength.

Density of stimulus: Pauses approximately 2–5 minutes.

Phase 3

Training objective: Improving quickness.

Types of Exercises:
- Throwing the medicine ball over the head using both hands (service).
- Throwing the medicine ball laterally using one arm (forehand).
- Imitating a serve against a stretch band (fore- and backhand).
- Swinging the arms back and forth with small weights (1–2 kg) and explosive changes in direction (fore- and backhand).
- Hitting training with weighted racket head (approximately 500 g) (fore- and backhand, service).

Particular Exercises:
- Forehand shot crosscourt from the backhand corner (trajectory flat under the rope, target area baseline).
- Backhand smash (after bouncing, the ball must reach fence height).
- Fore- and backhand with maximum hitting the tennis wall as with old, defective tennis balls or softballs as hard as possible (the training is done with a partner, who tosses every other hit).
- Smash steeply overhand with the highest possible jump.
- Cannon serves to the service area (the ball should reach the opposite fence as high as possible).
- Badminton: Fore- and backhand smash series with the highest possible intensity and maximum ball height and distance.
- Long throw with the tennis ball (service imitation).
- Long throw on the grounds with old, worn-out rackets (backhand, service).

Speed

Definition and Systematic Approach

In sports, speed can be defined as the fastest possible reaction to a stimulus and the highest velocity when executing a movement.

Speed can be divided into two components:
- Reaction speed,
- Movement speed.

Reaction speed is the ability to respond to a stimulus as quickly as possible (for example, the opponent's ball) with a purposeful muscle contraction (for example, start to the ball). Especially in return-play tennis, the reaction is very closely related to anticipation, so that an improvement of reaction time depends primarily on optimizing situation anticipation (for example, direction of the serve) and the subsequent response (for example, planning the spin of the return).

Movement speed is generally divided into acyclical speed and cyclical speed. Acyclical speed (also action speed) is responsible for velocity of individual movements (for example, jumping, pushing, or hitting). Cyclical speed (also basic speed) determines the rapidity of continuously progressing similar movements (for example, 100-m run after the acceleration phase, 50-m sprint).

In tennis, acyclical speed dominates; it can limit performance such as running speed and hitting speed in various game situations, and, as a result, it requires the highest level of expression. Maximum strength plays a central role in speed (quickness), when acyclical or cyclical movements must be carried out against greater resistances (for example, shot-put, acceleration in the first 5 m of a sprint start, or competitive rowing).

Hitting in tennis meets only limited resistance so that the maximum strength plays a subordinate role. Thus, it is understandable that even decidedly slender players can accelerate the ball exceptionally well (for example, Ivanisevic or Stich with the serve, and Noah with the forehand smash, or

Krickstein with the forehand shot). Hitting speed depends on the following factors:

- Contraction speed of the musculature that can be activated (individually differentiated muscle fiber),
- Intermuscular coordination (goal-directed cooperation of agonists and antagonists),
- Intramuscular coordination (number of motor units that can be activated at the same time).

Running speed in tennis revolves around distances that amount to only 4 m in one direction (distances over 10 m are extremely rare). As a result, for attaining high speeds, the acceleration requirement (against comparably high loads) plays a dominant role. In contrast to hitting speed, this does relate to the level of individual maximum strength. This is particularly important for special playing situations (explosive change in direction), for particular game strategies (for example, attack tennis) and for heavyweight players.

Recently, several authors have written about the programmatic character of speed mechanisms. Speed is seen as an elementary performance requirement, which is determined by the quality of neuromuscular control and regulating processes. The so-called temporal programs are developed in the brain and stored there. As a result, this type of speed is learned as an elementary ability and is, for the most part, largely independent of energetic components of strength.

Influence factors for realizing fast temporal programs include stimulus control and speed, reflex innervation and the proportion of fast twitch (FT) fibers in the muscle. The temporal program is characterized basically by the quality of neuromuscular mechanisms.

Elementary speed is developed through organization of general requirements, which model the temporal structure of neuromuscular mechanisms. In such a training program, comparatively low amounts of stimuli and stress levels are sufficient, and the regeneration rate of performance level is essentially more limited than when one trains under energetically limited performance requirements.

The development of elementary movement programs represents the first level of acyclical speed training and should, therefore, be integrated into the first phase of athletic training (basic training). As a second level, the movement programs are linked with discipline-specific exercises (for example, start to the ball and serve). At the third level, speed is developed in its full complexity (including quickness), and as closely as possible to competition-specific requirements of elementary movement programs.

In summary, elementary speed, concentric and reactive speed, and anticipation and reaction speed, as well as tennis techniques are primarily responsible for the quality of tennis-specific speed, according to current research (Fig. 91).

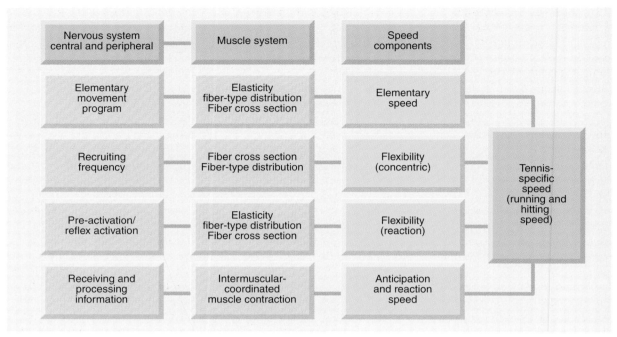

Fig. 91 Influence levels and manifestations of tennis-specific speed.

Thus, the speed of the tennis player can be developed optimally only through the systematic development of all relevant skills components on a neuronal and muscular level.

Importance of Speed

Running speed becomes more important as a performance-limiting factor in tennis competition if the opponent is under pressure and the court surface is fast.

Individual hitting speed is just as important (in close relationship with coordination). This is true not only for smashes and serves, which obviously win direct points with their speeds, but also for the fast forehand stroke (forehand

shot), which opens up the opponent's court or brings the volley to a definitive close. In addition, the quality of the return and volley game is essentially limited by hitting speed (in close relationship with the ability to react.

Because of the high speed of the ball (for example, on a return), limited distance from the opponent (for example, net play on doubles), and the complexity of play situations, reaction time is often insufficient. As a result tennis-specific ability to anticipate is of decisive importance for a quick and correct response.

Principles and Practical Tips for Speed Training

Speed training should first focus on the individual's level of strength and tennis-specific coordination (especially tennis techniques). For instance, strength plays a dominant role in starting and accelerating when sprinting to the ball. Similarly, the maximum hitting speed attainable strongly depends on the quality of the stroke-specfic coordination ability (for example, backhand smash).

The components of speed (reaction and anticipation time, running and hitting speed) require separate training methods because they are independent and because their deficiencies are unrelated, and they vary from individual to individual. On the other hand, tennis competition always presents multiple reaction possibilities. Depending on the situation, the player must make the optimum choice of reaction from the best of several possible actions, and do so in the briefest time (for example, when returning or hitting a passing shot). Reaction speed and acyclical speed are, therefore, generally not unrelated but taught in combination with other (tennis-specific) abilities.

Within the framework of reaction ability, improving the ability to concentrate is an essential parallel training objective. Training these together helps accelerate the development and stabilization of reaction speed. For optimizing anticipation, which is especially important, the player must have a certain sensibility. He must be able to pick up additional information (for example, on placement of his opponent's ball, on backswing motion, or on a standard playing situation) as early as possible, in order to then use it to prepare for his own stroke. In addition, the player should attempt to force the opponent into a particular mode of play through his own compelling actions. This assists the player to be able to react earlier and more successfully.

Intensity of Stimulus
The intensity of stimulus is always high or very high (90–100%), so that, as a rule, the movements must be executed as quickly as possible. This means, for example,

that the appropriate tennis stroke is executed at great acceleration with an explosive start-to-stop action. Absolutely necessary prerequisites for this are that the correct technique has been stabilized at the submaximal speed and is applied in keeping with the individual's own level in tennis. In addition, it must always be assured that signs of fatigue do not negatively affect the technical sequence of the necessary actions.

Duration of Stimulus
The duration of the stimulus should be the same as that in a competition. Because speed stimuli depend on the functional ability of the nervous system, as a rule, no fatiguing activities should precede speed training.

Density of Stimulus
For density of stimulus, the length of the pauses between the individual exercise units should be structured in such a way that the neuromuscular system can regenerate. If speed of movement falls off, the number of repetitions should be reduced or the length of the break between the individual exercises should be increased. The main form of speed training is thus the repetition method, which—in contrast with the interval method—allows for a most effective monitoring of performance.

Extent of Stimulus
In order to achieve a relatively high extent of stimulus in spite of maximum intensity, training should be carried out according to the series approach while varying the muscle groups involved.

Varying the training content avoids undesired "speed barriers" along with early (pivotal) fatigue with corresponding loss of performance motivation.

Principles for Training Children and Young People

Gifted young players distinguish themselves by an above-average level of speed and especially a greater ability to learn performance-determining skills. In childhood and adolescence, speed should be taught very early, so that the designated limited framework due to heredity can still be expanded before central nervous system development is complete.

Numerous studies show that the central nervous systems' limited ability to be influenced decreases qualitatively through early school age and puberty. The favorable situation of this developmental period is generally not taken full advantage of. On the other hand, one should guard against using this sensitive growth period, that is, this period of highest growth rate, for speed development. In this case, the various factors related to speed should be developed in different ways: Movement rate should be taught mainly in the early and middle school years, and typical speed training should be employed only in puberty and early adolescence.

Neuromuscular structures related to speed, acquired and reinforced through frequent exercise, cannot be altered later, or if so, only with considerable effort. In training adolescents (12–15 year olds), neuromuscular mechanisms can still be relatively firmly established. By making things easier, children can be given the opportunity to develop elementary movement programs. By doing this, the changes are directed toward performance requirements that are not yet sufficiently developed for the target program. In tennis, these are often deficiencies in strength requirements or fundamentals of coordination, so that in these cases, the two-handed backhand or playing on a minicourt and using soft (or Easy-Play) balls or a short racket are ways to promote speed early.

According to recent theories for optimal development of speed, one must first develop elementary speed through so-called short timed programs, in order to integrate this into complex speed requirements afterwards. Only at the highest developmental level should competition-specific requirements be considered. This sequence is especially important considering a long-term performance development program through childhood and adolescence. As an example, with 6–12 year olds, elementary speed is developed first. Afterward, depending on the training objectives and individual level of development, speed is taught in all its complex requirements, so that it can then be used optimally in competition-specific situations in connection with techniques and tactics.

Overall, very little is known about the ability of mechanisms to influence elementary neuromuscular movement programs in tennis. Even though the development of elementary movement programs in the sprint and jumping areas of track and field currently belongs to accepted practice, in high-performance training there are currently still no documented reports on the influence of tennis-specific running and hitting movements on speed. Optimum economy of movement should always be the focus. Interestingly structured training programs with varied training methods are necessary for the development of speed; otherwise, stagnation or even a diminution in speed occurs early on.

Training Examples

As a rule, reaction speed and acyclical speed are not isolated but are trained together (anticipation + reaction + start to the ball + stroke). At the beginner and advanced stages, it is advisable to train the repetitive running and hitting technique initially with submaximal execution, in order to avoid errors in technique and tense movement execution. At the beginning of a speed training program and when there are specific, individual deficiencies, it can be advisable to train the different speed skill components separately.

Reaction/Anticipation

Example 1

Sprint start in various directions (for example, forward, backward, laterally) for short distances (4–10 m), using an optical starting signal.

Example 2

Black/White: Reaction game for pairs (for example, starting point is 10 cm to the left of the center line).

Example 3

The player stands close to the tennis wall and intercepts all balls with his hands or feet. The partner stands behind him and throws the balls against the wall with varying speed, height, and direction.

Example 4

"Machine-gun" with different colored balls (yellow, volley to the right; orange, volley to the left). The one who is tossing continues moving closer to the net.

Example 5

The server varies the direction of serves, using forehand and backhand sides. Just before meeting the ball, the return player should indicate that she has recognized the direction of the serve from the server's follow-through movement, by appropriately turning her upper body.

Example 6

The server varies his serve in terms of aggressiveness, direction, and spin, so that the return player must constantly make adjustments.

Example 7

Return from a starting position, that is 1, 2, or 3 m in front of the usual hitting area.

Example 8

Smash volley: A lob is played from a volley dual on half-court, the following smash (precision rather than speed) should be placed into the opponent's court as a volley.

Running Speed

Example 1

Alternate foot hopping with short sprints.

Example 2

2 × 6 low jumps or combined low, wide, and high jumps (for example, jumping down from a 30- to 40-cm-high small box with the fastest possible finishing jump over a hurdle of variable height and breadth), with pauses of 5–8 minutes after each series. The rest periods should be kept as short as possible and done in at least half the number of series periods.

Example 3

Designated step combinations (for example, including cross steps and lateral steps) at very high speed in the in cross, rectangle, or triangle pattern as well as using the rope ladder. Floor contact times while doing this should be as short as possible.

Example 4

Explosive jump-running forward, short sprint up a (steep) hill or drag-running using a stretch band for increasing quickness, skipping, and sprinting uphill to improve speed of movement.

Example 5

2 × 6 shuttle runs for 12–20 m; for example, from the left singles sideline to the right and back again. Restart the runs again every minute, and pause after two series for 3–5 minutes.

Example 6

2 × 3 runs down the line (forward, backward, and lateral steps), with three or four change points; for example, half court-center to the singles sideline on the right, to the baseline, to the singles sideline on the right.

Example 7

4 × 4 starts to the ball; for example, the closely played ball must be reached as a low volley, followed by a lateral run to the baseline at maximum speed, and then a passing shot. Tossing should be such that approximately one third can be reached easily, one third are challenging, and one third are unreachable.

Hitting Speed

Example 1

Kneeling with both hands on the ground, in explosive motions, quickly clasp both hands and return, quickly touch elbows and return.

Example 2

Explosive long toss with hitting balls (of various weights) from the kneeling position or normal throwing position.

Example 3

Serve (cannon serve): The height of the second bounce on the opposite wall (fence) can be used as a rough measure for ranking speed capability.

Example 4

Backhand smash: The second bounce of the ball must exceed a designated height (for example, the height of the fence). Recommendation: Ten sets of three backhand smashes each.

Example 5

Serves with forward topspin (twist serves): The trajectory of the serves after bouncing at the opponent's baseline should be at least head high (return player or even referee serves as monitor). 5 × 8 twist-serves are recommended.

Example 6

Forehand baseline stroke: Forehand "winner" from the backhand corner low crosscourt into the opponent's backhand court. From the center of the baseline, 5 × 6 forehand strokes are hit, as balls are tossed appropriately from one's own backhand corner into the opponent's backhand court, after running around the backhand.

Example 7

Winners with fore- and backhand from half court: 10 × 4 forehand and/or backhand strokes are hit as "winners" down the line or crosscourt as balls are tossed short and high from the half-court.

Complex Exercises

Example 1

Training in return strokes as "winners" with quickest possible point of contact to a designated target.

Example 2

Running down a stop or lob with stroke execution appropriate to the situation.

Example 3

Two or three low volleys in succession with return each time to a designated starting point (for example, midline at the baseline).

Example 4

Baseline strokes while running (see also Training Coordination, Example 1, p. 123).

Example 5

Volley and smash (see also Training Coordination, Example 3, p. 124).

Flexibility

Definition and Importance

Flexibility or suppleness characterizes the range of movement in one or more joints. Flexibility depends mainly on the ability to stretch, or on the elasticity of the muscles. Generally, the maximum swing movement (breadth of swing) of a limb is the standard for the quality of movement.

However, this isolated way of looking at flexibility greatly oversimplifies the complex relationship of movement and an individual's speed and coordination skills in tennis. As an example, lightning-quick actions in difficult situations with a return or volley require evasive movements of the whole body, precise movement of the racket, and correct point of contact, as well as a high degree of flexibility, which is coupled to speed and good coordination.

Good flexibility (in the narrow sense) provides the tennis player with a favorable basis for maximum speed of movement (for example, serve and return), precise execution of movement (for example, low volley), and good economy of movement (for example, serve and backhand) by increasing the amplitude of movement. In other words, flexibility is important for executing movements that are both fast and technically correct. Furthermore, good movement protects against short-term and chronic overtaxing of structural elements that stabilize the joints (muscles, ligaments, capsules, and cartilage, etc.) and prevents acute injuries (for example, pulling and tearing of the abdominal or thigh musculature) and chronic overtaxing damage (for example, tennis elbow and tennis shoulder). The tennis player uses movement training not only as a prophylaxis for injuries but also as a regenerative measure after exhaustive training and competition stress. For a "muscle and limb hygiene," better physical and psychological well-being can be achieved this way as quickly as possible.

Stretching, especially of those muscle groups used in tennis that tend to shorten, is necessary to stabilize joints and forestall injuries. For this reason, stretching exercises for the following joints and muscle groups are important: wrist (flexors and extensors), elbow (especially extensors), shoulder (arm lifting and lowering muscles), spine (primarily in the area of lumbar vertebrae or back extensors), hips (flexors, extensors, and muscles that pull up the leg), and knees (extensors and flexors).

Principal Method for Stretching

Here we distinguish two principal methods in movement training:

- Static stretching (including postisometric stretching),
- Dynamic stretching.

The active-dynamic stretching exercises used formerly have been increasingly replaced in the past decade by passive-static exercises. Most recently, an equality of both types of stretching techniques has emerged. They are used regularly in appropriate circumstances according to the training goal. Most recent research results on improving flexibility come out against using a stretching technique as the only method.

Static Stretching

In static stretching, the reflex counterextension of the muscle is kept as low as possible, and at the same time, the stretching stimulus can operate for the longest possible time. Slowly feeling one's way to the optimal stretch stimulus end position, continuity of the stretch stimulus for more than 10 seconds, several repetitions and taking advantage of a contraction delay (tension-relaxation-stretching) creates the best conditions for this. Two principal stretching techniques proceed from this: maintained stretching and tension–relaxation stretching (postisometric relaxation).

With maintained stretching (passive stretching), the muscle stretches slowly and gently to the length that can be tolerated without pain. This phase (the easy stretch) is held 10–30 seconds or at least until the sensation of tension subsides considerably.

After that, the second phase (the development stretch) begins with a repeated stretch that is again held for 10–30 seconds without exceeding an interval of 40–50 seconds total during both phases. Various modifications are possible; however, overdoing it should be avoided.

With tension–relaxation stretching (for example, proprioceptive neuromuscular facilitating or PNF stretching), the musculature is tensed to the maximum immediately beforehand, thus exploiting the inhibitory effects of the tendon spindles on the stretching reflex. This leads to a relaxation of the muscle with an expanded stretching capacity. In practice, the muscle group is isometrically tensed for 3–6 seconds, completely relaxed briefly for 2–3 seconds, and stretched immediately afterward for at least 7–10 seconds.

Dynamic Stretching

Traditional gymnastics uses dynamic stretching to improve joint flexibility through a warm-up effect and activates the neuromuscular interaction. Exercises on imitation hitting are particularly advantageous for developing a sense of elasticity and stretching ability of the backswing movements and swing components for tennis players, which is especially true for the shoulder joint. By paying strict attention to a controlled and swift execution of movement, with a measured increase in the degree of stretching, the muscle stretching reflex, which interferes considerably with the stretching effect, is lessened. With this mode of operation, the disadvantages of dynamic stretching (danger of injury, poor final position due to inherent reflexes and resulting compensatory movements of neighboring joints), with its effect on reducing movement, can be reduced considerably.

According to current research, dynamic stretching is used as an auxiliary to special stretching exercises (chiefly as an injury prophylaxis and for muscle balance), and sometimes it works better than static stretching for a general and tennis-specific warm-up.

Monitoring Exercises

For objective evaluation of a player's current flexibility, and the effectiveness of training, standardized monitoring exercises are necessary.

Example 1

Shoulder flexibility: Shoulder level, with stretched arms, hands are holding a handkerchief. The least possible gap between the hands is measured.

Example 2

Spinal column flexibility (forward): Legs close together, bend the body forward stretching the legs. The distance of the fingertips from the upper edge of a small box stool is measured.

Example 3

Hip flexibility (backwards, specifically M. iliopsoas): While lying on one's stomach (with the knee bent), the thigh can be raised from the ground, if one has good stretching ability.

General Practical Tips

The quality of movement training will be influenced very positively if the following general practical tips are considered:

- Before movement training begins, there should always be a general and specific warm-up.
- An exercise program for tennis players is complete only when dynamic and static movement exercises are included.
- High ambient temperatures, heat therapy (for example, heat, [possibly a rub], hot baths) and massage have a positive influence on movement, while psychological excitement (for example, tension and fear) interferes with movement by increasing muscle tension.
- Longer, continuous periods of stretching (for example, 30 seconds of stretching) or high repetition rates, following the series approach, increase the success of movement training because it is the total stretching stimulus that essentially influences the muscle length.
- When one is fatigued, dynamic stretching exercises can increase the danger of injury, whereas static stretching exercises (perhaps in combination with limbering and mobility exercises) lessen the regeneration period.
- Overdoing movement training leads principally to a reduction in quickness and movement rate.

Training Examples

General Flexibility

Shoulder/Arm
- Shoulder circles (with racket and perhaps tennis bag).
- Stretching the large chest muscle as well as the upper- and forearm flexors (Fig. 92).
- Stretching the wrist extensors and pronators of the forearm (Fig. 93).

Fig. 92

Fig. 93

Lumbar Spinal Column/Hips
- Body circles.
- Standing jumps with continually changing position of upper body and legs.
- Stretching the lower back musculature.
- Stretching the seat musculature (Fig. 94).

Fig. 94

Hips/Legs
- Stretching the hip flexors.
- Stretching the thigh aductors (Fig. 95).

Fig. 95

- Stretching the knee extensors and hip flexors (Fig. 96).

Fig. 96

Tennis-Specific Flexibility (Combination of Speed and Coordination)

- Course of hitting training (for example, pairs volley on the half-court) with additional tasks (for example, simultaneous play with two balls, stretching 360 degrees, or passing the racket through the legs immediately after each shot).
- With someone tossing on the minicourt, returning every ball behind the back or between the legs.
- Serve and forehand and backhand topspin without a ball, with exaggerated breadth of motions in the shoulder, elbow, and wrist joints (including turning the forearm).
- Return against mid- and high-speed serves from 1 to 2 m in front of the baseline, placing the ball far outside.
- Low forehand and backhand volley or half-volley close to the net-starting position: "turntable" position as one's partner tosses or throws.

Home Training Program

Many tennis players do not achieve their highest potential because they have devoted too little attention to the harmonious development of their movement apparatus by strengthening appropriate muscle groups. At the same time, increases in the losses of injury-prone talented young players and internationally recognized top players has led to the opinion that neglecting to attend to muscles and joints of the body regions that are particularly used leads to problems.

In tennis, some areas in the body are particularly susceptible to injury: the back (especially the lumbar spine), thighs and knees due to (over) stress, and the hitting shoulder because of tennis' quite one-sided actions, as previously discussed. As a result, it is primarily a matter of strengthening the musculature in the problem zones cited and, at the same time, taking care to balance the one-sided loading demands.

An appropriate training program is necessary to protect against these dangers:
- Development and stabilization of the movement apparatus,
- Resolution of muscular imbalances,
- Prevention of tennis injuries.

Recently, a number of German fitness studios have started to offer an attractive array of equipment, and although their use by tennis players would be desirable, the acceptance by tennis players has been quite limited. The reasons for this could be mainly that the equipment and machines available do not focus enough on tennis-specific movements, and training tennis players in the fitness studio is frequently seen as boring. Besides, there is a high cost in time (traveling to and from the studio) and money. Therefore, more practical and economical (in time and money) training opportunities must be sought.

The selection of the following exercises is based primarily on three considerations: They should affect various, especially heavily used regions of the movement apparatus; require relatively little time; and be able to be done without auxiliary aids at the workplace and at home (home program).

The home program should be performed regularly, at least one or two times per week. In individual cases, we also recommend daily training. Normally, the course should not exceed 10 minutes.

We strongly recommend observing the following general principles for exercises that develop and stabilize muscle strength (for special tips for doing the stretching exercises, see p. 171):
- Continuous care to ensure that the exercises are being done correctly and functionally (especially regarding the pelvic area and spine).
- Beginners start with more limited stress, increasing first the length of the stress and then the extent of the stress.
- Several repetitions of individual exercises increase the effectiveness of the training.
- Increasing the diameter of the muscle requires high to peak stress stimuli (for example, via additional weights and more difficult performance requirements).
- The strength of the stimulus can be maintained by alternating the muscle groups.
- Stretching exercises immediately after the strength stress are recommended because they increase functionality and regeneration.
- Competitive tennis players in childhood and adolescence should be examined annually by an orthopedic or sports medicine specialist to monitor their structural and movement apparatus.

Practical Examples

Warm-up
- 5 minutes jumping rope with several variations (Fig. 97)
- Combination of running in place, knee-high steps and lateral jumping on one leg (perhaps on a soft mat).

Fig. 97

Abdomen

- Starting Position: Lying on the back, with legs bent at right angles on a chair (or gymanstics ball) and hands lying next to the rear.
  From the starting position, the spine is raised slowly, while the hands glide across the floor in the direction of the chair legs. In the end position, the shoulders and thoracic spine (upper back) should be raised noticeably from the floor (Fig. 98).

Fig. 98

- Starting Position: Lying on the back, with bent legs on gymnastic ball or chair and hands clasped behind the neck. First, the abdominal muscles are tensed so far that the lumbar spine is pressed against the floor, followed by a slow rolling with lateral turning of the spine until, in the end position the thoracic spine (upper back) has been raised from the floor (Fig. 99).

Fig. 99

Back

- Starting Position: While kneeling with hands on the floor, stretch one arm and one leg (on opposite sides) diagonally to a horizontal position (Fig. 100).
  In the end position, rotate the stretched leg gently towards the inside and avoid a hollow-back stance.

Fig. 100

● <u>Starting Position</u>: Lying on the stomach on a exercise bench, gymnastic box, or table, with the legs and hip joint outboard so hips can be moved freely, holding the upper body in place by holding on with the hands (Fig. 101).
Stretch both legs to a horizontal position, either together or one at a time. Avoid the hollow-back posture!

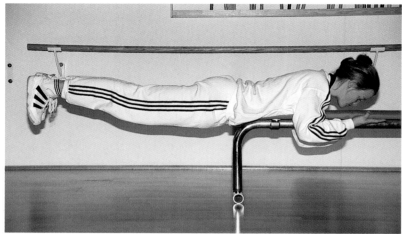

Fig. 101

● <u>Starting Position</u>: Lying on the back, with stretched legs, and the palms of the hands lying next to the seat. In the end position, the palms are pressed against the mat and the pelvis slowly raised from the floor. In addition, one leg can be raised approximately as high as the ankle or the toe tips of the other leg (Fig. 102).
For players with a limited strength level, the slow lifting of the pelvis does not work in the beginning. These players begin with repeated tensing without actually raising the pelvis from the mat.

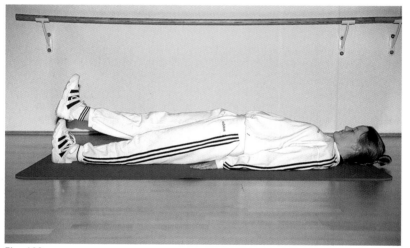

Fig. 102

Fig. 103

Pelvis (Stabilization)

● <u>Starting Position</u>: Lying on the back, with legs bent, and the hands lying next to the seat. From the starting position, the pelvis is slowly raised until the thigh forms an ascending line with the upper body; in addition, one leg is raised from the floor and stretched (Fig. 103). Here, half of the pelvis with the stretched leg may not be lowered.

● <u>Starting Position</u>: Lying on the back, with leg bent, the hands grasp the knee joint of the other leg and pull it in the direction of the chest.
Raise the pelvis slowly and push it upward as far as possible; at the same time, use the hands to pull the knee of the other leg as close as possible to the chest (Fig. 104). Here, the angle of the held leg must be maintained during the exercise; otherwise, there is the threat of hollow-back posture.

Fig. 104

Shoulder/Upper Body

● <u>Starting Position</u>: Lying on the back, with stretched legs, with the forearms propped.
Slowly push backward into the mat with the forearms, and at the same time, keep the body taut ("straight as a board") (Fig. 105).
In addition, one leg can be raised from the floor.

Fig. 105

Fig. 106

● <u>Starting Position</u>: Lying on the side, one leg is lying on top of the other, one arm is propped up, with the elbow located under the shoulder joint.
From this position, slowly press into the mat on the forearm and at the same time, keep the body stiff. In addition, one leg can be raised from the floor (Fig. 106).

Legs

- Starting Position: The upper body is supported against a wall, the knee joint angle is 100–120 degrees, the feet are separated as wide as the hips. From the starting position the foot of the free leg is placed behind the knee of the supporting leg; at the same time, make a transition to standing on one's toes (Fig. 107).

The following exercises are especially meant to prevent tennis injuries and can be done just before tennis training or competition. Their general character is always the alternation between tensing and stretching of the musculature.

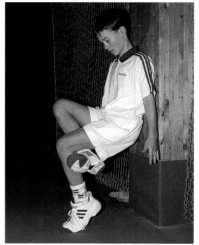

Fig. 107

Thigh Adductors

Tensing: Sitting against a wall or a partner with the straightest possible spine; both heels pulled to the rear, elbows are on the inside of the knee joints. Press the knees as strongly as possible against the elbows, which are preventing a movement toward the inside.

Stretching: While sitting upright, push both knee joints outward toward the floor, allow the elbows to gently force the stretching (Fig. 108).

Fig. 108

Wrist Flexors/Forearm Pronators

Tensing: While standing straight, with bent elbows, both hands are clasped with the palm and are facing the body. The grip is intensified, as if one wanted to squeeze a tennis ball.

Stretching: The hands remain clasped and are pushed away with the palms to the front as far as the elbows will stretch from the upper body. In addition, there is a final rotation inwards (Fig. 109).

Fig. 109

Knee Extensors/Hip Flexors

Tensing: Sitting on a chair, slide so far to the side edge that one leg can be bent to the rear, next to the chair seat. One hand grasps the moving foot, which tries to draw the holding hand downward.

Stretching: The foot is pulled to the seat without tilting the pelvis forward (avoid the hollow-back posture). The foot resting on the floor always keeps its starting position (Fig. 110).

Fig. 110

Wrist Extensors/Forearm Supinators

Tensing: With slightly bent elbows, one hand rests on the back of the other, which is closed into an inward-turned fist. The lower hand tries to lift the upper one (to the outside).

Stretching: After stretching the elbow, the wrist is bent as far as possible and the forearm is turned inward (Fig. 111).

Fig. 111

Back Extensors

Tensing: Lying on the back, with the head on the floor, both hands grasp the bent knee joints. The knees press against the hands holding them, and the head presses against the mat.
Stretching: The knees are drawn up as closely as possible to the upper body, and the head is rotated into the chest (Fig. 112).

Fig. 112

Training Conditioning

In the following, we present an example for the 10-minute home program. This program can be done daily after rising, after school, before tennis training, or during a television program. The selection of exercises and length of the session should be modified for each individual according to the training objective or weak points of the body (for example, lumbar spine, tennis elbow) or available time (for example, 5 minutes or 30 minutes).

Warm-up 2 Min.

Back I 4 × 6 Sec. (left & right)

Abdomen I 2 × 8 repetitions (30-Sec. break)

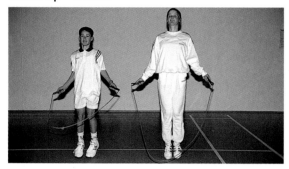

Back II 4 × 8 Sec. (left & right)

Pelvis (stabilization) I 4 × 10 Sec. (left & right)

Shoulder/Upper body 4 × 4 Sec. (left & right)

Pelvis (stabilization) II 4 × 10 Sec. (left & right)

Stretching and relaxing 2–3 Min.

Psychological Basics/Psychologically Oriented Training

Important Psychological Phenomena and Problems

Before, during, and after competitions, one often hears something like, "It just didn't work today—especially my forehand just didn't work," "Man, it just can't be that I blew such an easy volley," "He is playing like he's in a fog," "I know just what I'm doing wrong with my backhand, but I just can't change it in a competition," "I've already lost often with this kind of lead," "With wind like this, you can't win." Such remarks, heard so frequently, indicate that achievement in tennis is determined not only by physical, technical, and tactical circumstances but also by psychological processes, which are extremely important and can even be decisive for winning or losing in certain situations.

- There are players who always lose (and who always expect to lose) against certain opponents (the so-called nemesis) who are seeded below them.
- Many players refuse to let themselves be put in the role of favorite but feel more comfortable in the role of outsider or let themselves be very negatively influenced by defeats.
- Likewise, many players, mainly because of excessive nervousness in the pregame cannot find their usual game in the beginning phase of the match and cannot concentrate.
- Many players choke up depending on the situation; for example, they play well when relatively behind, but with the approach of tying, fear of winning suddenly occurs. They often fear specific game situations, especially tie-breakers.
- Individual players react poorly to external conditions such as court condition or interfering noise.
- Others lose self-control with unexpected events during play, such as perceived unjust referee's calls, so-called lucky balls and unexpected masterful actions of the opponent, and also his own unexpected mistakes.
- Basically, players let themselves be influenced to varying degrees by social conditions in which the game takes place. For example, many react differently to spectators or give their best performance during a competition only when the coach is present. Others react differently in singles play than they do in team competitions and the like.

Examples such as these show that tennis is a sport that is—if one plays competitively—to a great extent, psychologically demanding, even excessively so.

This is mainly related to the structure of the sport, the confrontation with an opponent, the high technical requirements, and the specific scoring system, which can often lead to dramatic action.

If one summarizes these examples of psychological stress and tries to find reasons for them, then the following leading problems are seen to occur in practice:

- Fear/stress,
- Poor self-confidence,
- Lack of concentration,
- Loss of self-control.

However, most players develop personal techniques of autosuggestion aimed at relaxing, but also at getting themselves to concentrate, gaining self-confidence and maintaining self-control. Thus, the serve often becomes a ritual; after the volley, a specific path to the next serve is preferred. Many players fire themselves up very loudly on the court and scold themselves; others talk to themselves quietly. Many prefer particular articles of clothing or a particular racket.

Such techniques of self-influence are considered, from the scientific perspective, "naïve psychological regulation techniques." They arise because of personal experiences—they are frequently linked to successful situations—and should be judged from the subjective view of the player (therefore, not objective). They can be thoroughly positive, if they actually aid relaxation and concentration, self-confidence, and trust by way of autosuggestion. However, they become problematic, whenever adhering to such ritualized approaches (and perhaps also on quirks) leads to inappropriate, unrealistic, and even compulsive interpretations of success and failure, and thus no longer allows any flexible adjustment to ever-changing competitive conditions. Therefore, it is important to supplement such naïve psychological control techniques with psychological training in which one tries to improve the personal conditioning that is important for success in competition, in a systematic, monitored, and objectively verifiable way.

Thus, it is important that each trainer develops and explores from her point of view practical forms of training that also correspond to valid psychological viewpoints; moreover, these psychological forms of training must be adjusted to the extent that they meet the individual needs of the players.

The following explanations should be thought provoking. In order to be able to develop practical psychological forms of training, there first must be the understanding of psychological principles. Some selected viewpoints that deal with issues of cognition, motivation, and stress are therefore laid out in the following discussion.

Psychological Forms of Training

Overview

Essential psychological requirements that are effective in an athletic competition are:

- Cognitive requirements (perception, attention/concentration, reflection, imagination, anticipation, thought, intelligence and skills and capabilities related to the specific sport, which are related to tactics),
- Motivational/emotional requirements (the will to succeed, anxiety/stress, attitude, etc.).

Psychologically oriented training aims to systematically improve and stabilize these psychological performance requirements; that is, through planned learning and practice to target those effects of training that can be used in competition to enhance performance.

Without continuous, systematic habituation through training, key technique and conditioning skills will not be available to apply in competition. The cognitive, motivational, and emotional requirements cited can be grouped into four types of psychological training (Fig. 113). With the so-called mental training, the direct influence of psychological conditions on movement is provided to a considerable degree by mental imaging of a movement sequence targeted for improvement, but the movement is not actually executed.

With perception and conditioning training, cognitive skills that determine performance, such as movement awareness and situational assessment, attention and concentration, anticipation, and tactically correct behavior are systematically improved.

Motivation training is concerned with working harder at training and improving poor attitudes toward competition and with changing negative motivations such as fear of failure and with realistic goal-setting and so on.

Psychological regulation training targets the optimal use of concentration, anticipation, game intelligence, stress readiness, the will to succeed, and so on in competition. Since psychologically stressful competitive situations lead to inappropriate psychophysical excitation and tension situations, psychological regulation training tries—with the aid of psychological exercises—to provide the activation level that is appropriate for the individual (neither too tense nor too relaxed).

This brief overview of the various psychological forms of training shows that there are close interactions with other forms of training, especially training of techniques and tactics. This leads to the conclusion that types of psychological training should be integrated into the training of techniques and tactics (for example, mental and concentration training integrated into technique training, and training in goal setting integrated into tactics training. However,

there should always be one dominant approach (see also *Tennis Course, Volume 1: Techniques and Tactics*).

Cognition

If a player, decides, say, for tactical reasons, when the score is 4:4 and 30:40, to run to the net directly after the serve, then a series of cognitive processes are set in motion. First, he will try to concentrate totally on the serve. In his mind, he will quickly execute the movement sequence of the serve, which he wants to play to the opponent high to the backhand side. He will decide to run forward as quickly as possible after the serve trying to anticipate as early as possible, where the opponent will play to and in what position he finds himself, so he can decide the best place he can play the ball to. Such processes, which, with planning and reflection, are connected with imagination and perception, are combined with the concept of cognition.

> Cognition is a comprehensive term for all the processes of perception, thought, imagination, and memory.

When the server initiates the volley, in which he plays an unreachable volley-stop and this confirms that he has a "good feel for the ball," then the usual idea "feeling" in this context is rather misleading because feelings generally refer to experiences such as joy and sympathy. More often, it is used primarily to refer to specific abilities. These abilities consist of being able to evaluate the ball hit by the opponent by its

Fig. 113 Types of psychologically oriented training.

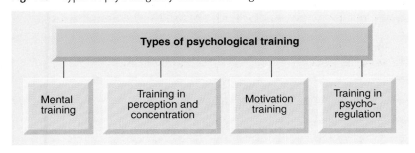

properties (speed, trajectory, spin) and to maneuvering into a favorable hitting position to move toward the ball (considering speed and direction of the racket movement as well as of the inclination of the racket face) in such a way that the goal of the movement (in this case, the volley-stop) can be reached. The perception component of these skills (and less of this feeling) is therefore based essentially on the visually (related to the behavior of the trajectory) and kinesthetically related perception of movement.

Above all, kinesthetic perception while executing technique, therefore the perception of the spacial, temporal, and tension movements via movement-sensitive receptors in the skin, the muscles, the tendons, and the joints is extremely important in directing and regulating coordination movements. Such perceptive capabilities, that is, such prerequisites for cognitive capabilities, can be taught, even if their trainability is certainly not great, as is the case, for example, with stamina. Some aspects of the examples mentioned are considered in the following discussion.

Visualization of Movement, Mental Training

Visualization of movement (for example, visualizing the movement sequence of the serve) is the result of perceiving other's as well as one's own serves, of storing these perceptions in the mind, and (frequently) describing them with words.

The oral and conceptual fixing of these visual kinesthetic perceptions is an important prerequisite for making it possible to grasp and structure the content of the image thoughtfully and to use them in deliberate actions. Mental training builds on such fundamentals.

Three types of mental training are given here:

<u>The player concentrates mentally on a movement sequence.</u> She visualizes, to where she must throw the ball for the serve, in order to meet it at the end of the main action at the highest possible point in such a way that the ball travels with a strong forward and slightly sideways lateral spin. As the specific skills are mastered, she is able to more exactly match the required elements of the total movement sequence to the trajectory of the ball, that is, gain a functional mastery of the movement (see also *Tennis Course, Volume 1: Techniques and Tactics*). The aim of this mental processing of the movement sequence by visualizing the movement is to picture for oneself the essential components of the technique and to imprint on the memory what the requirement for self-correction is.

The player visualizes the planned movement sequence intensively. This form of training, which is also called ideomotor training, is based on the knowledge that even the mere visualization of a movement leads to a neuromuscular excitation of the muscles involved in the visualized movement, so that this movement can be learned faster and grow stronger. Ideomotor training is made easier when the

player has an exact image of the movement he is trying to produce.

The player quietly verbalizes about the movement while picturing it. He gives himself command-based elements of the movement that are difficult for him (for example, "Throw the ball far to the left, to the rear," in order to be able to control the actual sequence of the movement better.

This form of training is also called subvocal training. The techniques of mental training are generally recommended for learning and improving movement skills. However, as psychological training, they are also appropriate for preparation for immediately following actions. In tennis, the preparation for the serve is especially appropriate for this, first and foremost because the serve can be the only stroke completely determined by oneself. Still, the serve, running forward to the rotating position and the first volley, can also be trained mentally as response to the expected return as "chain of action" and can then be practiced as a complete unit. It is also conceivable to mentally go through individual, smaller units (for example, a specific type of grip), to visualize oneself in the sequence, and to give oneself corresponding short commands.

In the course of training, it is therefore recommended that all three forms of mental training described be used together, and if possible, also adding the so-called observational training, that is, observing the movement sequence in other players, perhaps also on videotape. The video technique is also an effective way to show the player his own movement sequence, which can help improve the ability to perceive oneself, to visualize movement, and to make corrections.

A phenomenon connected to mental training is anticipation. This refers to the ability to predict the opponent's actions, to come to a deliberate decision during the sequence, and to let this influence one's own movement pattern. This skill is fostered in training, especially where waiting for the end of the opponent's action would no longer allow enough time for one's own reaction, as is the case, for example, with a volley as a reaction to a fast passing shot. The more often one practices correctly recognizing the opponent's intentions (and also his feints) in training, the earlier and more appropriately the player can react in competition.

Attention and Concentration

In general, the concept of attention is used as a generic term for focused perception. Therefore, attention is often compared with a spotlight. If the beam of a spotlight is directly concentrated on a particular situation, it illuminates it very brightly (concentration of attention). Thus, concentration can be viewed as an intensive form of attention, in which attention is centered on a narrow segment of the possible range of perception. This form of attention, that is, this concentration, in the narrow sense, is fostered in tennis,

especially where the fast-moving ball must be observed precisely. Before the serve, it helps to concentrate one's "internal spotlight" totally on the action at hand. The range of attention can be described in terms of the spotlight. When the baffle in front of it is opened, the light beam is more scattered. In this way, several things can be illuminated, although less brilliantly (dispersion of attention).

Therefore, applying this to tennis means, for example, that the doubles player must always have a greater segment of the court in view, in order to be able to adjust her actions to the fast-changing events. The question is, how many events can be perceived simultaneously and under which circumstances must the attention be shifted from one thing to another. Thus, she can direct the spotlight of her attention lightning fast (like an experienced lighting technician in the film industry) to different situations (shifting attention). Using the example of the doubles player, this means a sudden shift from the "disbursement" of attention to "concentration on attention" if she herself is played to. Generally, with voluntary effort, as happens in competition, total attention can be maintained only for a specific amount of time. The attention span is, therefore, limited. This leads to attention lapses, that is, involuntary shifts of the intensity of attention. High intensity, as is required in a longer tennis match, is connected with a high expenditure of "strong nerves." Therefore, the organism tends to keep shutting itself down, which leads to the

attention lapses mentioned earlier. It might be, then, that the player herself maintains control over her attention through well-placed breaks.

In spite of the variety of viewpoints cited, two standard situations can be differentiated in a general way:
- Attention paid before the volley,
- Attention paid during the volley.

To judge the ability to concentrate in competition, it is, therefore, important to know the conditions on which the concentration processes before and during the athletic action depend. The ability to be attentive—in particular, to be able to concentrate—is closely related to other cognitive and emotional/motivational processes. Therefore, strong emotional excitement (anger, rage, anxiety) interferes with the concentration process. The ability to concentrate is thus a gauge of psychological stability. The ability to concentrate in competition, therefore, is related to internal (mental) relaxation. Therefore, concentration cannot be voluntarily forced; such an attempt tends to lead to more tension. Every tennis player knows from personal experience that he cannot concentrate well if his thoughts are always wandering. This is especially true if he is preparing for a serve or return.

Based on this, it becomes clear that thinking can disturb the concentration process. Consider, particularly, self-reflection directed toward the past, on athletic actions that have just gone wrong, such as, for example, on a ball that has just gone wrong (often connected with anger, therefore with emotional excitement) or the if-then consideration directed to the future ("If I misplay this ball, I'll lose the whole set") impedes optimal concentration on the "Here and Now."

Finally, it should still be mentioned that the ability to concentrate depends, to a significant degree, on physical fitness. Therefore, among other factors, conditioning is vitally important for success in tennis.

Training for Concentration

Based on these general considerations on concentration, here are some tips for practical training:

- Before the volley, one should be sure to get into a state of relaxed concentration. Concentrate on the task without conscious effort and to ignore what does not belong to the task. In training, each player must explore for herself how much time she needs for this, how much her basic breathing rhythm helps her, which personal techniques help her succeed in getting rid of wandering thoughts and external disruptive stimuli (for example, ritualized actions before serving). To stabilize these techniques, it is advisable to use disruptive stimuli in a positive way (for example, on audio tape) now and then in order to simulate the stresses of competition.
- During the volley, the incoming ball should be followed as long as possible, even if this is possible only up to 1–2 m before contact with the racket face. This attempt, which appears banal, must be repeatedly made and controlled because many players observe the trajectory only briefly and, therefore, turn the head too soon in the direction of the opponent. However, this impedes control of the hitting movement when meeting the ball. Practicing keeping an eye on the ball may be easier with colored balls, which may more clearly reveal the ball's trajectory and spin.
- During breaks, it is helpful to systematically practice the shift from concentration while playing to relaxation and back to concentrating on the game, in order to prolong the ability to concentrate.
- If concentration is to be understood as a more intensive form of attentive perception, then concentration training can consist of having to perceive under difficult conditions and to react accordingly, for example, to balls coming in rapid succession from a ball-throwing machine or by hand from two opponents.

Because the ability to concentrate is especially impeded by psychological and physical stresses, corresponding stimuli should be incorporated into the concentration exercises; for example, concentration exercises should also include situations encountered in high training stresses, so that in a competitive situation, the player is still in the position to be able to concentrate at the end of the match.

Motivation

In order to be able to address motivational competitive problems in training, it is first necessary to be clear about certain fundamentals. Whenever players expend great effort and endurance to reach a certain performance goal, whether it is to play the ball over the net into the opponent's court or to win the match, during these performances, certain internal processes operate. These can be represented in a simplified way as follows (see Fig. 114, p. 187).

First, the player is given a task based on the events during play (or by his opponent). He then asks himself, more or less consciously, whether he has the necessary ability to carry out this task, how much effort (concentration, stamina, and will power) he must exert to carry it out, and to what extent external influence, which he cannot control (for example, the opponent's strength and also things that happen during play) will affect the results.

This evaluation of factors that can influence success or failure is known as assignment of causes. The assignment of causes helps to estimate the probability of success or failure, suggest hope for success and fear of failure, and to induce practical goal-setting to guide the action. If the designated goal is achieved, this is usually considered a success. Whether success or failure of an action also leads to a corresponding emotional reaction (therefore, elation on success or disappointment on failure) will depend on how much the

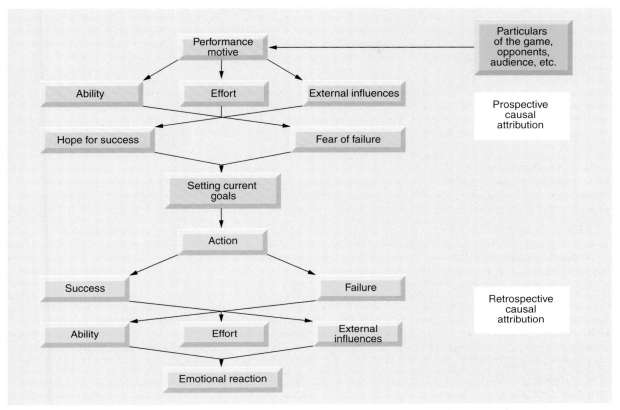

Fig. 114 Schematic for an exemplary representation of the sequence of the motivation processes in a performance situation (according to GABLER 1984)

individual feels responsible for the result of the action, for example, by confidently assigning causal factors retrospectively. The more one can attribute success to skills, the greater is the resulting satisfaction. On the other hand, concluding that poor skills are responsible for a failure despite effort produces disappointment and resignation because poor skills are relatively stable, so future failures will then be expected.

With respect to these processes, two emotions are especially important: hope for success and fear of failure. Because individual players have different histories of successes and failures, they can be differentiated between those who are success-motivated and those who are failure-motivated. This means that those who are success-motivated (hope for success) tend to be confident and optimistic, whereas those who are failure-motivated (fear of failure) tend toward anxiety and pessimism. However, one should not conclude from this that the fear-of-failure types do not strive for success. As compared with the hope-for-success types, who orient themselves to success, for the most part, because of their confidence and are concerned only very little with possible failure, the fear-of-failure types—because for them fear of failure is dominant—take pains to avoid this possible failure.

Research has shown repeatedly that both of these components of performance motivation, the hope for success and fear of failure, are interrelated with other components of performance motivation so that performance can be explained and predicted, in part on this basis. This affects a connection with practical goal setting. Those expecting success set predominantly realistic goals for themselves, that is, goals that lie within a medium subjective area of difficulty. Those anxious about failure, however, tend to set goals that are either very low or extremely unrealistic and loaded with conflict. Those who have set lower goals—because there is a good probability that the failure can thus also be avoided—exhibit a lower overall motivation. On the other hand, those who have set extremely high, even unattainable goals, providing an excuse for apparent failure, exhibit a strong overall motivation. However, there are significant interconnections between success and failure orientation with causal attribution. For those expecting success, gaining it may be attributed to their own capabilities, whereas failure can be assigned to poor effort or just bad luck. Thus, success tends to produce a positive feedback effect, whereas failure causes no pessimism. It is a healthy situation: more effort produces more success. Those expecting failure will be anxious and regard success as more a matter of luck than skill, while attributing failure to themselves.

The result is that pessimism and a lack of self-confidence are strengthened. It can be deduced from these relationships that self-confidence must be equated with a positive self-image. The more a player is convinced that she can carry out a given task, on the basis of her own capabilities, the sooner she will also reach her goal.

However, people who estimate their abilities (inappropriately) low, choose relatively easy tasks and give up rather quickly when, on pursuing the goal, they experience difficulties, that is, the length and strength of their efforts are rather limited. Such people also tend to have thoughts that digress from the action, which—as described earlier—often lead to lapses in concentration. A further aspect of performance motivation, which in Fig. 114 deals with the box "Actions" and is very important for the competitive sport, concerns the question of which conditions are necessary to keep the goal-directed action on track.

Therefore, it is also a question of the processes that operate because of athletic activity, particularly the ability to guide the action to the goal in spite of great obstacles. This ability to guide is called determination. Determination is the ability to marshall all the processes that are important for reaching the goals. The more obstacles that stand in the way of reaching the goal, the more important is the ability to overcome them through determination. In tennis, this ability to guide has two main aspects.

First, tennis players must be capable of "controlling themselves" in the face of stimuli that have emotionally negative effects, both internally and externally, such as anger at oneself or at the referee. Second, tennis players must have the ability to persevere, that is, they must be in a position to be able to

overcome barriers through elevated physical effort.

These barriers can be short-term or long-term:

- There are short-term barriers, for example, when it is necessary to play another stop, in spite of physical exhaustion after a long volley.
- There are long-term barriers, for example, when, if it is very hot in the third set, arms and legs become heavy and each step must be "willed." In such cases, one often speaks of a "battle against oneself," and when ending successfully, a "victory over oneself."

Self-control and perseverance are significant performance-determining factors in training as well as in competition. There are other concepts in this context that are close synonyms: determination, discipline, psychological toughness, tenacity, psychological staying power. Strongly expressed acts of the will can be attributed to three conditions:

- The more the player is motivated, the sooner he will succeed in maintaining and even increasing his commitment.
- The better the physical condition, the less likely that the player will give in to fatigue and lower his commitment.
- Finally, the ability to persevere ("to grin and bear it," to endure pain, to mobilize physical reserves) can be considered as a special personality trait.

Training for Motivation

The particular challenge here is that in training, it is difficult to simulate psychological problems, which show up mainly in competition. What is characteristic of a competition from a psychological point of view:

- One is under far greater pressure than in training;
- The goals that one sets for oneself are strongly influenced by the opponent, which often leads to an excessive fixation on the opponent (instead of on the task);
- Badly played balls (only with the serve is there another chance) cannot be repeated, as is usually the case in training.

Therefore, situations should be created in training that lead to psychological stress similar to those in competition. In this way, players learn to be ready even in training. A player who always practices in training without psychological stress runs the risk of being overtaxed in competition. Many players go through training with no psychological stress because they mostly play against opponents whom they know well, and the training progresses for the most part without serious participants. Competition, on the other hand, is serious, with unexpected situations that lead to uncertainty. Therefore, uncertainty must be provoked in training.

To simulate competitive stress, we recommend:

- assigning the player clear risk-taking tasks and goals (based on individual tactical training tasks or on a training match), but also letting him decide for himself.

- "Reward" the achievement of these goals or "punish" failure to achieve them through further training tasks.

Such tasks can mean accomplishing tactical tasks (for example, after each serve, the player must switch her racket to the other hand) or establishing handicaps (each game begins at 0:15) or confronting the players with a tie-breaker in the middle of the training match. "Rewarding" means that during training, players must have some form of rewarding themselves; "punishing" means that not achieving the goal has unpleasant consequences, so that even during training, the processes of performance motivation (see Fig. 114, p. 187) are experienced and are decided psychological stress.

Therefore, that means that the players in training must learn to set realistic goals and to develop self-confidence in their abilities and expectations to succeed, via appropriate causal attributions. They must learn to see the goal rather than the opponent, and the opponent himself as less of a threat, because to experience a challenge ("You are strong, but I am, too, and you have to show it first") and not always to equate success with winning and failure with losing, but to attribute success and failure to appropriate goal-setting and causal attribution. In motivation training, therefore, goals should be set that work psychologically like a competition, so that the players learn strategies afterward via conversations with the trainer, supported by videos and other monitoring measures, and, above all, by observing themselves—in

order to withstand such stresses in competition.

Finally, motivation training can refer to the training itself because it is frequently overlooked that motivation processes occur even in training. Even in training, players must learn to motivate themselves. The trainer can help them, while she is conducting a matchlike training program with continuous setting of measured goals, but is also leaving room for limbering up and relaxing forms of training, in order to avoid any kind of training monotony.

On the other hand, high physical demands should be made now and then (for example, in terms of conditioning-oriented training), so that the players learn how to combat internal and external resistances in the context of emphasizing the will in training.

Psychological Regulation

The physical and psychological stresses in competition often lead to psychological effects that are characterized by the term *poor competitive stability*. The player can no longer optimally incorporate concentration, perspective of the game, readiness for action, and the like into his game. He behaves as if stressed, tense, and also paralyzed) or as psychologically tired (also in conjunction with physical fatigue), that is, as if he is no longer in a position to exert himself. The types of experiences mentioned are related to an inappropriate internal excitement tension condition, which leads to decreased performance levels.

Psychological Stress

Psychological stress can at first be compared generally with psychological stress. However, the stress concept is increasingly used to characterize extreme demands. In competitive sports, such extreme demands mostly happen in the prestart situation in important competitions or with extremely high stress in training. In tennis, stress can occur and affect play not only in the prestart situation but also during the entire competition. This is because one can consider every situation before every new volley as an initial situation; in a three-set match, this happens approximately 180 times. Stress factors enter into the initial situation, such as unexpectedly leading or trailing behind, unexpected strength of the opponent, perceived or actual bad calls by the referee, unfortunate

position of the sun, and unfavorable wind and court conditions. In addition, one must consider that stress factors may also emerge occasionally in the course of individually longer volleys. The effects of great psychological demands, anxiety, and stress can be classified in three levels: the psychological, the emotional-motivational, and the cognitive-motor.

On the psychological level, there are side effects such as accelerated pulse, shortness of breath, dilation of the pupils, pale face, trembling hands, profuse sweating and elevated bladder and intestine activity.

On the emotional-motivational level, unpleasant, tense situations are evident. They are described with terms such as inhibition and excitement, paralysis and agitation.

Frequently, there is a sense of weakness. One's mood can be depressed, but may also be agitated. On the cognitive-motor level, the effects are especially varied:

- Perception is impaired. There is a narrowing of the perceptual field, optical illusions, faulty interpretation of one's own and others' movement sequences, and inappropriate analysis of situations.

- Thinking is disturbed by thoughts that digress from the action, that is, thoughts are concentrated less on the task itself but rather revolve around problems, the fact that they cannot be overcome, and the following assessment using the social environment. Thoughts also often wander or are "blocked"; the result is faulty decision-making.

- The ability to concentrate is significantly decreased.
- Because of their mutual influence, these effects, in conjunction with a muscular tension and tension due to stress and anxiety, lead to an essential impedence of coordination ability: Movement no longer proceeds "loosely." Play has more to do with power and less with technique; precision of movement decreases; movement stability gets worse because of high susceptibility to interference, and the ability to perform movements unconsciously that is so important for movements that run automatically is basically lost. In addition, there is the uneconomical expenditure of energy.

In summary, there is the following picture, as represented in the overview in Fig. 115. It becomes clear that two directions can be offered as reactions to stress. Either it results in a decrease in activity (hypoactivation), that is, the player has the feeling of being braked or paralyzed; or it comes to an excessive excitation (hyperactivation), that is, the player has the feeling of being tense. Scientific evidence shows that, in general, both limited and very great activation lead to lower capability. On the other hand, what is best for achieving optimal capability is a medium level of activation, which also contains what people call "starting fright," corresponding to "stage fright." What is meant as "medium level" of activation depends on the individual's abilities to control the activation level and on her temperament.

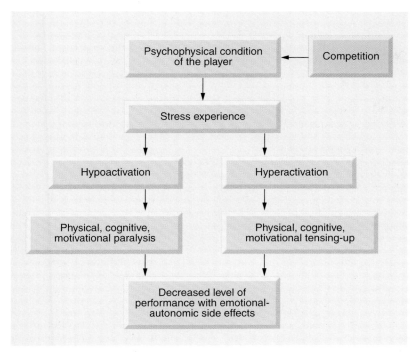

Fig. 115 Psychophysical factors that interfere with performance.

should be sparing with this form of mobilization, that is also, that one must practice it in training under suitable conditions, in order to be familiar with the reactions of his body (especially concerning intensity and moment of adaptation). Only then is it possible that mobilization techniques in competition can be decided on and employed quickly and effectively.

Psychological Regulation Training

Psychological regulation training is based on the following: With too low activation, it is necessary to mobilize oneself without tension. If activation is too high, it helps to relax without putting on the breaks. Therefore, psychological regulation training aims at teaching and systematically using mobilization and relaxation in order to achieve an individual's optimal activation level, as well as to influence and monitor one's own physical and psychological processes that normally operate involuntarily. Thus, one could infer that because of the close relationship among the motor, autonomic, and psychological (cognitive and emotional) areas, any change in one of these areas affects the others.

Mobilization

Mobilization is achieved mainly from the psychological area, and here, particularly, in the form of:
- Autosuggestion,
- Internal autocommand.

This is done in the hope that this mobilization also has an effect on the autonomic and, ultimately, the motor region. With many players, this mobilization can be observed when they drive themselves on after a long and tiring, or boring, match and "pull themselves together," as they breathe deeply, clench their fists, speak encouragingly to themselves, and the like. This self-motivation leads to an autosuggestive increase of adrenaline, to activation of the autonomic nervous system, as well as the circulatory system, and thus to mobilization of the musculature. However, one

Fig. 116 Self-motivation.

Relaxation

Concerning relaxation, there are a series of experiments that have already been carried out in sports and also in clinical medicine and psychology. The best-known procedure is <u>autogenic training</u>, according to Schultz.

In autogenic training, various exercises are done in autosuggestive form, such as, for example, the heaviness ("My right arm is very heavy"), which leads to relaxing the corresponding muscles, or the warmth exercise ("My left arm is very warm"), which causes relaxation of the corresponding blood vessels. Therefore, the action is again carried out by the psychological area, especially linked to the goal of first influencing the autonomic area. Internal verbalization of such exercise formulas in connection with general set phrases such as, "I am completely calm," while in a relaxed sitting position in a quiet place, with closed eyes. This autorelaxation, achieved through concentration might also influence bodily functions that are usually automatic. In a competitive sport, this method can be used only in a limited way. It can hardly ever be learned in a short time and should be learned if at all possible only under the professional supervision of a physician or psychologist. In addition, the main emphasis of autogenic training rests on general relaxation, so that activating components still have to be added if the technique is to be used in competition. Therefore, so-called relaxation-mobilization techniques that are based on the principles of autogenic training

Fig. 117 Relaxing during the break while changing sides.

were developed. However, there are even more sport-specific mobilization forms. Therefore, after the relaxation exercises, Frester, for example, recommends formulating intentions using set phrases.

Recently, progressive muscle relaxation is being used at an increasing level in competitive sports, according to Jacobson. This process starts in the motor area. Jacobson starts with the assumption that anxiety always leads to feelings of tension and corresponding muscle tenseness. However, if this is reversed and one achieves muscular relaxation, this is not the same as experiencing anxiety.

The benefit of progressive muscle relaxation is, therefore, to achieve an increasing relaxation of the whole skeletal musculature via the systematic alternation of tension and relaxation of individual muscle groups. This

tension and relaxation of the individual muscle groups proceeds according to the sequence: hands, arms, face, neck, shoulders, back, chest, abdomen, lower body, legs, feet.

Finally, this is followed by an overall tensing and relaxing the body. The instructions proceed as, for example, "After you have relaxed, clench your right fist, clench it tighter and tighter and simultaneously observe the tenseness in your right fist, your hand, forearm. . . . And now relax. Let the fingers of your right hand loosen up and observe the different impression. Let yourself go completely and try to relax your whole body."

Jacobson training is attractive for the tennis player for several reasons:
- It can be learned relatively quickly (also with the aid of audio cassette tapes) and does not take too much time to do.
- It is similar to conditions in competition and, therefore, motivates players to learn.
- Relaxation reaction can be called upon quickly just before play begins or during a change of sides. This is possible, because in Jacobson training, the players learn to shift from tension to relaxation, while also learning to relax without the preceding tension.
- The players must be in a position to concentrate mentally at the end of the relaxation phase on that which they intend to do after changing sides. Jacobson training is also effective in this respect, because the relaxation

that is achieved is aligned more with a physical relaxation and less with meditative processes (as in transcendental meditation) or to a state of suspended attentiveness (as in autogenic training).

- Jacobson training makes it possible for the players to become sensitive, by emphasizing concentration on the sensations that arise during tension and relaxation for the muscle tone of individual muscle groups, which they can also use for individual play situations, that is, particularly before each volley.

- This sensitization can also help them succeed in relaxing during breaks when changing sides, to such an extent that there is no decrease in tone below a threshold value, which impedes the readiness to act which is necessary afterward. On the other hand, the players can also be able to mobilize themselves (when fatigued).

Psychological or Psychologically Oriented Training?

Previous understanding of psychological training was that the psychological performance requirements (such as perception, thinking, motivation, and stress-stabilization) can be systematically improved and stabilized through training. However, training of techniques and tactics and psychological training overlap to such an extent that it is not clear which is the proper place of psychological training. Thus, we can assign the mental training that is oriented toward movement sequence per se to technique training. Consequently, it can be asked, can tactics training—in which perception, judgment, and decision processes are to be optimized—also be considered as psychological training? In

differentiating among technique, tactics, and coordination and psychological training, it becomes clear in many cases that the psyche is fundamental to each of them.

Therefore, in the practice of training, the term *psychological training* should be replaced by the term *psychologically oriented training*. At first, it helps to differentiate among psychologically oriented conditioning, technique, tactics, and competition training (Fig. 118). These forms of training clearly show the overlap. Thus, for example, technique and tactics training are very closely related. However, the expression of the various forms of training is oriented toward the focus that the trainer establishes. Corresponding to this focus, she gives her instructions and corrections. Psychologically oriented means that visualization, decision, concentration, and stress management processes are in the foreground.

Fig. 118 Psychologically oriented competitive training as a supplement to the conditioning, technique, and tactics training.

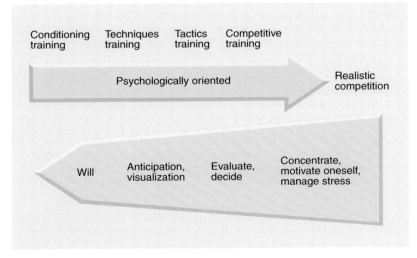

Conditioning training   Techniques training   Tactics training   Competitive training

Psychologically oriented → Realistic competition

Will   Anticipation, visualization   Evaluate, decide   Concentrate, motivate oneself, manage stress

In order to be able to better understand the similarities and differences of psychologically oriented training of techniques and tactics, as well as psychologically oriented competitive training, it is advisable to differentiate between <u>learning</u> and <u>training</u>. To learn tactics means learning basic tactical patterns and practicing them. To train tactics means using these learned basic patterns under difficult conditions in matchlike situations.

For the trainer, the following tips are helpful:

- Move behind the player (as his "shadow") in order to be able to put oneself better into the player's perception and decision processes. If necessary, interrupt the action, in order to discuss these processes with the player.
- Create problem situations, and thus improve the ability to decide among two or three possible modes of action.
- Present strategic concepts and let the player use them in various ways.
- Watch videos of opponents and, using the interruption-of-play method, have the player predict the opponent's actions.
- Stop videos of the player and discuss (video-feedback).

The more the training is directed to the demands of a real competition, the more important the psychological processes become, especially concentration, motivation, and stress management processes.

Before psychologically oriented competitive training is discussed, it should be made clear that

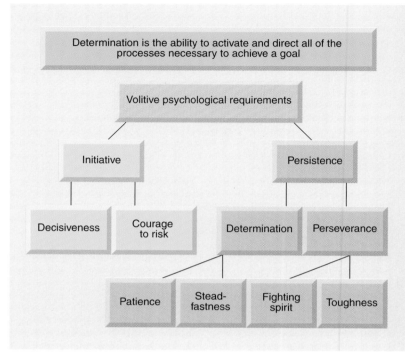

Fig. 119   Volitive psychological requirements.

analogous to technique and tactics training, players must first learn how to regulate these psychological processes completely, before they are in the position to use them under the stressful conditions of a competition. This means:

- Psychological skills, such as the ability to be aware of oneself, relax, concentrate, and motivate, must be learned. This can take place off the tennis court or on it in playing <u>with one another</u>.
- Training psychological skills means using the learned skills under difficult or psychologically stressful conditions in competitive

situations. This occurs on the court during playing <u>against each other</u>.

Psychologically oriented competitive training (Fig. 120) logically takes place on the tennis court. Here, two situations in training can be differentiated from each other. Training can be related to behavior while playing and to behavior during breaks. In "playing against each other," it can first be a matter of concentrating on the individual volley. Psychologically oriented training of individual volleys means, then, to focus not so much on techniques or tactics, but rather very specifically on the

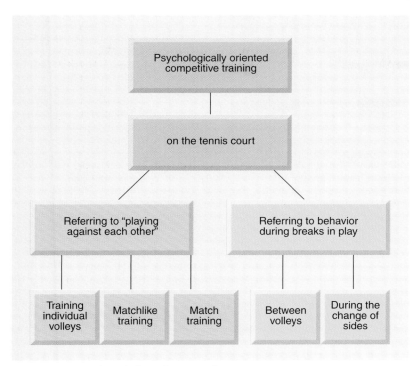

Fig. 120 Types of psychologically oriented competitive training.

volley under psychological pressure. Here are three exercise examples:

- 20 volleys are played. The players' task is to call out words like "hop" or "come" just as the ball bounces, and "hit" or "on" just as they meet the ball with the racket. This promotes perception and concentration, as well as a sense of rhythmic movement sequences. The trainer counts the volleys, so one of the two players wins the game. (Playing against each other.)
- Again, 20 volleys are played. The players now have the task of exhaling aloud just as they meet the ball, for example, saying a long "Aaah." This also promotes the ability to concentrate and assists timing.

- One of the two players has the task of measuring his energy and strength output on a four-step scale, during the hitting movement as the trainer calls out. "1" means low and "4" means high, as can be seen in the variations in speed of the balls. With this exercise, the players optimize their ability to perceive themselves and also their ability to use activation and relaxation flexibly, depending on psychoautonomic conditions or tactical situations.

Psychologically oriented matchlike training focuses on providing psychologically stressful competitive tasks that simulate a tennis match but can also exceed the regulation match rules. To provide competitive tasks here

also means "to play to win" in the narrow sense.

- Who wins, for example, the 21st point? Scoring is the same as in table tennis. The ball is put into play without a serve (that is, tossed underhand). Stops and volleys are not allowed. Attack players and all-round players are especially required to produce a good mixture of safe and risky baseline play. Therefore, the ability to put into play a difficult tactical concept under psychologically stressful conditions is the main lesson taught here.
- The tie-breaker also represents a special scoring method. The trainer can suddenly declare that tie-breakers are to be played; these require flexibility and psychological strength.
- "Playing to win under difficult conditions" can also mean that handicaps are introduced, for example, playing only with the forehand, or having only one serve. These exercises can also help to develop abilities under stressful conditions.

With match training, the goal is, for example:
- To maintain the ability to concentrate throughout the entire match,
- To pay particular attention to the shift between activation and relaxation,
- To prevent possible stressful situations.

That is, the focus of one's efforts lies not in the area of techniques or tactics, but in that of psychological processes, which operate under the pressured conditions of a seriously played training match. The development of practical sports psychology in tennis was at first directed toward confronting the players off the tennis court with psychology, teaching them relaxation techniques, and the like. They once concentrated more intensely on what happened on the tennis court itself and on behavior during play. Prompted by the American sports psychologist and tennis expert, J.E. Loehr, behavior during breaks has also recently taken on greater significance. Thus, it is often noted that the proportion of the average playing time, that is, the periods in which volleys take place, is approximately 1:2–1:5 of the total length of the match, depending on the court surface. A volley on clay courts takes 10 seconds on average, and on fast courts sometimes only 2–3 seconds; the following break takes an average of approximately 20 seconds. Using a three-set match as an example, this means that there are approximately 180 pauses between volleys and approximately 15 breaks for changing sides. Therefore 180 breaks between the volleys means 180 initial situations occurring approximately every 20 seconds.

The Four-Phase Program Between Volleys

Because 70–80 percent of the time in competitive tennis is used for sitting, waiting, and preparing, the time in the breaks between the individual volleys can be used for psychological measures. With inexperienced players, psychological problems occur most often during this period because they clearly show their anger and disappointment after badly played balls, lose their composure over bad calls by the referee, or let spectators irritate them. Conversely, top players distinguish themselves mainly by using this time to their best advantage to relax after the preceding ball and to concentrate on the next one.

The four phases of the program between volleys can be described as follows:

Phase 1

How Should I React to the Previous Volley?
There should be a positive reaction directly after the volley, if at all possible. This is also quite easy after winning an important point. Thus, the "Becker fist" was not only a widely recognized image of success in tennis; it is the expression of joy and pride in one's own performance and also confirmation and acclamation, in which one demonstrates his own strength for himself and others.

However, dealing with serious mistakes (especially those caused by oneself) is more difficult. It is worth recommending here that the player should forget the mistakes as quickly as possible. That is, she should put what has happened behind herself in order to be able to concentrate completely on the next volley. At the same time, it is important to show—both physically and mentally—that she is "above it all" and in control. Therefore, in the case of a volley error, for example, the player should turn away very deliberately from the place of the error, return energetically with erect posture to the baseline, and say to herself, "It doesn't matter!" In this way, negative thoughts and self-doubt can be prevented. The faster anger and disappointment can be worked out, the more energy is spared and more time remains for the next phase between the volleys.

Fig. 121 Concentrating by contemplating the racket strings.

Fig. 122 Self-motivation.

Phase 2

How Can I Reach the Medium Activation Level?

As discussed, a medium activation level is an important prerequisite for optimal performance. After the volley is finished, the second phase can serve either the physical or psychological relaxation or mobilization. To do this, one can, for example, shift the racket to the other hand while walking back to the baseline, in order to relieve the hitting hand. Behind the baseline, the player moves back and forth slowly, while always moving and loosening up overall.

For relaxing, it is also worth recommending that the player should breathe especially deeply and concentrate mentally on calming thoughts (for example, "Be calm," "Relax"). In order to avoid being distracted by external stimuli, it is wise, for example, to contemplate the strings of the racket.

Breathing can also be used for mobilization, should the situation arise that the player finds himself in a phase of weariness.

Phase 3

How Do I Prepare Myself for the Next Volley?

This phase begins as soon as the player has relaxed enough or has mobilized (so far as this is necessary), or when she goes to the baseline for a service or return. This preparation for the next volley can include:
- Motivating oneself mentally through positive thinking and convincing oneself, as well as externally, through appropriate body language,
- Preparing oneself by visualizing the approaching movement action, or
- Preparing oneself appropriately through tactical thinking, that is, devising problem-solving strategies or playing things through in one's mind.

Phase 4

How Do I Concentrate on the Service and on the Return?

This last phase is characterized by habituated rituals that increase concentration. It begins at the instant in which the player finds himself in the correct starting position for the service or return.

It is recommended, for example, that the serving player let the ball tap at least two or three times, and at the same time, just before the last tap, to pause briefly in order to avoid a hasty serve.

Before the return, the player can either move slightly in place (dancing around or jumping) or rock the body back and forth. It is important here to observe the opponent's movements exactly. In this phase, attention should be very concentrated, all thoughts (for example, on techniques and tactics or on possible consequences of a lost point should be switched off. Instead, the player can visualize a clear, graphic image of the impending action.

The following remarks can be made as a summary of this program:
- The borderline between the individual phases is fluid. If necessary, a method of transition between the phases (for example, relaxation) is recommended.
- This also means that, under some circumstances, some phases can be skipped. The criterion for this relates to whether there is a problem situation, which should be dealt with in such a way in the pause between the volleys that

Closing Remarks

Some general tips for practical use of psychologically oriented training are given here (in part, as a review):

- An essential prerequisite for the effective use of psychological training measures is a positive attitude of players toward these measures. Only a voluntary and active willingness to participate promises positive effects. A prerequisite for this can be that, at the beginning, the players are also informed at the beginning of the basic psychological issues concerning the competition, before they have to deal with corresponding training activities.
- A prerequisite for learning the processes themselves is sensitization (for example, the ability to be sensitive) for the internal cognitive, emotional, autonomic, and muscular processes that arise with psychological pressures.
- The individual processes should be done in steps.
- The goal of practicing is to learn and train the individual forms of training in such a way that they also remain stable in difficult situations and, therefore, function relatively automatically where used.
- Because what is learned can also be unlearned again, it must be practiced again and again, even if a real occasion does not always exist.
- Therefore, psychologically oriented training is also a component of a long-term training structure.
- The individual psychological forms of training have been described separately only for

internal balance can be restored. At any rate, Phase 4 cannot be skipped—it is indispensable.
- Depending on the situation, the length and content of the individual phases can be varied, depending on where the preceding volley ended (for example, at the net or behind the baseline), whether this

volley was won or lost, how long and how dramatic it was, what the score is, whether there are ball retrievers, and whether it is singles or doubles.
- The game regions for one's own strategies in the context of the individual phases are large and should also be stabilized in training. At any rate, they decrease until Phase 4.

practical reasons. In practice, they are closely related; for example, forms of relaxation and mental training are related as are forms of relaxation and concentration training.

- Basically, all psychological forms of training are integrated as closely as possible into the usual techniques and tactics training (and if necessary, also into conditioning training). This is particularly true for younger players.
- Particular attention should be given to how similar to competition the situations are.
- Because psychological problems are always expressed more or less individually, the corresponding measures must also be varied according to the individual. Therefore, there are no "recipes"; it depends rather on trying out the various measures and using them again according to the individual effect.

- Psychologically oriented training should not be emphasized too much, if the player has no problems dealing with her ability or if she can do this because of "naïve" measures.
- However, if she has bigger problems that cannot be solved even with the help of her trainer, then a sports psychologist should be brought in for consultation.
- Concerning the use of psychological training measures with young people, it is apparent that, for example, training for concentration and goal setting is particularly important in youth. Therefore, using psychological forms of training depends on the problem, the performance level, age, and level of intellectual development and can be determined only for each individual case.

In conclusion, we again emphasize the overarching goal of psychological training.

The players should be in a position to prepare themselves for competition in a concentrated manner, mentally and emotionally (in conjunction with a midlevel autonomic and muscular activation in such a way that they have the sense that "everything is running on automatic"). They should be "dead sure" that they are "playing as in a dream." No doubt, distracting thoughts, muscular cramping, and similar diversions destroy the synthesis of attention, consciousness, and action. The players participate totally in the action. This is a sign that all performance potentials are being used optimally in competition.

Planning for Training and Competition

Planning for training and competition includes long-term training development as described in the chart on page 107 (performance training). In addition, short-term and midlength training measures and competition planning are also oriented to annual planning. In this section, general tips for annual planning (and also cyclical scheduling) are discussed.

Cyclical Scheduling

The term *cyclical scheduling* generally refers to longer time segments—6 months to a year—even if tennis-specific shorter segments are taken into consideration.

No tennis player can maintain his highest level of performance uninterrupted over 12 months. He cannot always be at his individual limit of capacity. Therefore, it is interesting, that tennis players must also plan their yearly cycles in such a way that they are at their best form exclusively in the time period that is important for them as individuals.

The capacity of the athlete fluctuates several times throughout the year. The annual cyclical scheduling takes this into consideration.

1. Preparation Period

Phase of development or dealing with increasing pressure (lasting approximately 4–6 months). This is divided into two stages:
- General preparation stage,
- Specific preparation stage.

2. Competitive Period

Phase of relative stabilization, of stabilization of pressure (lasting approximately 2–4 months).

3. Transition Period

Phase of temporary loss of form, of reduction in pressure (lasting approximately 1–2 months).

This classic division of the year into a monopolar or bipolar cyclical scheduling, which is based primarily of the experiences of track-and-field, weight lifting, swimming, and other types of sports, does not work for tennis without modification.

The competitive player, not just the world-class player, has several particularly important high points in the year; therefore, cyclical scheduling must be alternatively adjusted to the designated seasonal high points. For example, one can cite the four grand-slam tournaments for a world-class player (Paris in May/June, Wimbledon in June/July, U.S. Open in September, and Australian Open in January) or the Davis Cup rounds (March, August, October, and December).

To compete in all of these, a top player strives for four to eight peaks in a year, that is, she would have to be in absolute best form in possibly six periods, which is impossible physiologically. It is no different for national or regional classes, or for young people. Again, the experience of the experts helps here. Based on experience, approximately three peaks are possible. An alternative tennis-specific proposal of a three-peak cycle for a world-class player take on the following form.

Three-Peak Cyclical Scheduling

The following division can be made, based on specific athletic requirements:

1. Preparation Period

Phase of general and specific skills development.

2. Competitive Period I

Phase of optimizing match and tournament rhythm.

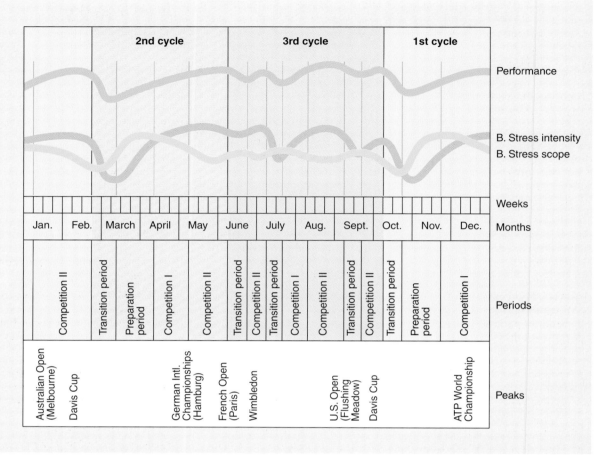

Fig. 123 Example of a three-peak cyclical schedule in tennis in three cycles.

3. Competitive Period II

Phase of maximum capability.

4. Interim Period

Phase of slight regeneration or reduction of skills level and new or intermediate development.

5. Transition Period

Phase of active regeneration. As a first step, the particular peaks, in which the player wants to or has to achieve his top performance level, must be reflected.

In the pattern presented in Fig. 123, the top competitive period (competitive period II) should be included in the following time periods:
- From mid-January to the beginning of March (Australian Open, Davis Cup),
- In May and June (German International Championships, French Open, Wimbledon),
- In August and September (U.S. Open and Davis Cup).

Accordingly, competitions of the competitive period I must happen in the following periods:

- December,
- Approximately from mid-April to mid-May,
- From mid-July to mid-August.

The brief intervals are then planned for:
- Mid-June,
- To mid-July,
- Mid-September.

The longer preparation periods are:
- Beginning of March to beginning of April,
- End of October to the end of November.

The transition periods can then be:
- End of February to mid-March (14 days),
- Mid-October (14 days).

As can be seen, for a top player a three-peak cycle is also not ideal, because relatively little time remains for the regeneration phases.

If one considers that the players do not make it to the finals, that they take a short break in between times or are injured, and that while traveling to tournaments, training conditions are not ideal, short regeneration breaks automatically occur several times a year.

This makes careful planning all the more necessary for top players, in order to put the individual's top competitive period at the right time and to deal with the available limited performance capacity. Figure 123 also shows that the intensity curve agrees, for the most part, with the performance curve and the scope curve dips where the intensity curve rises.

We can assume from this that the maximum of the tennis player's optimal capability is achieved three times in a year. From these explanations we can assume: (1) that tennis-specific cyclical scheduling must take into account the current state of the sport of tennis in the world and (2) that one pays attention to the fundamentals of sports science and is realistic in planning and training.

It should be emphasized that the peaks within the individual periods must be selected according to the player's playing strength and age. If, for example, Wimbledon is the peak for one player, for another it is the Davis Cup, U.S. Open, the league championship, or a combination of one or more of these with other tournaments.

For young people, the peaks are different. The younger they are, the more important is the priority given to systematic training and development before competition. Again, the competitive situations must correspond appropriately to the playing strength of the young person. A healthy mixture of easier and more difficult tournaments—and later, a mix of youth and adult tournaments—is very important because successes that one experiences against equal or somewhat weaker players must be paired with experiences from losses to stronger opponents.

Basically, however, up to about 13 or 14 years of age, the general motor- and tennis-specific development is most important, whereas after 14, playing matches is much more strongly emphasized. That means that the individual preparation periods for younger players must be stretched out and annual planning must be limited to a two-peak cyclical scheduling.

With 13 and 14 year olds, the three-peak format can be planned, but the length of the competitive period, especially competitive period I, should be shortened in favor of the preparation period.

For 15 year olds and older (assuming the appropriate playing strength and ability) planning gradually approaches that for adults.

Managing Training

In order to be able to regulate the training in keeping with the planning objectives, the periods should be divided further. The individual periods, then, include:
- Training units,
- Microcycles (3–8 days),
- Macrocycles or possibly mesocycles (3–6 weeks).

Training Units

The training unit is, for the most part, identical with the daily training curriculum. In high-performance tennis, especially, this unit is further subdivided into phases. One speaks of a one-, two-, or three-phase training program. With current demands on the scope and intensity of training for high-performance tennis players, a two-phase training plan is an urgent necessity; for training camps, a four-phase training plan is encouraged because a 3- to 4-hour training session without short regeneration phases is impossible, especially when technique training is paired with conditioning.

Each training unit should have a methodical development (see Table 12, p. 204). When one trains two or three times a day, this division should be maintained in each phase. In this, the introductory segment before the first phase (up to 30 minutes) and the conclusion after the final phase should be expressed especially strongly.

Segment	Tasks	Content
Introduction	Systematic preparation for the main section: • Physically: muscle warm-up, limbering, increased organic and metabolic adaptability • Cognitive/psychological: Directing attention, thoughtful and motivational attitude	General warm-up by running or a short game (soccer, basketball, hockey). Stretching exercises, limbering exercises, easy gymnastics. Sprinting practice
Main Section	Further development and stabilization of the training level. Note: • In the sequence, positive carry-over of effects of training • Regularity of stress and regeneration	Elements of technique, speed or coordination exercises, types of tactics, etc. Note the sequence: • First, conditioning (strength, stamina) followed by a 3- to 5-hour break or as an independent daily unit. • Then, techniques, tactics, coordination, flexibility
Conclusion (if necessary and possible)	Introduction and acceleration of regenerative processes. Bring the body back to normal functional level.	Run or play at a slow pace winding down the exercise

Table 12   Training

Besides introducing regeneration via cooling down by running or playing at a slow pace, a short sauna or massage session, whirlpool, or the like should be planned to accelerate regeneration.

The sequence of the capabilities to be trained include:
• Flexibility,
• Coordination,
• Speed,
• Strength,
• Stamina.

However, new studies in sports science report that intensive strength or stamina training immediately following technique training has a negative influence on the results of the technique training because the fine-motor patterns of the technique training in the muscle and nerve cells can be destroyed.

Therefore, it is recommended that the trainer plan training in such a way that either (1) on the day of the intensive strength or stamina training, which mainly takes place in the preparation period, there is no technique training or (2) strength or stamina training is included in the plan, for example, for the morning, and technique training after a 3- to 5-hour interval and recuperation for the late afternoon.

In addition, short exercises for coordination and technique should be to follow the strength training in order to stimulate the corresponding nerve and muscle cells and thus reactivate them. This prevents a possible loss of capacity in this area. However, these exercises must not be considered as principal coordination or technique training.

Microcycle

The microcycle is best executed by a weekly training plan. Practically, this is the most important time interval for directing and planning a training program because only over a period of several days can one build a meaningful harmony between requirements of the various areas of technique, tactics, and conditioning on the one side, and the necessary recuperation periods on the other.

The following principles should guide detailed microcycle planning in tennis:
• Consideration of the period. (preparation period of the first and second segments, competitive period I, and competitive period II);
• Determining the long-term peaks and objectives based on the calendar age, training age, strength, capability, resilience, level of training, play readiness, future tournament program, and individual's weaknesses and strengths;
• Consideration of the individual's chronological training alternatives;
• Consideration of environmental influences (parents, friends, travel, school, work, profession, etc.);
• Consideration of the training sites and associated trainer;

- Establishment of the peaks in the beginning, middle, and end of the week;
- Fine-tuning of conditioning areas and factors according to the principles of supercompensation;
- Consideration of the personal characteristics of each individual player.

The following recommendation is offered as a detailed interpretation of a microcycle for tennis players:

It is understood that, for example, strength or stamina is trained throughout the entire week to a limited extent, that speed and coordination are improved daily because of training in techniques or match training, and that the ability to react is practiced every day. In detail planning, all conditional factors must be reviewed at least twice a week in order to guarantee the supercompensation effect, although the individual's goal setting also allows for individual fine-tuning in the planning.

Serious mistakes in micro-planning at worst can have disastrous and irreparable consequences in the building-up process and, at minimum, cause a considerable diminution or stagnation in certain areas.

Macrocycle

The macrocycle contains several microcycles and can extend from one to several months. Therefore, a few mesocycles can also be included. Macrocycles are meant to manage stress and regeneration, thus to compensate for weeks with a high level of pressure with weeks with more limited pressure.

Thus, an important characteristic of a macrocycle is the alternation of scope and intensity pressure.

A macrocycle, particularly in the tennis player's preparation period and, depending on circumstances, in the competitive period I, begins with broad scope and mid to more limited intensity. In the course of the first and second cycles, the scope is first increased to the maximum. The intensity also increases, but to a much more limited degree. Only toward the end of the preparation phase, therefore in the second or third macrocycle, is the proportion reversed. At the end, the scope should be more limited, but the intensity should be very high. It should reach its maximum in the competition period.

This fact must be understood within this time frame in terms of setting the focus and content of the training. At the beginning of the preparation period, it is primarily a matter of instruction in the basics and developmental training in all areas. Here, individual requirements, general aerobic stamina and muscle development training in the area of conditioning are most important, as is a broadly aimed technique training program (weakness, expansion of the stroke repertoire, stabilizing existing techniques). All these areas demand a broad scope of training with lower intensity.

Intensity will be increased only in the course of the preparation period or the second or even the third macrocycle. At that point, strength, intramuscular coordination, elasticity, anaerobic stamina, speed of movement, dexterity, reaction speed in the motor area and habituation and

stabilization of the situational movement sequence are most important. All these areas require high-intensity training. However, the scope must correspondingly decrease somewhat.

During the competitive period, training intensity is very high, and the scope is further reduced. With a broad scope, there is a deep draw-down of energy reserves, and this requires a long regeneration period. This is not advantageous during the tournament period, in which—depending on circumstances—a match is played every day over a period of weeks, and the player must be in top condition and readiness for the competition throughout.

Because the player must maintain the current level of technique and conditioning, or even improve it somewhat—which happens only with daily training, even on a game day—this must be structured in such a way that a maximum effect is achieved with a minimum loss of energy. This is possible only through a significant increase in intensity accompanied by a simultaneous reduction in scope. The regeneration period is shorter after very intensive and shorter training units.

How long a macrocycle is and how many macrocycles make up a period again depend on individual planning.

Training with Various Target Groups

Even if the findings of training pedagogy described in previous chapters are generally applicable, specific viewpoints should be considered when conducting training with various target groups. As with teaching tennis with various target groups, the choice of target group based on criteria of age, gender, and ability can correspond to the appropriate goal. Proceeding from this statement, and considering practical experiences, three specific target groups can be identified (talented children and youths, women, and senior competitive tennis). These will be discussed later.

Talented Children and Youths

Talented children and young people represent a specific target group, whose objective is to achieve a high level of performance in tournament tennis. Looking at this group from the point of view of practical experience, the following tasks and problems become apparent:

- Development of tennis technique,
- Importance of the two-handed backhand,
- Improvement of footwork,
- Improvement in understanding tactics,
- Psychologically oriented training methods,
- Problems of retraining,

- Introduction to current world-class tennis,
- General independence of young people.

The following remarks are also helpful for other target groups but are particularly meant for talented children and young people.

Development of Tennis Technique

Talent is systematically scouted and selected somewhere between the ages of 8 and 10 (see p. 105). The main criteria sought are speed, flexibility, coordination, ability to learn, feel for the ball, performance motivation, and psychological stability. Based on the particular viewpoint that high skills level should be achieved later, the principle of versatility must now be considered, especially when teaching tennis techniques. That is, the variety of tennis techniques must be developed from the beginning. Various tasks relating to placement, trajectory, and speed of the balls to be played from various positions, point-of-impact heights and in pressured situations show the child early on how important a versatile tennis technique is. Development of technique should begin with ground strokes, followed soon afterward by variations in spin (slice, topspin), before the ground strokes are established in the stabilization phase. Development of technique should roughly follow these steps:

- Ground strokes, simultaneous volley and serve, lob and smash; versatile coordination exercises should be included; aspects of bilateral tennis

should be considered in particular.
- Variations in spin, stop, and half-volley.
- Further differentiation of techniques, for example, variations of serve, smash from a jump, and backhand-smash.
- Stabilization of techniques in various play situations. This goal should be achieved sometime before the end of puberty.
- Somewhat after puberty, there should be particular attention to expression of personal style and play situation. On the one hand, successful shots should be accepted; on the other hand, imitations that promise little success and few preferences (for example, too many stops) should be discouraged.

Importance of the Two-Handed Backhand

In the context of teaching tennis techniques to talented children and young people, the two-handed backhand is particularly important (especially for girls). With two hands, the racket accelerates quickly in spite of inadequate arm strength, allowing for good hitting control. Basically, the one-handed and two-handed backhand should be considered equal. The decision to develop only one of these techniques or both simultaneously should depend on the individual's talent (constitutional) and motivational qualifications (play situation, etc.). When introducing (or trying out) the two-handed backhand, the following variations, which apply to right-handers, can be tried out:

- Two-handed backhand with lead-in and hit with the right hand; the left hand supports and merely guides the hitting movement. Experience shows that it is easy for older children to switch over later from this two-handed backhand to a one-handed backhand.
- Two-handed backhand with initial strong support by the left hand; after meeting the ball, the left hand lets go of the racket.
- Two-handed backhand in the version of a left-handed forehand. If this variant is emphasized too strongly through puberty, relearning later is difficult. However, this form of a two-handed backhand frequently develops into a strong "weapon" (especially when combined with topspin and good ball control).

It would be advantageous if children and young people would learn to use these variations depending on the situation. That is, that the young player learns, for example, to use the third variant (a left-handed forehand) for a topspin short crosscourt or a topspin-lob and the first variant (left hand supports and merely guides) for a volley or down-the-line ball.

Improving Footwork

Those who have perception problems, that is, cannot judge ball speed, spin, behavior of the bounce and distance from the ball correctly, have problems with footwork. However, those who are generally stiff or "not adept at movement" also have problems with footwork.

In principle, footwork technique is simple (see *Tennis Course, Volume 1*). Very many talented children and young people automatically move correctly on the tennis court and have problems only when they try to use certain set combinations when they consciously think about footwork. To improve footwork (besides learning perceptual ability), it is necessary to know various ways of moving on the court. For this, one can observe players with outstanding footwork (for example, Steffi Graf and Pete Sampras) and compare one's own footwork (on video). After that, different variants of footwork are tried out in prescribed situations in which the ball is tossed precisely; footwork that better suits the player is selected and used in training and competition.

The student must also learn, in particular, to observe and check his own footwork. The following points are aimed at improving footwork:
- Moving the legs constantly, always ready to move.
- Jumping into the straddle position (ready position/split step) when the opponent meets the ball (in doubles, both players).

- Checking start and running speed, length of steps, and running techniques and rhythm (for example, three-beat rhythm in a baseline duel to appropriate hitting positions).
- Assuming a hitting position that is correct for the situation, being careful about the distance between the feet.
- Checking the weight shift and using a good step sequence when hitting on the run: tango step (crossover backward) or continue running normally.
- Working out an effective end step after the stroke and the running technique to the next good court position; to achieve this quickly, players often execute a cross step first (crossover forward) followed then by the sidesteps.

Basically, as with all movements on the tennis court, the trainer must be careful that the players have good balance, as often as possible. In particular, players must also keep their upper body and head as steady as possible while running in order to be able to execute steady backswing movements.

It should be emphasized once more that footwork should be practiced "isolated" only very rarely; more often, it should be taught and trained as part of complex techniques-and-tactics exercises (for example, as part of a training program based on modeling).

Improving Understanding of Tactics

Children and young people should understand as early as possible the concept behind tennis. They can get to know the tactical dimensions such as security, placement, and positional play by throwing and catching the ball (thus eliminating the aspect of hitting technique) on a minicourt. Tactics should be developed parallel to techniques (and linked with technique), as far as is possible. In connection with the call for a variable technique related to play situations, talented children should learn from the beginning to use appropriate tactics in play. This means that plays are practiced as soon as possible and are used in small competitions (particularly in small-court tennis).

Teaching specific stroke combinations involves teaching basic tactical knowledge as well.

After that, teaching basic strategies is added, such as, for example, attack play, defensive play, consistent ball control. Then from puberty, play-related work is required to a certain extent.

Early on, even in childhood, learning the fundamentals of tactics means avoiding inappropriate theorizing of instruction. In addition, perception and decision skills can be taught systematically here, where videos provide an especially good opportunity to observe one's own game as well as others.

Psychologically Oriented Training Methods

Psychological training consists of systematically improving psychological skills requirements (such as perception skills, attention/concentration, anticipation skills, performance motivation, will, and the ability to manage stress). This is

Fig. 124 Overcoming stress.

accomplished through well-planned teaching and then practicing what has been learned in training sessions that can be used to increase performance in competition. The player who does not systematically improve such skills and abilities in training, cannot expect that she will be able to use them in competition (such as technique and conditioning). The earlier children and youths acquire such skills and

abilities, the more stable they are in the face of internal and external disturbance factors that occur in competition.

When teaching children and youths, the instructor should be very careful to integrate such forms of mental training, concentration training and relaxation techniques as closely as possible into the usual training in techniques and tactics (perhaps also into conditioning training), so that the term psychological training can be dropped in practical instruction.

The Problem of Retraining

In the course of tennis-specific development, even talented children and youths get used to certain idiosyncrasies that can lead to limitations in the long term. These learned limitations affect technique as well as tactics. With respect to technique, it is mainly a question of an unconventional grip, a fixation with the two-handed backhand, and individual expressions that crop up in the backswing and the follow-through movements. However, concerning tactics, it is a question of one-sided adherence to tactical concepts, (for example, those who "stick" to the baseline and those who always seem to storm the net).

Retraining is an extremely difficult process. It is long-term, requires understanding on the part of the student and trust in the instructor, and takes patience as well as the willingness to even accept backhands. Before a tennis trainer deals with the thought of retraining, he must take a good look at the development of the student and try to find out what has led to these idiosyncrasies.

A typical baseline player with this mentality will not let himself "switch" to a serve-and-volley player and vice versa. Consequently, the key idea is to train such players in the context of situations that are unfamiliar to them so that they become more versatile. In this way, it becomes a matter of learning something new rather than retraining. If the young player has developed into a baseline player because he plays with extreme grips and therefore has no success at the net, then a switch-over to an all-round or grip player is possible and wise. However, a change of grip should be done only in extreme cases and then always as required by the situation (point-of-impact height, court position, target, technique).

Players who hit two-handed should learn the slice and volley one-handed. Individual expressions during the backswing and follow-through should be left as they are, if they do not negatively affect success. Playing under time pressure (with higher speed of the toss or a faster surface) automatically regulates the spatial range of the movement of the transitory dynamic structure of the hitting technique that is suited to the situation. In no case should a successful technique, which is, however, a "false" one in the eye of the beholder, be readjusted without hesitation. However, the instructor should be able to assume with high probability that the adjustment will succeed and

lead to an overall better play situation and that the student will feel comfortable with this new technique after the switch-over. Experience shows that retraining, if introduced at all, is very different from the old (for example, from an extreme forehand grip to a central grip or from a high overhand arc in the backswing movement to a relatively straightline).

Experience also shows that switching over often succeeds in training, but then does not work in competition because stability is too limited, that is, players lapse into their old movement patterns. Therefore, as mentioned earlier, one should try to use the corrected technique in competition (even at the cost of temporary losses).

Introduction to Current World-Class Tennis

In a careful analysis of world-class players who, despite difficult movement tasks have achieved a high level of hitting technique, one can see that in world-class tennis, technique is not only distinguished by a certain expression of the individual, but also complies with the fundamentals described in this curriculum.

Therefore, it would be wrong to assume that this master technique is the result of rules and principles different from the technique of average players. Even the world-class players go through the various levels of technique in their year-long development regimen, from the fundamentals described in this

curriculum to their individually expressed virtuoso world-class technique.

Through the individual expression on the one hand, and the strict orientation to basic principles of technique on the other, they can reach their tactical objectives, even in difficult situations. Above all, they can combine high running and hitting speeds with excellent precision and economy. For this reason, they are also in a position to limit themselves to the essential. In this way, the impression can develop that there are great differences between the techniques of the masters and the average players.

When training talented children and young people, the tennis instructor should concentrate on the features of current world-class tennis and should strive for this goal. Basically, world-class players operate at significantly higher speeds than average players. In spite of that, they also achieve great security and precision. High speeds are reached in baseline shots when they are in keeping with biomechanical principles to a certain degree. Thus, the top players essentially use more frequent and considerably stronger body rotation; in addition, they push off relatively powerfully when they jump. In this way, they rotate even more into the direction of the stroke with the right shoulder and hips (for right-handers). The rotating radius of the shoulder can be more than 200 degrees. Top players also use a strong rotation of the upper body for the backhand, so that the direction of the follow-through runs parallel to the baseline or even beyond it.

The open hitting position is increasingly preferred because it guarantees a considerably better extension of the musculature involved and storage of the necessary energy; it also saves time. This is true not only for the forehand (which in practice is dominant in all performance classes even in the youngest age groups) but also for the backhand, particularly the two-handed backhand.

High ball speeds are also achieved when:

- The balls are played as early as possible
- The player does not let herself be forced back from the baseline, and
- The player rotates in place using body rotation, and long balls that bounce just in front of the baseline are hit in a rising arc or as half-volleys.

And use of the wrist action is best in top players; it allows them to achieve a greater acceleration of the racket without having to use more strength, which is very important, especially with the shorter hitting sequences in difficult situations described earlier. (See also *Tennis Course, Volume 1.*)

All this requires a very high level of coordination. Because top players express such an extremely high level of coordination, they can also carry over power impulses optimally to different situations, even with much shorter hitting sequences.

This shows again why the training of general and tennis-specific coordination skills is so important for talented children and young people, and why it can not

be ignored at any level of ability.

Practicing and expressing coordination skills also lead to a corresponding ability to improvise, which is visible again and again in world-class tennis. The ability to improvise is also evident in masters, particularly in difficult situations in which they even develop certain artistic capabilities. In such situations, they are capable of reducing the ideal balance when hitting to a minimum time span (precisely the point of impact) because they must hit accurately far too often while running fast, while jumping high, and in quite difficult body positions.

The technical skills and capabilities described provide the basis for fulfilling the conditions of today's world-class tennis from a tactical point of view. At first, the tactical pattern must be learned and trained (baseline play, attack play, defensive play, service, return, passing shots). The current trends should then be considered:

- Structuring plays from the baseline,
- Provoking short balls from the opponent through one's own (fast or placed) play,
- Using the opponent's short balls for offensive play (mainly for a net attack) sideways from his place through corner play, thus opening up the court, allowing for more offensive play.

General Independence of Young People

Unfortunately, it happens all too often that children and young people are placed with a tennis instructor for training and coaching, and people expect that she should make them master players as quickly as possible. As a rule, this only happens—if at all—when the young people also become independent on their own.

However, the young people often let the instruction proceed uncritically; sometimes they are enchanted by the tennis instructor. Only now and then do they rebel, that is, against the individual exercises and then do them only unwillingly because they do not understand the purpose.

In order to lead young people to independence, the instructor should allow room for their natural ability and give them opportunities to find their own ways of dealing with assigned tasks. She should also encourage them to express their opinion and to give them a real say in shaping the training. The ideas and goals of young people must be discussed and moderated to a realistic level.

When young people do exercises (1) straightforwardly and (2) as a matter of simple habit, they have taken the first step toward independence and self-motivation. Young people then know why they are practicing something, and can now also complete the required tasks without constant supervision. That means that they continue training seriously, even if the instructor must work more intensively with other participants in the group for a short time.

In addition, the young people should be encouraged to train independently more often and be given a choice of exercises and individual checks on achieving their goals. Initial supervision of this independent training is gradually built up until young people are able to train completely independently. The tennis instructor can always be consulted as advisor. Even in competitive tennis, the development to independence should be introduced early. Trainers and parents can help a lot here if they leave things up to the children and interfere only in cases of extremely unsporting behavior and ask the tournament director to have the play supervised. Very early on, children and young people should take on refereeing activities in their competitions.

When observing competitions together, the trainer can either assume the role of commentator or coach to a player. In this way, the young people get an idea of competitive leadership and learn to judge opponents and situations for themselves.

Videotapes of their own competitions can also be discussed. Here, the trainer gives advice for the students' own control of techniques and tactics, with the goal that the young people learn to coach themselves to a certain extent. Finally, young people should be enlisted to help with organizing and conducting tournaments. By doing this, they get to know the problems that are faced by the players in

tournaments (from catering to reserving courts) and are then much more independent in their own tournaments.

Training with Women

Women's tennis is different from men's in a few particulars:
- Women do not serve as hard and thus concentrate more on the return. In women's tournament tennis it is therefore more difficult to win the serve.
- Men play with more spin variation and over larger angles.
- Most importantly, men attack more often than women; particularly, the transition from the baseline to the net is easier for them.

Such differences in techniques and tactics go back to biological differences between men and women. In general, women are smaller and use less strength (particularly elasticity); however, they play on the same courts with the net at the same height and mostly with the same balls as men. On the other hand, however, these gender-specific differences are also related to socialization; that is, boys learn to deal with balls more intensively than girls. This is especially evident in the throw, which is the basis of the serve.

Such differences lead to girls and women being less often in the position to judge the volley quickly. On the other hand, they often have to try to place the ball

in such a way that they force their opponents to make a mistake. However, such differences also lead to most girls using both hands for the backhand; and this influences the variability of the play situation, especially the transition from the baseline to the net.

Basically, there have to be serious differences between women's and men's tennis because the men hit harder and have a greater ability to jump. Men are also in a position to run around a ball that has been hit hard and placed and to hit it back hard. In training with girls and women, the following implications should be noted:
- In all phases of long-term training programs, increased attention should be paid to the serve.
- The same holds for the transition from play at the baseline to net play.
- This requires the development of the broadest possible play situation, including net play, even if specific basic strategies are individually preferred in a match.
- Even if there is generally no "best of five" matches in women's tennis, conditioning training in women's tennis should be given the same value as in men's tennis.

Because physical fitness is the basis for training techniques and tactics, one should also be careful to have a corresponding nutritional program.

In women's tennis there are comparably fewer doubles tournaments. Therefore, in training, doubles should be played more often, especially because the requirements in doubles (serve-attack combination, net play, etc.) also work out well for singles play.

Girls have the chance even in their early years to compete successfully in women's tennis. This is encouraging; however, there is the risk that the girls will concentrate too soon on a specific play situation and that this will become firmly established (for example, baseline play with a more defensive character in order to avoid failure). In training, this tendency should be countered by practicing variable techniques and tactical patterns.

Activities that are connected with training should also be included. It is natural that fluctuations in ability often go along with menstruation. However, they are not as great as often assumed. A professional medical opinion may be sought in questionable cases.

Concerning coaching women in tournament tennis, many trainers report that personal problems are often the cause of disruption in the course of training and tournaments. Men can apparently separate their private life from the athletic more effectively. It is also reported that women's teams are more difficult to manage than men's. Therefore, when conflicts arise, it appears wise to initiate individual conversations before having a team discussion. Finally, it should also be mentioned that women prefer men as trainers. On the whole, the reasons for such sociopsychological differences are not altogether clear. However, they should be considered. Because the psychological requirements in tournament tennis are not in principle different for men and women, one should try to equalize such gender-specific elements.

Training in Senior Competitive Tennis

The number of middle-aged and older tennis players who remain active competitively is steadily increasing. The specific training recommendations for this group should be geared to the personal situation.

With the majority of players engaged in senior-competitive tennis, we are dealing with people who have been connected with the sport since their youth. Thus, they can build on a well-developed and stable tennis technique that is often different from contemporary technique in strokes with reverse spin or topspin.

In the area of physical conditioning, as one gets older, one must cope with a continuous decrease in strength, flexibility, and stamina. The decrease in maximum strength and maximum resilience in connection with a less offensive play situation leads to the volley lasting longer than with younger players. Along with that, the importance of resilient stamina and (aerobic) stamina in the older age group is increased. At the same time, a good aerobic capacity protects against possible overtaxing of the circulatory system in intensive and long-lasting tennis competitions, especially in unfavorable climatic conditions. In order to avoid injuries, it is recommended that the player maintain the flexibility that is reduced because of age through flexibility training, enhancing it with comprehensive strengthening exercises.

The following recommendations present details for a (competitive) tennis training program in advanced age:

- Technique training, as a rule, stabilizes the tennis technique acquired long before. Intensive learning and relearning of individual hitting techniques is, in general, not necessary. However, this should not mean that in the second half of life learning new techniques is no longer possible.
- Technique training is supplemented by a match-training program, which should take on a broader role in tennis training for seniors than for younger players. In this training program, the player tries to maintain or even improve his level of performance.
- Training to improve conditioning is very important with older competition-oriented tennis players. Foremost is the improvement of aerobic stamina, resilient stamina, and flexibility. In addition, a good level of general fitness, resilience, and speed should also be specifically taught.
- As a rule, conditioning is improved off the tennis court. In this way, aerobic stamina is best improved with quiet long walks. Resilient stamina and flexibility can be taught, for example, within a functional gymnastics program (see the "Training Conditioning" section).

Senior competitive tennis requires individualized and very specific training (see page 212).

Competitive Coaching

Introduction

The goal of competitive coaching is to advise and influence the players in such a way that they are able to realize their personally best performance levels in competition.

- Competitive coaching begins with preparing for the competition.
- It continues in the competition (coaching during the competition), so far as contact is possible between the player and coach.
- It ends with the debriefing, in which at the beginning and end of the competition coaching, there are fluid transitions from and to the general training activities.

Training should be considered as a long-term activity for preparing for competition. All activities, from travel to the site of the tournament to finding the best prestart situation are included in short-term preparation for competition.

Coaching in competition is limited to all those situations in the competition in which direct contact between player and coach is possible. In team competitions, there are various activities directly after the tournament for physical and psychological processing of the competition, and others will

be tried later at the training site to develop training programs to process other experiences of the competition.

In contrast, competition coaching in the narrow sense is limited to the competition itself and in German-speaking areas is referred to as coaching. However, in English-speaking areas, "coaching" refers to all advising and coaching activities in training and competition.

Short-Term Preparation

Short-term preparation can be divided into two types of activity. The external factors, from travel to the immediate preparation for the competition belong to the one type; whereas the other includes the individual components of the immediate preparation for competition, from getting up, through the last meal before the tournament, to warming up immediately before the competition.

Dealing with External Circumstances

The larger and more important the tournament is, the earlier one should arrive. Basically, things

must be structured in such a way that there is enough time for recuperation from the rigors of the trip. This is especially true when players must adjust to a climate or time change. In order to become acclimated to high temperatures, players are advised to work out several times a day.

Even the accommodations should be selected in such a way that there are no unusual or unnecessary stresses.

Particular attention should be paid to nutrition (see p. 243).

If possible, there should also be medical and physiotherapeutic coaching. Next, it is wise to check out the external conditions of the competition, such as court surface and lighting and whether play will be indoors or outdoors. If the player is to arrive early, it is also best to find out how this will affect training. In the context of her training, she should consider specific technical/tactical factors that have been determined in regard to the strengths and weaknesses of the opponent.

In addition, the player can get used to the established brands of balls and even test the degree of the tension appropriate for the surface of the ball. Finally, planning free time wisely can also be a part of the job of coaching—particularly with younger players.

Immediate Preparation for Competition

The goal of the immediate preparation for competition is to achieve the best <u>prestart situation with midlevel energizing</u> (see p. 191) in order to be able to fully employ all the individual performance requirements in competition. Depending on when play begins, the individual activities of this preparation should be scheduled as in the following two examples:

Play begins at 9:00 A.M.

6:00	get up
6:15	relaxed running, gymnastics
6:40	breakfast
7:10	leave for the competition site
7:30	training
8:10	relaxation, regeneration
8:30	prepare equipment
8:40	final warm-up before competition
8:50	mental and psycho-regulative preparation
9:00	prematch warm-up

Play begins at 1:00 P.M.

7:30	get up
7:45	relaxed running, gymnastics
8:30	breakfast
9:10	leave for the competition site
9:30	training
10:45	light snack
11:15	relaxation, regeneration
12:15	prepare equipment
12:30	final warm-up before competition
12:50	mental and psycho-regulative preparation
1:00	prematch warm-up

This time frame should serve as a guideline that changes according to competition demands and the personal characteristics of the players. It is especially useful for the sequence and interval of the individual segments.

Some of these segments are considered in more detail below. It is the job of the coach to structure these segments into a meaningful whole.

Getting Up

For physiological reasons, the player should get up at least 3–4 hours before the tournament. This time is also necessary for sufficient preparation directly before the competition. We strongly caution against a catnap during this period.

Warming Up

Two goals are linked with systematic warm-up:

- Performance potential should be improved.
- Injuries should be prevented.

The principal effect of the warm-up is the elevation of body temperature and the release of warmth. This release of warmth triggers a variety of processes:

- The intracellular friction is reduced and the loosening up of the musculature is increased.
- Because of the improved loosening up of the musculature, there is an improvement of the coordination capability.
- The release of warmth also leads to an improvement of physiological capability.

The reasons for the positive effects are: circulation is stimulated; metabolic processes in the cells are accelerated; the central nervous system is activated, which leads to an increase in the ability to concentrate and motivation; and performance-enhancing hormones are secreted.

Because the most important goal of the warm-up is to supply the entire musculature with blood, the <u>forms of warm-up</u> must be sufficient for the sport-specific requirements. The warm-up therefore also consists of exercises from beyond the tennis court in the sequence: warm-up, general limbering and stretching, stress through running uphill, executing specific stretching exercises, cooling off.

Warming up beyond techniques training should take at least 10–15 minutes. The <u>intensity</u> should not exceed 60 percent of maximum capacity. That is, heart rate should not be more than 160 beats per minute, but the players should break a sweat.

Factors influencing the effects of warming up can include, for example, play beginning in a short time, meteorological factors, training level, or time elapsed since the last competition. Above all, the coach should be careful that the warm-up is learned systematically, if it is to be used effectively. The interval between the last warm-up and the beginning of the game should not be more than 10–15 minutes; the warm-up effect must be maintained with clothing that is dry and warm.

Training

In training, all important strokes must be systematically played first, especially in reference to the strengths of the player. Sometimes, as a preparation for the planned tactical approach, specific strokes and stroke combinations can be practiced. At the end of the training session, depending on the time available and the time left before the beginning of the scheduled match, some games should be played (for example, two service games).

Preparation of Equipment

Preparing the equipment consists of assembling and checking the following items in particular: warm-up clothing, tournament clothing, racket, ace bandage, grip wrapping, towel, replacement shirt(s), replacement towel, sweat bands, tournament food, and mineral drink.

Mental and Psychoregulative Preparation

In the last phase before going to the court, the player should achieve his personal best state of activation. If the activation is too low, he must mobilize himself without tensing up; if it is too high, he must relax without braking. The corresponding mobilization or relaxation exercises should be linked (as a mental preparation) with a review of the tactical considerations that have been developed for the impending match. The coach can often be helpful here.

Prematch Warm-Up

The prematch warm-up serves primarily as a sport-specific warm-up shortly before the match so that the player can find his own movement rhythm. This includes running through strokes at the baseline and the net, as well as the serve (next to the return) in a manner that combines relaxed muscles and psychological concentration. Only as a second objective should one try to prepare particularly for the opponent. Because the warm-up period is limited, the player should know exactly which strokes need the most practice; however, the serve should always be included.

Coaching in Competition

Coaching in competition has two prioritized functions, so far as is allowed:

- In the case of passive external influences, it is enough if the coach sits on the bench and gives the player the feeling that he is not alone in the match, that is by being able to make eye contact now and then, being able to turn to him when there are perceived or actual bad calls and being able to express himself while switching sides. The activities of the coach are limited to, for example, offering drinks, a towel, and congratulatory or encouraging remarks.

- In the case of active external influences, the coach tries (beyond eye contact during play) to give technical and tactical advice during the pause and when changing sides and to strengthen or correct the player's motivational level and processes or to calm and encourage him (which is more often the case).

Requirements of a Coach and Coaching

Especially when setting the goals for active external influences, it is important that the coach brings with her specific prerequisites in

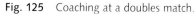

Fig. 125 Coaching at a doubles match.

order to be able to achieve these goals. Such prerequisites are:

- The coach must be accepted by the player. It is good when both are at least receptive toward each other, so that, if possible, no conflicts arise that are amplified by a general tension between them.
- The coach should know the player as well as possible, especially his technical and tactical idiosyncrasies, potential, his motivations, temperament and ability, in order to be able to work through physical and psychological stresses.
- In order to be able to judge the player appropriately in actual play situations, the coach must use empathy and observational skills.
- The coach should have expansive tennis-specific knowledge about techniques, tactics, and competitive psychology and should have long-term experience as a competitive player; however, her own performance level is of secondary importance.
- Because coaching should be viewed as interaction between coach and player, the coach should also consider the importance of playing, that is, the various forms of interaction must be learned and stabilized in training and competition.
- The coach can fulfill these requirements and use them in competition only if she herself is fully engaged.

Using the example of coaching a player individually, the following sections deal with the various forms of active external influence (advice on technique, tactics, and

motivational coaching). It can also be noted that, in the context of passive external influences, nutrition (and especially considerations of mineral- and water-balance) during competition plays a particularly important role.

Tips on Technique

Advice concerning the technique of the player being coached should be as sparing as possible; in particular, corrections that refer to the main action of the technique should be avoided. Such corrections can hardly be processed by the player due to the overwhelming stability of the main action. At any rate, it can be that under the strain of competition, some auxiliary actions (see *Tennis Course, Volume 1*) reveal actual deficiencies that can be corrected.

Tips such as "Move more," "Stand more to the side," "Bend your knee more," and "Watch the ball longer when you toss it," can most often be processed. However, what should be considered is whether the player is in the situation because of age, experience, and/or motor flexibility.

Tips on Tactics

A central component of coaching is to give appropriate advice on tactics (see also the chapter "Training Tactics"). Therefore, it is important from the beginning to observe one's opponents and analyze their strengths and weaknesses. If the suggested tactic proves worthwhile, the player should be appropriately encouraged. However, if it does not, then whether the tactic

should be changed must be examined (at the latest, after the last set). Here, one must consider whether the player being coached is also in the position to process the new tactic (or whether she is overwhelmed by it) and how the opponent will most likely react to the change. Basically, one should also remember that a too-frequent change of tactics sometimes confuses the opponent less than it does one's own player.

Motivational Coaching

Motivational coaching depends first on the action and score. If the game is going successfully, the player should be supported by praise and agreement. Sometimes however, he should also be warned against underestimating his opponent and risking a loss. If the player is trailing, the reasons for that should be examined. Often the player (and coach) overlook the fact that the opponent's skills are simply better.

If this is not the case, the coach should consider whether actual deficiencies are to be rectified, if there is no mid-level activation, that is, if the coach must help the player to mobilize or to relax, if the player exhibits a lack of concentration, or if there is a lack of proper attitude toward the game (see the chapter entitled "Psychological Basics/Psychologically Oriented Training," p. 181).

If the current performance motivation is the main problem, one should consider whether the player is more motivated by success or more motivated by failure (see p. 186). Because those who are motivated by success ascribe failure to external factors (beyond the individual), the coach must make it clear to them that they themselves are also responsible (perhaps in a demonstrative tone) and give appropriate directives. Because those who fear failure blame internal factors, one must emphasize their good skills and praise them appropriately while also making external factors responsible for lost points, especially the strength of the opponent. One should weigh both of these reasons in such a way that the motivation by success gradually gains dominance over the fear of failure. At any rate, the influence of motivational coaching cannot be overvalued because both components of performance motivation—the motivation by success and the fear of failure—are relatively stable personality traits and are difficult to change.

Coaching Activities During the Change of Sides

When sides are changed, there are 90 seconds available from the end of the last point to the next serve. This important break can be divided into six phases in connection with the concept "pause between volleys" (see p. 196).

(see p. 196)

Phase 1

First, the player should take enough time to dry off, to take a drink, and, as a reaction to the finished volley or the last

play, to express herself and "let off steam."

Phase 2

Then the player should relax and recuperate, using a chair that is comfortable and suited to relaxing. The legs should be extended. At the beginning of relaxation, deep, regular breathing exercises should be done because such breathing leads more quickly to a state of relaxation.

Phase 3

In the second part of relaxation, the player should prepare herself mentally for the actions after the change of sides. She should be supported in this by the coach, who offers advice and sometimes directives.

Phase 4

At the end of the time on the bench and while going to the baseline, there is a brief tension (mobilization), perhaps linked to set phrases that the player says quietly or mentally in order to be able to reenter the game energized.

Phase 5

Just in front of the baseline there is the practical mental preparation for the next volley, particularly for the serve and return.

Phase 6

The break is completed with the backswing position, with concentration on the serve and return.

The time distribution of these six phases can vary from person to person; it also depends on the previous play and on the score.

On the Behavior of the Coach

Because the behavior of the coach during the break at the change of sides, during the volley, and during the breaks after the individual volleys is very important, it will be discussed next:

- Speaking during the change of sides should be directed first to the particular demands of this break. Therefore (in phase 3) as little as possible should be said; the essentials should be stressed. The proposed sequence of the break suggests holding back one's own speech at first, which is difficult for many coaches.
- If player and coach do not agree on the tactical measures, the coach should not try to push his point of view because the player could then inform the coach that he (the coach) is wrong. The reverse, that is, if the coach allows the player to try out her own ideas and she (the player) fails, the player would have to admit to the coach that she herself was wrong, which is good preparation for accepting future advice. However, the long-term goal of coaching is basically to make the player independent of the active external influence of the coach.
- A special problem of coaching is the question of how the coach should behave when the

referee has made a bad call. Should he protest or behave passively? Because every player must count on an average of three bad calls in a match, and these usually apply equally to both players, the player being coached should be prepared to be able to deal with them without protest and without stress. If this amount is exceeded, and particularly if it goes against one's own player, the coach should then intervene, especially in the case of important scores.

- Even for the coach, competition is often a heavy psychological burden he cannot work out through his own physical activity (like the player). Many coaches are so little in control that they behave like their players after lost points, that is, they might grasp their head demonstratively or express themselves verbally in a negative manner. Such behavior can also have a negative effect on the player—independent of the question whether it is appropriate to the role of coach. Therefore, the coach should practice some psychoregulative exercises himself now and then, in order to make a calm impression, which he can transfer to the player. On the other hand, if the coach sits on the bench looking bored and transfers that impression to the player, he would not be engaged enough for his job.

Coaching After the Competition

Coaching after the competition must be concerned with the course of the competition (concerning its length and drama) and its outcome. The greater the physical and psychological stresses were, the more comprehensive and intensive the regenerative phase must be.

Physical Regeneration

For physical regeneration after the competition, activities such as cooling down for 10–15 minutes or, if possible, hitting balls loosely for 15–30 minutes are recommended. This renewed <u>active warm-up</u> is an important requirement for a more active regeneration because metabolic waste products are removed more quickly from the musculature as a result of the continuing increased circulation.

With a passive warm-up in the form of a hot shower, a warm bath, or one or two short sauna visits, increased circulation in the musculature is less likely. In fact, there will probably be a strong increase in circulation in the skin, causing an outbreak of perspiration. This causes excessive warmth. The passive warm-up should be considered a psychological health measure that leads to physical and psychological relaxation, similar to massage.

This, in addition, accelerates the regenerative processes of the muscles.

Psychological Coaching

Psychological coaching after the competition essentially depends on the outcome of the competition. After a victory, there is normally praise and approval. There can also be criticism, if the victory came about in spite of shortcomings in playing and to correct euphoric, unrealistic self-assessment as well as faulty setting of goals. After losing, the player should first be calmed and consoled, as much as his psychological condition requires. In such a case, there should first be a general analysis of play, when the player has calmed down enough that his self-assessment is not all too subjective, that is, not determined too much by his emotions. Then the coach should consider to what extent the loss should be considered a failure, that is, that realistic goal setting was not achieved—because a loss to a far superior opponent can also be considered a success, if the player has performed well in his own view and that of the coach.

When judging the loss as failure, it should again be considered, whether, for the player being coached, it is a question of being motivated by success or motivated by failure, since the assignment of cause (causal attribution) is fundamentally influenced by this (see p. 187). Because those motivated by success ascribe responsibility for failure more to external causes, the coach must make it clear that they should also feel personally responsible, in order to be able to derive fruitful results. Because

those who are motivated by failure tend to make themselves solely responsible for the failure, the coach must emphasize their positive abilities and make it clear that external factors (for example, the opponent's strength) are also responsible for the loss, making a positive motivation for future training and the next competition possible.

Independent of this, if a victory or a loss is analyzed, it is good for the coach to have a colleague or other player occasionally go through an objective observation of the competition (see p. 237), because it nicely supports the objective discussion with the player and can even provide the player and coach with important information as the basis for training and preparing for the next competition.

Coaching Several Competitions in One Day

There are often planning problems at a tournament, if:
- the beginning of the match is considerably delayed,
- matches are interrupted because of rain,
- several competitions must be completed in one day (for example, two singles and a double).

In such cases, the coaching measures described earlier (especially the direct preparation for competition and coaching after competition) must be adjusted to the current situation. Particular attention should be paid to nutrition (see p. 243).

Comprehensive Coaching

The more the coaching involves several competitions and extends over several tournaments, the more comprehensive are the coach's responsibilities. They can then include tasks such as reserving training sites, booking hotels and air flights, and speaking with parties to contracts. Thus, the role of coach becomes a complex one, in which he must assume the jobs of a trainer, a manager, a private confidant, and (especially with year-round tournament players) also a teacher.

Sports-Medical Aspects

Sports-Medical Coaching

As a recreational sport, tennis is considerably different from the competitive version of the sport in terms of training level, motivation, and performance goals. As a result, the range and intensity of stress differ markedly between the competitive sport and the popular sport. This gives rise to different results in the sports-medical assessment of the player's ability to withstand stress, as well as the type of sports-medical coaching.

Coaching the Recreational Sport

For those tennis players interested in recreational sports, sports-medical research aims to record all existing health-related injuries or illnesses in order to use this to consult on the type and scope of tennis-specific stresses. This affects all recreational players who want to begin tennis in middle-age or older, and for all seniors who compete in tennis tournaments (mostly in teams). From the viewpoint of preventive medicine, detailed advice on a healthy lifestyle (good nutrition, sufficient recuperation, avoidance of nicotine and substantial alcohol consumption, etc.) is as important as individual details on the quality and quantity of athletic activity.

Coaching the Competitive Sport

For tennis players involved in the competitive sport, sports-medical coaching has as its purpose to support the optimal development of abilities, to protect against illnesses, and to treat injuries and illnesses optimally. Working with players and trainers, one also tries to protect against overtaxing and the resulting limitations on health and performance. This is frequently possible only through continuous monitoring of the scope and intensity of training. Sports-medical support represents an important means for the optimal development of skills and, at the same time, it offers an effective protection against damage caused by overtaxing in tennis.

Nationally and internationally ranked players must then be examined at least once a year from a sports-medical perspective and must also be coached more intensively with this in mind.

Before taking up a competitive sport and undergoing the training that goes with it, a player should receive a full medical checkup specific to the sport. This sports-medical aptitude test should reveal physical weak areas, latent illnesses, or injuries and provides the basis for evaluating the effects of these on the player's health in training and competition. As a rule, sports-medical aptitude tests should be done separately by internists and orthopedic specialists specializing in sports medicine. In addition to taking a health history, this examination consists of examinations by the internist and orthopedic specialist, as well as various laboratory tests.

The sports-medical check-up (health exam) in the course of preparing the tennis player for competition looks for the known physical weak spots or existing injuries; in addition, the examination tries to discover deficiencies and conditions related to overtaxing and to combat them through prophylactic measures. With comprehensive and continuing sport-medical coaching of competitive players, the annual check-up is sufficient. However, if the sports-medical coaching is poor, a second annual check-up will not really change things.

Sports-medical coaching includes measures related to methods and psychotherapy to maintain health and to prevent injuries. It provides individual advice for nutrition, and involves diagnosis of skills potential and managing training. Especially with competitive tennis players, sports accidents due to a sudden event (for example, ligament tears or muscle pulls) on the court happen relatively seldom; however, lately there have been more injuries because of chronic overuse. This usually involves the back, in the lumbar region, the shoulder of the hitting arm, the thigh musculature, the abdomen musculature, and the Achilles tendon.

Based on information from players, trainers, physiotherapists, and sports-medicine physicians, the following measures can be used to avoid the injuries due to overtaxing mentioned earlier and the mechanisms that cause them:

- Massage, physiotherapy, and relaxation baths to combat muscle tension and to prevent its occurrence.
- Ongoing systematic warm-up and a cool-down phase.
- Regular strengthening and stretching of the muscles to prevent muscular dysbalances; perhaps also training to develop the overall body musculature.
- Regular balance training and gymnastics (for example, stretching) to develop and regenerate the tendon-ligament apparatus and the joint cartilage.
- Protection against high training scope and intensity on unfamiliar surfaces, especially nonslip hard courts.
- Guaranteed correct relationship between stress and regeneration in the course of a training unit or a training day or in the context of a microcycle.
- Individualized nutrition suited to the load, including vitamins, minerals, trace elements, and fluids.
- Athletic lifestyle (avoiding nicotine, etc.) under special consideration of the regeneration phases (sleep, etc.).

Injuries in Tennis

Compared with other recreational sports such as gymnastics, track and field, and alpine skiing, injuries in tennis are relatively rare and mild. The risk of injury for tennis players is also considerably smaller than with other ball sports, such as soccer, handball, volleyball, and squash.

In spite of this, tennis players must reckon at any time with acute or chronic damage as a result of an injury while playing tennis. The growing number of older tennis players also necessarily leads to an increase of the total number of tennis injuries. The prerequisite for correct prevention is knowledge of all of the basic tennis injuries, as well as their sources.

In addition, the coach should be familiar with the most important fundamentals of first aid for the most frequent tennis injuries. This will have less to do with serious injuries, but rather with the lesser ones that cause problems for the trainer and the first aider.

As an example, the differential dynamics of overextending, pull, and partial tear of a muscle requires detailed knowledge and many years of experience. As a result, some basic knowledge of the individual tennis injuries should be taught. However, it cannot be the goal to present all the types of injuries specific to tennis in detail and to discuss different therapy strategies according to current knowledge. This type of operation must remain the purview of the physician ("First Aid from the Physician").

Explanations of Concepts

Sports injury is the general designation for all events that injure the integrity of a tissue during an athletic activity. Examples of this include bruising, pulling, tearing, or breaking, as well as inflammation and degeneration. Injuries that occur before, during, or after playing tennis are tennis injuries.

Tennis injury is caused by a tennis-related accident; and damage, by tennis (primary tennis damage). If the injury occurs as a result of a sudden, one-time event, it is an accident, such as tearing the outer ligaments of the ankle while moving to the tennis ball. However, if the event that caused the injury happens slowly or several times and is low-grade as a microtrauma, it is a primary injury, such as tennis elbow (Hinrichs 1989).

Tennis accident and primary tennis injury lead to secondary tennis injuries (sports damage) under certain circumstances, such as previous damage, serious injury, errors in diagnosis and therapy, and insufficient follow-up. Under favorable conditions, results of accidents and primary tennis injury heal completely to integrity of the tissue and its function. In principle, they can be reversed. If no complete healing of the tennis accident or the primary tennis injury can be achieved, the persistent injury condition is defined as secondary tennis injury or delayed damage caused by tennis.

The most frequent tennis accidents are discussed later, differentiated according to the various tissue types—skin, ligaments, and muscles—along with the best-known primary tennis injury, tennis elbow. The description of the individual symptoms also includes the cause and diagnosis; however, the focus is on prevention and immediate action (first aid).

The most important general advice for preventing tennis injuries is presented comprehensively later.

Tennis Accidents

In the general legal definition, the accident is defined as an event that endangers health through sudden force and can lead to physical and psychological damage. There are many causes of accidents in tennis. However, as a rule, individual, internal causes (for example, age and personal attitude, athletic experience and the level of training, warm-up and regeneration, as well as general lifestyle, including nutrition, sleep, and alcohol) are most important, whereas external causes such as athletic facilities, condition of the surface or sports equipment generally play a lesser role.

The most frequent tennis accidents involve the following organ systems and/or structures:
- Injuries to the skin,
- Injuries to the ligaments,
- Injuries to the muscles.

Injuries to the Skin
The most frequent injuries in tennis (resulting primarily from minor accidents) are limited to the skin. Here, it is basically a question of superficial wounds; contusions and lacerations are relatively rare. Injuries to the skin are usually caused by a fall and sometimes by a hit or a kick. With tennis players, injuries to the skin also appear as blisters (an accumulation of tissue fluid in the uppermost layer of the skin) and calluses. Blisters are caused by one-time playing that lasts too long after a longer break (for example, blisters on the palm of the hand or on the transition to the fingers) or by new shoes (for example, blisters on the heels or

toes). Calluses develop because of frequently repeated play over a longer period (for example, calluses on the fingers and palm).

Diagnosis
If the smallest capillaries are injured, the bleeding occurs in drops; with the less-frequent injury of veins, the blood is dark red, and blood from arteries is bright red and spurts quickly. Because of the possibility of an injury to the important, deeper tissue structures, such as nerves, tendons, muscles, and bones, a precise function test and further diagnostic measures must be done by a physician.

Emergency Measures (First Aid)
Superficial wounds are covered with a simple adhesive bandage after being disinfected. At the same time, inoculation against tetanus must be verified or administered immediately if there is a doubt. If there is obvious contamination by the court sand, the wound should be carefully cleaned first with special cloths that have first been saturated with a disinfectant. The popular spray bandages and application of ointment or powder are often unsuitable because they adhere to the wound and cannot be removed for several days without reopening the wound. If necessary, the wound can also be cleaned under running water. Wounds that are gaping must be stitched or stapled by a physician.

Wounds that are bleeding heavily are stanched by placing a pressure bandage and elevating the affected limb. A spurting artery requires a tourniquet on the affected limb; however, this obstruction may not be applied for more than 60–90 minutes.

With blisters, self-help should begin immediately after the first indication (pain/redness). The affected section of skin should be covered with a protective bandage; on the foot (heel), a foam patch with a hole in the center is best because it leaves a space immediately around the blister while relieving pressure on the damaged area. On the palm and fingers, narrow strips of tape or even a thin leather glove are useful because regular adhesive tape is too thick and usually slips out of place. These aids will help avoid tearing the blister and the intact skin will prevent an infection. If the blister is swollen full with fluid, it can be opened carefully to relieve pain using a sterile needle after the covering skin has been disinfected.

Calluses are harmless and form a good protection for the skin against excessive wear and tear. For cosmetic reasons, they can be softened by regular application of salicylic acid.

Preventive Measures
- Good footwork and corresponding good level of conditioning.
- Firm fit in shoes with functional soles for every type of court surface.
- Break in new shoes first in training.
- At the beginning of the outdoor season and after each longer interruption in play, adhere to the highest levels of training and competition (for example, maximum 90 minutes).
- Booster shot for tetanus (protection against tetanus).

Injuries to the Ligaments
The stability of a joint is assured through active and passive factors. The musculature is responsible for active stability, and the ligaments of a joint are principally responsible for the passive stability. A ligament injury occurs when a joint exceeds its natural extent of movement because of direct and indirect effects of strength. This can involve a few fibers or the ligament as a whole.

In tennis, primarily, the ligaments at the ankles are at risk. A partial ligament tear involves only a part of the ligament; the stability of the joint is often not influenced by this. With a complete ligament tear, all or almost all fibers of the ligament are torn, and the joint loses its stability.

Generally, each ligament tear is accompanied by bleeding in the surrounding tissue, so that a bruise is visible. A ligament injury inside the joint (for example, a crucial ligament) or the joint (for

example, capsule) usually leads to bleeding into the joint. Ligament injuries of this type can also be accompanied by damage to the cartilage surface.

Diagnosis
The following symptoms indicate a ligament injury:
- Bruising, swelling, and spontaneous pain, or pain when the area is touched or when the player moves.
- Occasional bleeding into the joint.
- Pain related to movement.
- Instability of the joint, depending on the extent of the injury.

With ligament injuries, the affected joint should continuously be tested for stability. To rule out injuries of a serious type, as well as to employ early therapeutic measures, an immediate visit to the physician is absolutely necessary.

Emergency Measures (First Aid)
Immediately after one stops playing, a cooling pressure bandage is applied and the extremity is elevated for relief and support. An elastic bandage and ice pack or ice water, or sometimes a sponge, are necessary. An ice spray can also be used on the ice-water soaked pressure bandage (not directly on the skin, because of the danger of frost damage), so that a constant cooling is achieved. This mode of treatment, according to the PICE rule (Pause, Ice, Compression, Elevation has been advocated for two decades.

Most recently, however, ice therapy is viewed with critical distance and at least partly replaced by administration of medicines especially for alleviating pain, retarding inflammation, and promoting regeneration. For further clarification of the diagnosis (for example, testing the joint's stability) and for the purpose of early therapeutic measures (for example, taping), the patient is brought to the doctor with the extremity elevated.

Preventive Measures
- Equal strengthening and stretching of all those muscle groups that stabilize the ankle and knee joints.
- Finding and eliminating as fast as possible elevations (for example, lines) and ruts in the tennis court surface.
- Removing tennis balls lying around in the playing area.
- Preferring clay courts over hard courts (court surfaces must not be too slippery and should have a granular surface).
- In exceptional cases, using prophylactic taping, a joint bandage or orthoses, or special shoes as protection against repeated ligament injuries.

Injuries to Muscles and Tendons
Muscles and tendons form a functional unit. Basically, injuries occur in this area of the muscle source, the muscle body, the transition from muscle to tendon, and the tendon itself and at the bony attachment point. In tennis, the player is especially at risk when stopping suddenly (eccentric stress), when accelerating quickly (concentric stress), and especially when combining braking and accelerating movements, for example, on every change in direction while running under time pressure.

In tennis, muscle and tendon injuries occur most often with sudden, powerful, or uncoordinated muscle actions. The reason for this is frequently that a muscle has not properly been warmed up, has cooled down since the warm-up (for example, with doubles in the cool of the evening), or is overtired. In combination, deficiencies in tennis-specific hitting or running technique, as well as an insufficient level of strength and flexibility, play an important role. Also, muscular dysbalance (for example, insufficient ability to stretch) of the agonists and not enough strength of the antagonists are important causative factors.

Muscle tears occur especially often in muscles attached to joints at two points, such as at the back of the thigh; this musculature is subject to a special neuromuscular control. The situation is similar for the musculature on the front of the thigh and on the back of the lower leg, which are particularly vulnerable when untrained with regard to stretching because they react predominantly as tonic muscles by contracting when insufficiently trained.

Diagnosis
In general, the different types if muscle and tendon injuries are as follows:
- Muscle pulls occur because of overextending and often occur in the superficial portions of a muscle or close to the muscle source or attachment point.

Anatomical structure is unaffected by a pull, but function is disrupted.
- Blunt muscle bruises result from a compression of the muscle through the immediate effect of an object, such as one's own racket, usually with no injury to the skin.
- With a muscle fiber tear, muscle fibers in a small region are torn. There is usually intramuscular bleeding that requires special therapeutic attention; it is hard to the touch and one would not expect a bruise that is visible externally.
- With a muscle bundle tear, the tearing of muscle fibers involves all of a muscle bundle (quantitatively different from a muscle tear). Bleeding is within the muscle and the amount of bleeding varies, depending on the scope and location. External bruises can be expected, in general, to be distal (toward the periphery).
- Muscle tear causes complete separation of the muscle, so that bleeding can be recognized early, also externally.
- Muscle tear causes an acute stabbing pain that forces one to stop playing immediately. The pain can be clearly localized. An early palpation will indicate a more or less definite fiber break that appears as a depression where there are extensive fiber tears. Subsequently, the muscle depression fills with blood and fluid; at the same time, there is a significant increase in tension in the whole muscle bundle, culminating after approximately

24 hours. This should be considered as a protective reaction of the muscle. However, if there are problems with sensation, a physician must be consulted immediately.

The differential diagnosis between muscle pull and muscle tear (particularly, level 1) is often difficult at first. Because it is so important for the success of the treatment and the course of healing, the most important differences are summarized here.

In the superficial musculature, a muscle tear will have clearly palpable gaps (depressions), bruises last one or several days, and there is a significantly longer recuperation compared with a muscle pull; the muscle pull often heals through careful stretching.

However, the palpable depression, particularly in the strained musculature, can be filled in a few hours after the injury by a bruise or accumulation of fluid, so that diagnosing by touching no longer works.

With a fiber tear, it is sometimes possible to feel a (very small) muscle depression. With a complete tear, the complete separation of the muscle body can be palpated. In this case, the muscle can also pull itself back to the tendon and is visible as a knotty lump.

With tendon injuries, we differentiate the partial and total tendon tears. Compared with muscle injuries in tennis players, tendon injuries are rare and mostly involve the Achilles tendon.

Total tendon tears often occur when one has degenerated tendons. They are often found in older players who are taking up the sport again after a long training hiatus or who allot insufficient regeneration phases to the tendons. Incomplete tendon tears are not always recognized and are misdiagnosed as inflammation or overuse.

Emergency Measures

Emergency measures (first aid) first aim to stop bleeding. The following measures should be initiated immediately: The affected musculature is relieved through immediate support and appropriate positioning, keeping it above the center of the body. At the same time, cold is applied to the injured area, in combination with compression. An ice-cold pressure bandage (for example, with an ice-water soaked cloth) is suitable for this because it cools the injured musculature extensively in approximately 20–30 minutes. The immediate treatment in the first 10 minutes is extremely important for the length of time it will take to heal. Based on experience, a treatment that is delayed 1 or 2 minutes within the first 10 can cause a day's increase in rehabilitation time. After another thorough examination, the diagnosis should be refined, and further treatment should be introduced. Until the definitive diagnosis is completed, the limb should be supported, especially because each counter effect or renewed strong muscle contractions (for example, uncontrolled movement) presents a risk that bleeding will start again within the first 24–36 hours. In contrast to a muscle tear, with the muscle pull, a substantial but simultaneously careful stretching

treatment (for example, postisometric stretching with 10–15 repetitions) is recommended in direct connection with ice therapy for a prompt recovery. Recently, the effect of ice therapy after blunt muscle injuries, bruises, or dislocations in the joint has been viewed extremely critically because cooling alleviates pain; in contrast to earlier thinking, there is no indication that it has any significant influence on bleeding or inhibiting inflammation. In the first minutes and hours, besides compression and appropriate cooling, a sport gel that is effective in inhibiting inflammation and promoting regeneration is recommended. After about a day, as a rule, there is a functional treatment with taping.

Massage should not be used in the first 3 days after a muscle injury because it can cause new injuries. Lymph drainage for swelling, and massage of the muscle areas that are not injured may have a positive influence on healing.

Stretching should be done before ice therapy and helps detone the muscle and also make a diagnosis. If the pain diminishes, the problem is a pull; if it becomes worse, a muscle tear. After the subsequent 20–30 minutes of ice therapy, different types of therapy are available; they are quite varied and in professional circles are rated differently, so that their choice must be left up to the decision of the treating physicians and physical therapists.

Preventive Measures

- Warm-up of the circulatory system and principal muscle groups (including stretching exercises) before every training session and competition.
- Regular strengthening exercises equally for all muscle groups that are important for function, including antagonists.
- Flexibility training for the musculature responsible for main functions.
- Prevention of cool down during training and competition (for example, thoughtlessly taking off warm-up clothing) and between individual training units (for example, sitting unprotected on the terrace in the club restaurant).
- Protection against muscle fatigue during training and sufficient regeneration phases between the training units.
- Treatment of every muscle injury.

Tennis Injuries

Types of injuries involving the movement apparatus that occur in tennis and have no apparent effect on power are defined as primary injuries, which manifest themselves through pain and disrupted functions.

Primary tennis injury is characterized by the fact that, with sufficient treatment, along with changing and reducing stress, there can be a return to complete capability and freedom from symptoms.

On the other hand, secondary tennis injury is characterized by persistent defects and a persistent decrease in stress. Because the transitions are fluid, clear demarcations are not always possible.

The appearance of a sports injury is likely to happen in all those places and types of tissue where there is an imbalance between stress and the ability to withstand stress. This can result in applying the wrong amount of pressure or too much; or perhaps capacity becomes diminished because of various factors, such as heredity, environment, or illness. Very often, the metabolically inactive (bradytrope) tissues such as tendons, ligaments, cartilage, and scars are affected. For tennis players, the most likely places for an injury are the elbow, shoulder, lumbar spine, and Achilles tendon.

Because of the very high frequency—approximately 40–50 percent of all tennis players have had problems such as tennis elbow during the course of their career—and because of the close relationship of this syndrome and tennis technique, tennis elbow will be discussed comprehensively.

Tennis Elbow

With tennis elbow, we are dealing with various pathological changes in the elbow joint that occur because of overtaxing and are characterized in soft tissues by degenerative changes in the tendon base region of the muscle attachments located at the elbow with adiposity and splintering of the tendon fibers. The great majority of cases (approximately 80 percent) involve external (lateral) bony knots on the extensor muscles of the wrist and pronators of the hand originate. The inner (medial) bony knots on the wrist flexors and hand supinators are painful in only about 20 percent of the cases. With competitive tennis players, the percentage of the medial problems is higher, but the number of affected players is relatively low.

Tennis elbow often occurs with activities or jobs that rely on intensive work with the hands (especially turning movements). Housewives in earlier times were especially at risk because of wringing wash; today, activities of the construction worker, such as paving or turning screws against great resistance provoke tennis elbow.

For the tennis player, an uneconomical technique—mostly on the backhand side (extensor muscles)—is most often responsible for this overtaxing or incorrect stress; thus, preventive measures must be introduced first of all with the backhand technique.

In spite of the essential significance of an uneconomical tennis technique for causing tennis elbow, other factors must also be considered. Therefore, one must look for connections between elbow problems and emotional disturbances, as well as with ossifications at the roots of the arm nerves related to the cervical spine.

Even more important are age-related degenerative changes in the region of the muscle attachments at the elbow joint, which contribute to the fact that the tennis elbow syndrome begins most often in the middle of one's 40s and reaches its peak in the 50s and 60s.

Diagnosis

Tennis elbow causes temporary (at the beginning of play) or continuing pain in the region of the joint condoyles at the elbow (when touched and especially while hitting the ball). Most often, the pain is centered in the root area of the short wrist extensor, which lies toward the thumb. In an extreme case, the patient cannot raise a cup of coffee or turn a newspaper page. Tennis elbow patients can be recognized right away when greeted because they avoid a firm handshake. If the external joint condoyles is affected, these pains occur when hitting backhand; with the inner condoyle, the forehand and a quick backswing movement are painful. The decided preference for the backhand side as the point of origin for the pain results from the fact that the strength of the flexors (principal musculature for the forehand) is considerably greater than that of the extensor (principal musculature for the backhand). In addition, the forehand grip allows a better transfer of effort because the palm is situated behind the racket grip.

Therapy

Tennis elbow is primarily treated by a physician. However, it can also be managed by a tennis instructor—if at all possible, in cooperation with the physician.

The focus for treatment via the tennis instructor is the decrease in overloading the working muscles by making the tennis technique more economical. The tennis instructor can reduce the overall expenditure of effort significantly through appropriate movement tasks and advice on technique. At the same time, he can work out a transfer of the muscle work to other muscle groups (for example, shoulder and trunk musculature).

In addition, the instructor will be able to get rid of exogenic disturbance factors (tennis rackets, lacing, balls) and endogenic factors (for example, training level of the arm muscles) through consultation.

Practice has shown that regular stretching of the affected arm muscles (for example, wrist extensors and hand pronators or wrist flexors and supinators) before and after training—perhaps after an adequate break of 1–4 weeks—leads to success in many cases. Applying an elbow bandage can also lead to a noticeable decrease of symptoms because this decreases the amount of muscle contractions, resulting in a reduction of the overload.

Preventive Measures

All preventive measures have the common goal of preventing simultaneously increasing strength and elasticity. Basically, this involves three different starting points for preventive measures:
- Economizing tennis technique,
- Eliminating exogenic disturbance factors,
- Strengthening and stretching the working musculature.

Economizing Tennis Technique

To decrease the effort, attention should be paid to the following errors in technique:
- Point of impact is too late (includes too-late backswing or too-early forward shift of the body's center of gravity).
- Poor transfer of effort in the case of a timely point of impact (includes faulty forward shift of the center of gravity due to incorrect grip, poor swing technique, or eccentric point of impact).
- Limited backswing of the racket from the return point in the loop to the point of impact (includes open hitting position or short backswing movement).

The deficiencies in technique cited previously hold for both forehand and backhand. Because tennis elbow problems are localized primarily in the outer condoyles on the joints, economizing the backhand technique is particularly valuable. Because the two-handed backhand might unburden the overtaxed working musculature considerably, the two-handed technique should be viewed as an important preventive measure for players who are prone to tennis elbow. However, this is related to a greater effort on footwork and, often, coordination difficulties in changing position. Therefore, at more advanced ages, the two-handed backhand can be used only in a limited way as a preventive or rehabilitative measure.

Eliminating Exogenic Disturbance Factors

Exogenic disturbance factors can be eliminated through careful selection of materials (balls and rackets) that can be responsible originally for the occurrence of tennis elbow.

Important exogenic disturbance factors include:
- Heavy racket,
- Top-heavy racket,
- Too-thick (or slender) grip,
- Hard racket with limited vibration damping,
- Too-taut strings,
- Nonelastic strings,
- Heavy (wet) balls,
- Hard balls (for example, "long-play" balls),
- "Fast" court surface,
- High speed of opponent's balls (particularly on the service).

Strengthening and Stretching the Working Musculature

With systematic care for the muscles, in conjunction with health-conscious behavior, the occurrence of tennis elbow can be avoided. The following individual measures help:
- Strengthening the overall musculature of the forearm,
- Stretching exercises specifically for forearm extensors and pronators as well as wrist flexors and supinators,
- Relaxation of the hitting muscles between strokes and after the stress,
- Warming up the working muscles and keeping them warm.

In summary, it can be established that tennis elbow can occur because of a group of several causative factors. Ideally, tennis elbow is therefore treated jointly by a cooperating physician and tennis instructor. The tennis instructor is most competent and responsible for treating tennis elbow.

Advice on Preventing Tennis Injuries

The most important advice on preventing tennis injuries is summarized systematically in the following sections:
- Suitability for the sport, physical constitution, and mental attitude,
- Training level,
- Preparation for training and competition,
- Regeneration after stress,
- Behavior in dealing with injuries and after illness,
- Technical equipment on the tennis court.

Suitability, Physical Constitution, and Mental Attitude

Health is the basic requirement for the highest performance in tennis. In addition, physical constitution, mental attitude, and spirit must be developed in such a way that they grow to meet the specific requirements of the sport of tennis in training and competition and can continue to develop. For this, there must be a check-up—including orthopedic aspects—at least annually, especially in childhood and youth by a sports physician.

Training Level

After physical constitution, the current level of training plays the next most important role in preventing tennis elbow. In tennis, the following are extremely important: general coordination and tennis technique, as well as conditioning factors, such as strength, speed, stamina, and, not the least, flexibility. These factors must be adequately considered when formulating a training plan, as well as when applying to tennis tournaments. They are most important for children and senior players.

Preparation for Training and Competition

Faulty preparation for competition and training is one of the most important reasons for injuries. A systematic and comprehensive preparation has the goal of putting the circulatory system and muscular metabolism on an elevated performance level. This can be achieved through systematic tennis training, such as a warm-up routine. In addition, the overall movement apparatus (neuromuscular coordination, mobility of the joints, ability to stretch the working musculature and its antagonists) must be prepared for some extreme stresses, such as the fastest possible switch of concentric and eccentric muscle contractions, uneven spots in the court surface, and nonslip subsurface. An intact intra- and intermuscular coordination is achieved by systematic repetition of the individual hitting sequences, even under competitive conditions. The joints that are especially taxed, such as the shoulder and spine, are prepared through specific swinging exercises. (Be careful to carry out the movements precisely.)

In addition, all ligament structures that are very highly

stressed (such as the ankles) are properly conditioned for tennis. This is accomplished by jumping rope, high-jumping, and sideways jumping, and especially through appropriate training on the tennis court (tossing: left/right, short/long).

The effect of the warm-up program is enhanced by the right kind of clothing. Normally, outer clothing that is considered to maintain warmth (such as a sweatsuit) is taken off toward the end of the warm-up phase, in order to prevent an unnecessary elevation of body temperature and an excessive loss of fluids. At the same time, the player gets the correct feel for the competitive situation.

Because the elasticity of various tissue structures is reduced as one ages (for example, muscles, ligaments, and joint cartilage), tennis players in the young-senior and senior classes—compared with children and young players— must complete a longer warm-up program with a corresponding shift in emphasis. A positive mental attitude toward content and stress demands in training adds to the prevention of tennis injuries. This mainly concerns the correct attitude toward the player's performance (perhaps under consideration of external influences such as opponents, condition of the court, and weather), motivation to the best possible performance, and concentration, as well as mental identity with the basic goals of training and competition.

Regeneration After Stress

After strenuous training and grueling competitions, a measured cooling of the body with simultaneous relaxation of the mind leads to recovery and the fastest possible regeneration so that previously arranged training and competitive periods can be dealt with in a rested state. Cooling down or moderate hitting training after the competition and limbering gymnastics with stretching, as well as physiotherapeutic and balneological measures such as massages, baths, and sauna contribute to accelerated regeneration, whether used individually or in combination. Nutrition that is adequate for training and competition is also very valuable in connection with this.

The processes of autogenic training and progressive muscle relaxation (see also p. 192) belong to the psychological methods of recovery. The knowledge of such processes is of great value for players and trainers.

Sufficient sleep (also between individual training units and competitions) and a regulated sleep rhythm support physical and psychological regeneration.

Behavior in Dealing with Injuries and After Illness

Tennis injuries heal at various rates, depending on the degree of severity and location, as well as the individual's circumstances (predisposition and behavior). A complete recovery requires that the physical therapist has a basic knowledge of healing processes as much as specific related experiences in tennis. Only under these circumstances can rehabilitation programs that are effective in different ways be used, so that an early and successful return to training and competition is possible for the athlete.

Basically, the prescribed breaks from stress after an injury should be strictly observed, and there should be an absolute ban on tennis during the typical healing period. However, prescribing a break from stress in no way means complete rest. Finally, there are several measures, such as contralateral training, muscle development using exercise, and elastic bandages, etc. that promote and shorten the healing process. Even the slightest indication of an injury (for example, muscle pulls as a precursor of a muscle tear or a muscle-fiber tear, as well as pain in the shoulder or elbow when moving, after a comprehensive training session) must be given special attention and, when there is doubt, must be dealt with by a visit to the physician. False pride on the part of the players and their personal circle (for example, parents) often have serious consequences for health and performance capability.

After bacterial or viral infections (for example, a festering tonsillitis or general viral illnesses), the player must be alert that the illness does not last too long and that the infection does not spread to important organ systems, such as the heart.

Taking blood to determine lactate level.

Technical Equipment on the Tennis Court

The correct selection of tennis racket for the individual (materials, sweet spot, weight distribution, and size of the grip), of the strings (tension, elasticity), and of shoes (foot bed, sole profile, heel fit, toe space, and comfort) can play a significant role in preventing tennis injuries. Frequently, the necessary acclimatization on a new court surface is given too little attention. The different surfaces (clay, granulated material, artificial grass, and hard surface) require not only different play tactics, but most importantly, different running tactics with (suddenly) changed stress conditions for the joints. Well-cared-for clay courts are basically much safer for the movement apparatus than nonslip surfaces.

Monitoring and Testing Performance

The Importance of Monitoring Performance

Tests for performance are indispensable instruments for managing and regulating the process of training and competition. Here, the individual decisions to change training (consciously or unconsciously) build on the results of the previous performance diagnosis.

The various monitoring procedures in competitive sports are also viewed as research procedures, diagnostic procedures, measurements, monitoring performance, or, generally, a test. In tennis, observation (systematically or unsystematically and with or without documentation) and the test for sport-specific motor skills (especially the conditioning test) are the most frequently used monitoring procedures.

The complex processes of performance/skills diagnosis on the basis of previous analysis of the sport-specific demands profile, as well as planning, execution, and supervision of the training are designated in training science as monitoring and testing athletic performance or simplified to training management or performance/skills management. For performance/skills management, the trainer constantly needs new information on the current training status of his athletes and players. Only with this can he structure the training in such a way that it guarantees the optimum stress (and stress distribution).

Also in tennis, the trainer obtains this information by monitoring his players (in the broadest sense). This means that he also manages putting the plan into practice. Performance/skills management are not limited to training because the lessons learned in competition under the higher physical and psychological pressures provide practical directives that are very important for managing a training program. Under genuine competitive conditions, the individual performance components can often be increased only with the greatest difficulties (for example, start and running speed), or perhaps even not at all (for example, anticipation/reaction). Besides, it is precisely a characteristic of tennis that, with each competition, variable factors (court surface, storms, opponents, etc.) limit the reliability of the control values.

In summary, performance/skills management in training and competition has two objectives, which are usually linked:

- Precise diagnosis of strengths and weaknesses in components related to performance, and also in overall performance.
- Objective checks on the success or failure of a training program and of the training content and methods used; this often provides a practical basis for determining the trainability of an individual so that more objective predictions for future development of potential can be made.

Specifications for Monitoring Procedures

The most important step before making recommendations for performance and training is setting up a list of priorities for increasing potential, where the training goals are refined and prioritized. However, ranking factors that determine performance potential on the one hand, and training goals on the other, must not be identical. Factors that determine performance potential are valuable training goals only if they can be trained in a worthwhile manner. Weight training goals, therefore, depend on seeding and on trainability.

The identification of levels of influence is especially difficult in tennis, since the possibilities for compensation (for example, quality of serve or net play on the one hand and ground strokes on the other, depending on the type of player, etc.) increase considerably in such a complex sport. The current density of demands in world-class tennis and the high quality and scope of training indicate the value of performance/skills monitoring because even minimal improvements of detail factors can mean decisive progress.

However, it must be made clear to the trainer which skills components the monitoring procedure should cover and which results she can derive from the monitoring. Results from performance/skills monitoring must be compared with average and target values. Norm-specification profiles with

Fig. 126 Flow chart of a performance management situation and its consequences.

representative comparison and reference values can be drawn up only after comprehensive and systematic capture of data. This allows an objective evaluation of individual test results from diagnoses of skills based on practical training results. Because of the complexity of tennis and the ability to compensate for individual capabilities, it is important to allow a tolerance where there is a deviation from the statistical norm.

The results of performance/skills monitoring can be useful (Fig. 126) only when the procedure used for the criteria of a test (objectivity, reliability, and validity) is sufficient. As a rule, information from performance/skills monitoring cannot be worth much if the method of checking does not stand up to the cited scientific factors. The most important, and simultaneously

most difficult, criterion of a performance/skills test is validity. This determines the level of accuracy with which the monitoring procedure actually records the feature (relevant to the particular sport) that it is supposed to determine. For example, the person who wants to monitor, for example, the general aerobic stamina of a tennis player in the midst of a 1000-meter run may choose a procedure that does not apply well to the task desired. The running capacity over 1000 meters (and with a 6-minute run) depends on the anaerobic stamina capacity and various psychological qualities (performance, motivation, will) in addition to the general aerobic stamina. Determination of the anaerobic threshold via a stepped test with checks on blood lactate is the much better procedure for the desired objective.

Objectivity characterizes the level of independence of the results of the monitoring procedure compared to influences during the procedure and the evaluation. For tennis, this means that a test is objective when different observers or trainers give the same test result after independently administering the test at the same time and perhaps another place. Detailed specifications of precise guidelines when evaluating the test (especially with tests of technique) and a standardized execution of the test are thus an indispensable requirement for a high level of objectivity.

Reliability of a testing procedure characterizes the level of accuracy with which an ability or a quality of an athlete is measured. Like objectivity, the reliability of a test can be determined numerically through a correlation (R). With this, we can determine if the test result is invalidated by inaccuracies in the measurement procedure, accident, and effects of practice. Particularly in tennis, the reliability of a test often depends on the stability of the tested quality. For example, tests for technique have a relatively low reliability, especially for beginners and advanced players, because the quality of the execution of a movement on these levels is subject to wide fluctuations. Thus, reliable results in a techniques test can be expected only when the tested technique (for example, serve or forehand-topspin) is largely habituated.

Direct and Indirect Monitoring of Performance/Skills

Performance/skills can be monitored directly or indirectly in training under specific conditions. If the complex athletic skills and/or the factors that determine capability within a competition are registered, this is considered a direct monitoring of performance/skills.

In contrast to more simply structured sports, such as the 100-meter dash, shot putting, or 1500-meter freestyle swimming, there are significantly greater difficulties in data acquisition in tennis because the complex capabilities depend on numerous factors. On the other hand, if the trainer builds specific situations into the training program,

wherein particular movement sequences are to be executed (for example, successful forehand-topspin in specific situations or a 10-meter sprint), this is an indirect monitoring of performance/skills. As a rule, this allows for testing of skills components.

The test for athletic motor skills (for example, the general test for athletic motor skills for 6- to 11-year-old children or the conditioning test for young tennis players from 11 years old or the Cooper test) is an example of a method of indirect monitoring of performance/skills because the demand for standardization of the test situation rules out using it in competitive situations. Sports-medical laboratory tests, psychological tests, and biomechanical tests are also indirect monitors of performance/skills. The indirect monitoring has the advantage of a relatively high level of objectivity, accuracy of measurement, and reliability of results for the individually tested skills components. On the other hand, it remains doubtful, whether these results (for example, the 10-meter run) can be carried over to actual performance in a tennis competition because some factors, such as recognizing the play situation, are not considered in this test.

With direct monitoring of performance, this is directly reversed. However, as a rule, the actual competitive situation presents difficulties in measurement methods (complexity and speed of the action, measurement instruments that disturb players) and produces various psychological variables, which, in combination with the

considerable influence of the opponent's performance, invalidates the individual's results.

In addition, the complex play situation seldom allows isolated skills components (for example, anticipation, hitting speed, aerobic capacity) to be evaluated because they merge with other factors in a holistic tennis performance. The question of correct procedure occupies trainers and theorists. Should the judgment rest on concrete training test results or on subjective evaluation? Both possibilities have advantages and disadvantages; therefore, a good trainer should let her personal observations and experiences in training and competition, as well as various objective measurement results in isolated training situations and complex competitive events, influence her judgment and the corresponding management of the training program.

Scheduling Performance/Skills Checks in the Training Process

The increasing interest in monitoring skills in the past few years has led to a better level of training and skills development for the athlete, and, as a result, training programs can be structured more economically. Based on this, athletic training managed to develop from an untested, accidental influence on success or failure to economical processes that promote optimal performance.

Performance/skills checks are made at the following times:

- Performance/skills check at the beginning of a training period: It is a basis for establishing the individual's performance level and thus, for setting up appropriate training groups aimed at giving each participant the correct level of stress. The more precisely the beginning level in the abilities to be trained is known, the more effectively the tennis player can be challenged.
- Performance/skills check during the training cycle: It provides on-going supervision of skills development in connection with the continuous monitoring of the effectiveness of the training measures and the possibility of fine-tuning, such as increasing or decreasing the training load.
- Performance/skills check at the end of the training period: Its goal is to test the effectiveness of the training methods and stress norms and to determine future training and competition planning authoritatively.

Monitoring performance/skills must always have a predetermined goal so that it can contribute to clarifying specific questions. Unnecessary use of performance/skills testing should be avoided.

The Spectrum of Monitoring Performance/Skills

The variety of influences affecting performance in tennis demands multidisciplinary procedures. These come directly from training practice and science or can be related to the established fundamental scientific disciplines, such as psychology, medicine, biomechanics (Table 13).

The focus of testing procedures in training practice and science is the diagnosis of performance criteria related to technique, tactics, and conditioning of a specific sport. Examples include athletic motor skills tests to evaluate conditioning and coordination capabilities or to test technique as well as to observe the player in a systematic way.

Athletic motor-skills tests usually have a close relationship to competitive activity. The value to playing is a result of the close relationship of training content and monitoring procedures. This means that results of techniques tests (for example, technique grids or hitting statistics) are usually more complex than those for conditioning tests and, as a result, are more difficult to interpret. Typical examples for athletic motor-skills tests in tennis are the shuttle sprint (22 m), the three-legged hop, and the two-handed medicine ball distance throw. For coordination, there are the ball-legs-wall test, target throwing, and the obstacle course. More examples of these can be found through tennis associations in your area.

The systematic observation of players has a special place among monitoring procedures because it observes the student in actual training and competitive situations and provides precise "hard" data at the same time. In contrast to the other monitoring processes, it is not done under special test conditions beyond the competition. Basically, one can differentiate between systematic observation of the player ("scouting") and observation where the judgment of performance is made unsystematically via cell phone or

Table 13   (Training) scientific testing processes

Evaluating performance in tennis				
Training science/ training practice		(scientific) Basic disciplines		
Motor skills test	Systematic observation of the player	Psychological test	Medical test	Biomechanical test
e.g. • standardized testing of technique • general and specialized conditioning tests: age 6–11 "Conditioning Test-Tennis"	e.g. • quantitative: – hitting success – hitting direction – spin • qualitative: – video analyses	e.g. • Concentration • Motivation • Stress	e.g. • State of health • Reactions and adaptations in training and competition • Stamina	e.g. • Running speed • Acceleration • Lead-in with racket • Racket speed • Racket acceleration

video camera. With the first procedure, the player's capabilities are systematically written up according to a prescribed grid and the results are prepared statistically.

A special form for observing players uses an electronic data processing system that allows direct evaluation of the data immediately afterward ("on-line"). Individual weaknesses involving technique and specific situations (for example, Becker's too-low forehand-volley in the Wimbledon finals against Edberg in 1990) can be investigated this way (Fig. 127).

Video recordings also enjoy a special position. The tape can be made either systematically or unsystematically. Coupling the computer and video recorder (interactive video system) makes a systematic video analysis possible (Fig. 128). The qualitative analysis of play is possible via computer-assisted observation of a selection of clips from the match (for example, frequent mistakes with a specific hitting technique). This process is especially useful for visually oriented trainers and players because they can follow the developmental history of the technical and tactical strengths and weaknesses on the screen as "hard" data without having to give up objectivity and precision.

Psychological test results capture psychological performance factors (for example, the ability to concentrate and the motivation to perform). However, their transferability to tennis applications is not certain. Therefore, one should systematically directly observe the behavior of the players in training

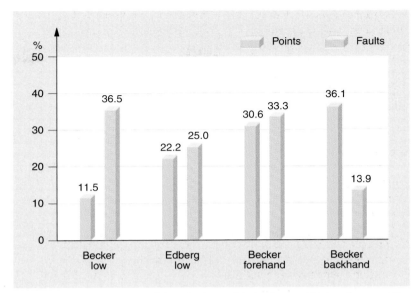

Fig. 127 Comparison in % of the winning and losing low and high volleys, and the forehand and backhand volleys, in the 1990 Wimbledon finals.

Fig. 128 Model of function and sequence of a systematic video analysis by trainer and assistant (Ferrauti/Weber 1991).

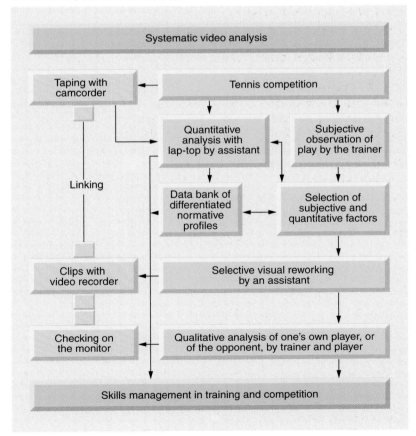

and competition. If possible, the players can also be questioned directly about the psychological factors that represent the background of their behavior.

Medical testing procedures allow the objective recording of numerous parameters of the circulatory system and muscle metabolism, as well as the movement apparatus. The data can be used to monitor health status and to register performance stamina, strength, and movement of important muscle groups. Lactate diagnosis especially allows field research under sport-specific pressure conditions directly at the training and competition site, with immediate analysis of the results. Further parameters, such as urine, ammonia, iron, and magnesium open up further opportunities for a precise measurement of stress (intensity and extent of the stimulus) and recuperation (regeneration, overtraining). With their subdisciplines—internal medicine/cardiology and orthopedics/traumatology—these medical fields are increasingly involved with wellness and pathological aspects of health, as well as capability in sports.

Biomechanical testing procedures use very different measurement procedures and make it possible to record numerous cinematic and dynamic measurements. High-quality video cameras with extreme slow-motion replay, electronic procedures to determine body angles, telemetric data transmission, and power instruments are examples of typical and reliable biomechanical research methods. In tennis particularly, multidimensional cinematic analysis of technique

(for example, tossing the ball up for a serve, racket swing and point of contact when serving, as well as anticipation, movement of the racket and angle of the wrist), running style, and speed are finding more and more practical uses.

Finally, it should be noted that this monitoring process should include training documentation, in the broadest context. Training documentation consists of the systematic registration and recording of all training content, scope, and intensities, as well as various training methods and relearning techniques. Injuries and illnesses and other particulars, such as climatic factors, should also be listed. In addition, the time and results of all skills tests and competitions should be noted precisely.

Tennis Under Extreme Conditions

Training and Competitions in Hot Weather

During difficult muscular work, the release of heat via vaporization is the most important regulating factor. In order to maintain a balance in temperature under normal conditions, a tennis player must give off approximately 600 kcal/h over her body surface. With total evaporation of the perspiration, this would correspond to a production of 1000 ml/h. However, because, on the average, only 40 percent of the perspiration produced is totally evaporated, a production of 2.5 l/h would be necessary.

In tennis training and competition, the body weight drops 2 lbs. on the average (for women, approximately one third less)—mainly through release of perspiration. Because at most half of the perspiration evaporates, the release of heat via evaporation is approximately half of the amount of heat produced so that the body temperature rises. The demand for the production of perspiration and its evaporation through light clothing, as well as continuous intake of fluid (and staying in the shade during the change of sides), prevent an extreme rise in body temperature, which can be dangerous to health and harmful to performance capability. Loss of fluid in larger amounts limits endurance and the will to perform and is sometimes linked to muscle and stomach pains, as well as a dazed state and weakness. With a fluid deficit below 6 percent of the body weight (for example, 2 kg weight loss for a 40-kg child), thirst, weakness, irritability, aggressiveness and in some cases, muscle cramps, can occur as primary symptoms. From a fluid deficit of more than 6 percent (for example, 3.5 kg for a 50-kg youth after training twice daily without taking in any water) there may be apparent weakening of the physical and mental abilities. Tennis competitions and prolonged training sessions in high ambient temperatures thus require regular intake of fluids. As a point of reference, 150–200 ml water for every 15 minutes should be sufficient.

Two singles matches under competitive conditions or two training sessions (for example, 9:00–11:00 and 3:00–5:00) on hot and humid days cause losses of 3–6 liters.

In this process, in addition to salt (approximately 20 g NaCl/l of perspiration), other electrolytes such as potassium and magnesium and important trace elements such as iron are excreted. Under today's competitive training conditions (two training sessions daily, training camps in southern regions, tournament sequences in humid countries), water loss and the deficit in electrolytes and trace elements must be compensated. Potassium, magnesium, and iron (especially for women) are particularly important for maintaining capability.

Subsequently, before signs of the deficiencies appear, one must consider whether special nutritional variants or specific replacements (such as iron or magnesium tablets) can prevent a loss of capacity. Commercial preparations ("isotonic thirst quenchers") are not recommended for competitive athletes because, generally, they contain only a small amount of magnesium and potassium and no iron (see Table 16, p. 248). With an elevated external temperature, the lactic acid concentration in the blood rises earlier because the working muscles are provided with a limited blood flow and less oxygen in favor of increased circulation in the skin. Subsequently, the tennis player activates anaerobic metabolic processes under heated conditions, even at midlevel training intensity; this causes an increased production of lactic acid with an earlier onset of fatigue. As a result, training in intensive heat should be less intensive (limited strength and density of stimulus) or shorter in length. A systematic acclimatization is recommended in the case of training trips to humid countries. To become acclimatized as soon as possible, the tennis player should exert himself physically several times a day, at the level he would do at home. Thus, the tennis player must train more often each day, (for example, three or four times), but for shorter periods (for example, 50–60 minutes) than he would in a moderate or cold climate. In addition, carrying out a general warm-up program before breakfast and beginning training

immediately after breakfast have been shown to be worthwhile.

Tennis players who are used to the heat and those trained for stamina have a better thermoregulatory reaction in the heat than nonathletes. They produce considerably higher amounts of perspiration and thus maintain a lower skin and body temperature. At the same time, the concentration of salt and other mineral matter in the perspiration decreases.

Health-Related Problems

In athletic competitions, heat exhaustion is the most frequent health-related problem because of loss of fluid in the extracellular area. In extreme cases, it results in heat stroke.

With <u>heat stroke</u>, there is a thermal buildup because of the effect of high external temperatures in connection with physical exertion, accompanied by an insufficient release of heat. As the body temperature rises, there is an acute circulatory disturbance with subsequent dulling of consciousness leading to loss of consciousness.

Typical signs of heat stroke are:
- Accelerated breathing,
- Pulse considerably above 100 beats/minute,
- Rectal temperature above 40°C,
- Headache, dizziness, and nausea,
- Dulling of consciousness leading to loss of consciousness,
- Gray skin and bluish lips.

One should differentiate between the red and the gray stages. The red stage is characterized by reddened skin. The heavy circulation in the skin represents an attempt by the body to release more heat through radiation or perspiration, causing the body temperature to decrease. In the gray stage, there is not enough circulation in the skin.

First-aid measures aim to lower the elevated body temperature and to cool the head. The following individual measures can be used:
- Lay the person flat in a shady, well-ventilated place and open any clothing;
- Cool the head, neck, and extremities by applying cold compresses;
- Continually check breathing and circulation;
- Place the person on her side if she is unconscious (do not administer fluids!).

Sunstroke is an irritation of the meninges and occurs mainly when the head and neck are not protected from the sun's rays. This happens when there is no breeze during training or competition (for example, in deep center court) and can be prevented by using special sun hats with neck protection or turning the visor around 180 degrees. In some case, sunstroke is accompanied by heat stroke.

Signs of sunstroke include:
- Head is hot and bright red,
- Nape of the neck is stiff because of irritation of the meninges,
- Irritability, nausea, dizziness,
- Muscle cramps,
- Loss of consciousness.

First-aid measures are essentially the same as with heat stroke.

Heat cramps occur during or after prolonged tennis competition when temperatures are very high. Higher levels of perspiration (sometimes resulting from the activity) help, sometimes in spite of administering greater amounts of fluids. The cramps are more likely to occur in the area of the working muscles (particularly, calves and thighs; and less so in the forearm and fingers). Treatment consists of stretching the affected muscle area to the extreme and replacing the lost water and electrolytes. The only effective preventive measure is maintaining proper balance of fluids and minerals (in training and early in competition). In persistent cases and where the player is predisposed, treatment may include administering magnesium for 4–6 weeks just before and during the heat periods.

Training and Competition Under Ozone Concentration

Numerous tennis players are exposed to an elevated ozone concentration up to 5 hours in the course of their matches. This results in a general uncertainty concerning what causes an ozone concentration and what general and specific dangers might arise for tennis players. In addition, it is interesting to know what measures can be taken to reduce the risks related to ozone concentration.

Formation and Occurrence of Ozone

Ozone is a three-atom oxygen molecule (O_3) with a strong oxidizing effect. Depending on the concentration of the gas, it is colorless to blue. When evaluating the ramifications for human health, one must differentiate between the ozone content of the atmosphere near earth (troposphere) and the ozone shield at a height of approximately 15 miles (stratosphere).

In the stratosphere, oxygen molecules absorb shortwave UV light and are split. The oxygen atoms that have been set free combine spontaneously with molecular oxygen (O_2) to ozone (O_3). The concentration at a height of 15 miles is more than $30\ \mu g/m^3$.

From a health standpoint, this ozone layer is of tremendous positive importance, since it absorbs the shortwave UV portion of sunlight and thus represents an indispensable protection against possible dermatological problems. The increasing emission of fluorochlorocarbon hydrogen compounds is causing the breakdown of these ozone molecules ("ozone hole"), which also allows the radiation intensity to increase and thus also increases the risk to human health.

On the troposphere, the direct splitting of oxygen molecules can no longer take place because of the limited UV-rays close to earth. Especially in polluted air, the UV-absorption occurs via nitrous oxide (NO_2) and partially via carbohydrates, which gives rise to atomic oxygen and then ozone. Thus, the extent of ozone generation in the troposphere essentially depends on the level of air pollution. This can present a health-threatening concentration for humans when there is extreme radiation from the sun and high concentrations of auto exhaust.

Limits for Tropospheric Ozone Content

According to the World Health Organization, on days with maximum 1-hour averages of less than 100 µg/m³ of ozone levels, there are no effects that cause health problems.

In the course of a day, the ozone concentrations are highest between 2 P.M. and 5 P.M., and can reach 300–450 µg/m³. In the U.S., it is recommended that athletic instruction be discontinued in schools when ozone levels exceed 360 µg/m³.

Depending on the sensitivity of one's bronchial system, the ozone effects can be clinically perceptible even with levels below 200 µg/m³ because of coughing, restricted breathing, and pain in the chest. With the lowest ozone concentrations at 160 µg/m³, a decrease in lung function was observed where there was significant physical stress for more than 6 hours. However, practical experience, especially in competitive sports shows that beyond these concentrations athletes with the highest volumes of breaths per minute generally have no problems.

To sum up, the problem of a unified definition of a limit for ozone rests on the fact that besides ozone concentration, the type of physical activity, the duration of the effect, the amount of air taken in, and, most importantly, the sensitivity of the individual must also be taken into account.

Because tennis players achieve only a midlevel breathing capacity, which is below the level of typical (intensive) endurance demands, they are less at risk outdoors than typical endurance athletes such as cyclists and runners.

Effects of Tropospheric Ozone

The tiny ozone molecules push deeply into all the respiratory passageways with each breath. The effects of chronic high ozone exposure can be summarized as follows:

- Restriction of the trachea branches when at rest as well as under physical pressure,
- Triggering an inflammatory reaction in the pulmonary alveoli,
- Decrease in physical capacity.

The most important factors concerning the extent of impairment due to breathing ozone—besides the actual ozone concentration—are the depth of breathing and the duration. Theoretically, with only limited ozone concentrations (approximately 160–200 µg/m³), there can already be irritations of the mucus membranes of the eyes and respiratory passages. Symptoms such as burning of the eyes, tears, scratchiness in the throat, increasing cough and chest problems related to breathing—

and also headache and nausea—can occur with ozone levels exceeding 240 µg/m³. People who suffer from asthma or chronic bronchitis are more at risk; however, endurance athletes with continuously deep breathing over a longer period should also avoid periods of the highest concentrations.

Ozone warnings must therefore be taken seriously by all people with hypersensitive bronchial systems. For the healthy recreational and competitive athlete, there is still no reason for dramatizing the ozone problem. Establishing the limit specifically for tennis players does not appear wise because the individual's sensitivity and the demands in competition are not easily determined. Extenuating circumstances, such as extreme heat, high humidity, and the severity of the individual's existing medical conditions (such as pollen allergy, diabetes, and coronary disease) play a very important role in deciding for or against a ban on play.

Recommendations for Training and Competition

Tennis Training

When weighing the value of physical activity against the risks associated with chronic or acute ozone problems, it is not merely a question of whether tennis training should be discontinued, but rather how the training should be structured. With the goal of reducing the depth and frequency of breathing, perhaps by limiting the time spent outdoors, the following possibilities are worth recommending:

- Avoid the highest stress stimuli, such as speed and drill training.
- Reduce the training session to 90 minutes or, at most, two instead of three training sessions per day.
- Shift the educational content to the areas of techniques and tactics, while eliminating the conditioning component.
- Reduce the level of stress by limiting the volume of activity (for example, halve the court for singles instruction or increase the number of players on the court in group instruction).

For children and youths with asthma or a hypersensitive bronchial system, the precautionary measures should be taken particularly seriously. In such cases, an additional consultation with the house doctor or sports physician is recommended.

Recreational players with flexibility in reserving their courts should shift their tennis training to the early morning or later evening on heavy ozone days. When burning of the eyes, coughing, headache, or pain when taking a breath occurs, the player should reduce or discontinue the stress intensity (for example, doubles instead of singles) and the duration (for example, 1 hour instead of 2 hours).

Tennis Competition

In tennis competition, the effective stress period during the volley is only approximately one fourth of the total playing time, so that the tennis player achieves only a midlevel breathing capacity. The number of breaths and their depth or ventilation are not included in the capacity-limiting factors. Thus, with normal sensitivity, an accurate health risk or reduction in capacity should not be expected in competition.

According to current research on the actual health risks, an official limiting of team competitions does not seem to be appropriate. However, if on especially hot days in the summer months there is the opportunity to reschedule, one should move play to the morning (early morning hours are best) or later in the evening.

Training and Competition in the Cold

In comparison with heat, lower external temperatures present much less of a problem for the capacity of the circulatory system and the muscular metabolism. However, coordination at the beginning of the training session is more aggravated in cold ambient temperatures, and the risk of tennis injuries (particularly, muscle pulls) increases.

For a person at rest, the ideal ambient temperature is approximately 65–70°F. With increasing muscular activity, the optimal ambient temperature level decreases. As a result, intensive tennis training can have an ideal ambient temperature at approximately 60°F or less; for doubles, it should be at least 65°F. The combination of cold and wind multiplies the sensitivity to cold. For example, for the body, 35°F with a high wind speed is as unpleasant as 5°F with no wind.

Health Problems

The main problem for tennis players is avoiding the gradual change in temperature and sudden cooling-off, and thus avoiding catching cold. This danger is particularly prominent when training or play is interrupted (for example, by rain) in colder seasons, as in spring or fall. Special attention must be given to suitable clothing and careful behavior.

Because metabolism increases 10- to 20-fold with intensive training as opposed to resting, each tennis player should take off his warm-up clothes for intensive training, so that in the coldest gyms (for example, on January mornings), the level of perspiration can fit the situation.

Thus, the choice of clothing must ensure that the evaporation of perspiration will not be hindered. Otherwise, capacity will be impaired and the danger of catching cold will increase. Of course, in the case of the recommendations cited, one has to choose between intensive tennis training or strenuous singles and doubles to avoid running.

At low temperatures, even the tailwind (especially with perspiration secretion in the lumbar region) can present health problems, a chill threatens reactions of the intervertabral discs, the sciatic nerve, or the kidneys. This is also the case, for example, when there is a strong wind in the cool of the evening and it hits the tennis player's sweaty back during a less-active doubles match with short playing periods, or on the club terrace (while not wearing appropriate warm-up clothing). Wind from the front is less dangerous because the face, stomach, and bladder react well to cold stimuli and trigger earlier warning signals.

Nutrition for the Tennis Player

Optimal nutrition for the tennis player should be healthy, natural, and suitable for her needs. Because no food contains everything necessary, and foods complement one another somewhat, nutrition must be as varied as possible. The food itself should be tasty and should be served in an appealing way so that not only the nutritional value but also the visual impression and the individual's taste can lead to an accelerated regeneration of the body and relaxation of the mind.

Healthy Nourishment

This is necessary because only a healthy body can perform at the highest levels. Competitive tennis players, especially, are exposed to the health risks of the foods of a modern civilization (high fat content and little roughage) due to substantial consumption of meat and deficiencies in vitamins and minerals and trace elements due to "empty" calories such as in lemonade, sugar, or food that has been warmed-up several times. Tennis players frequently eat in fast-food establishments and (club) restaurants with easily prepared foods, and at home they prefer ready-made meals because it saves time.

Natural Foods

Natural food is currently much discussed among those interested in nutrition, and even athletes have developed a keen interest in it. According to the concept, food should be left as natural as

possible. In other words, it should be processed as little as possible (for example, whole grain instead of white flour). The likelihood that a food contains all the elements necessary for life is greater if the food is processed less. Even food in gourmet restaurants is prepared according to these basic ideas. Food is natural when all the required nutrients are present. In addition, a total of five balances must be taken into consideration: energy, nutrients, vitamins, minerals and trace elements, and fluid.

The term *natural foods* covers a type of nutrition that basically consists of grains, milk products, the freshest possible fruits and vegetables, and seeds and vegetable oils made from them, supplemented by herbs. Vegetable products are preferred, and the consumption of meat is reduced. Fish is a desirable supplement (for example, once or twice per week).

With prolonged use of a vegetarian diet, which excludes all food coming from animals, there is a risk of deficiencies, particularly for children and youths who are training for competition. The main problems are possible protein deficiencies as well as an undersupply of minerals (for example, iron and calcium) and vitamins (for example, vitamin B).

In contrast, the ovolacto vegetarian diet, which permits milk products and eggs, should be considered adequate. If there is not enough variety in this diet, one should expect no disadvantages for those participating in tennis as a competitive sport. However, the amount of time required for preparing the food is considerably greater than with a conventional diet.

In summary, the following basics should be followed:

> Eat a variety of appealing foods, alternating types and taste, and selecting primarily on the basis of a carbohydrate-rich mixed diet of unprocessed foods (cereal as whole-grains, potatoes, brown rice, etc.) with a significant amount of fresh vegetables and fruit, as well as milk and milk product. Use vegetable and (lean) animal proteins and fat only sparingly.

The amount of food depends primarily on the requirements in training and competition, as well as one's optimal performance weight. Checking weight daily on a scale and making sure that it is in keeping with one's personal feeling of well-being are better indicators for the amount and level of food than nutritional programs and calorie charts.

Need-Based Nutrition

Need-based nutrition is directed qualitatively and quantitatively as precisely as possible to the particular type of stress or actual need. Tennis competitions and training have an acyclical sequence with demands that alternate in waves; these require stamina and resilience as well as coordination. Intensive (high

levels of stimulus strength and density) long-term demands at intervals reduce the carbohydrate supplies so that an immediate resupply of the glycogen reserve is necessary. Elastic movements with a high demand for coordination require a sufficient intake of proteins. In current competitive tennis, the necessary broad scope of training (for example, two or three training sessions in a day) require a high caloric intake, which can also be satisfied in these cases by an increased intake of fat.

The energy requirement of world-class male competitors is approximately 3500–5500 kcal, depending on the intensity and scope of the training unit; thus, with an average breakdown of 55 percent carbohydrates, 17 percent protein, and 28 percent fat daily, the increase of approximately 500–750 g carbohydrates, 200–250 g protein, and approximately 120–180 g fat is necessary. Recreational and fitness athletes manage on approximately two-thirds of the calories and amounts of food cited. The type and scope of stress are different in the different training and competitive phases, so that nutrition for a specific fine-tuning requires:
1. Nutrition in the training phase (basic nutrition),
2. Nutrition before the tennis tournament,
3. Nutrition immediately before and during a competition,
4. Nutrition during the competition,
5. Nutrition after the competition.

Nutrition in the Training Phase (Basic Nutrition)

Nutrition while training should be varied, nourishing, suited to one's needs, healthful, and appetizing. Nourishing fresh food with a clear preference for carbohydrates, in combination with a lot of fruits, vegetables, and raw fruits and vegetables are central to nutrition, in order to guarantee the basic requirements for vitamins, minerals, and trace elements, and including roughage. In addition, there should always be enough (if possible, low-fat) supplements, such as low-fat yogurt, fish, and poultry available. At the same time, those foods and preparations should be avoided that contain mostly "empty" calories, with none of the necessary substances such as vitamins and minerals. In particular, young tennis players are often served food that is too rich in fat, such as chocolate, ice cream, grilled sausages, sauteed chops, and french fries; and they prefer drinks and sweets with low nutritional value (comparison of vitamins and minerals with the calorie content of food). This comparison is based on the one hand, on the necessary requirement (energy deficit), on individual cravings (for example, cola drinks, lemonade, ice cream, cookies), as well as on the chronic shortage of time for young people and their parents. This leads to preparing foods in the shortest time possible and eating in club restaurants and fast-food establishments.

Carbohydrate-rich, whole-grain fresh food can be modified, depending on the training focus (for example, techniques, basic stamina or strength), and the scope of training (for example, one, two, or three training units per day). With strength and speed training, the protein increases, and with training that stresses stamina, the carbohydrate share increases.

Tennis training is usually accompanied by profuse perspiration, which under specific climatic conditions can be a considerable amount. As a result, one always has to be careful to take in enough fluid with the necessary mineral content, as well as vitamins and trace elements.

Minerals and Trace Elements
These are the indispensable components of vitamins, hormones, and enzymes and control the metabolism of foodstuffs. Iron is especially important for building up the red blood cells. Potassium, sodium, magnesium, and calcium are essential for controlling the function and sensitivity of the muscle and nerve cells.

A high output of perspiration on the one hand, and bottlenecks in providing minerals and trace elements on the other, cause deficits, particularly, magnesium, potassium, and iron (especially in women) in tennis players on a healthy diet. Therefore, tennis players must become familiar with those foods that are especially rich in potassium (lentils, spinach, potatoes, fish, meat, bananas, tomatoes, apricots, etc.), magnesium (oatmeal, brown rice, whole-grain rye, spinach, cow's

Food	mg/100 g	Food	mg/100 g
Cocoa powder	414	Sole	73
Peanut butter	410	Pasta	67
Cashew nuts	267	Spinach	58
Boullion	264	Rye bread	35
Soy beans	247	Mackerel	31
Beer yeast (dried)	230	Roll	30
Almonds	170	Gouda cheese	28
Peanuts	163	Trout	27
Brown rice	157	Pork	20
Hazel nuts (Filberts)	156	Beef	19
Rye, whole grain	140	Veal	15
Oatmeal	139	Corn flakes	14
Milk chocolate	104	Chicken's egg	12
Whole-wheat bread	92	Cow's milk (3.5% fat)	12
Pumpernickel	80	Apple	6

Table 14 Foods with a high magnesium content. Magnesium content is given in mg/100 g of the edible uncooked portion.

milk), and iron (pork and beef liver, millet, soy beans, wheat germ, lentils, spinach, chocolate, etc.). In connection with this, there is also an important practical tip, that the usual type of nutritional tables frequently give a false impression because they are almost always organized according to weight (mg/100 g), although the content per serving for the user is much more important. Thus, cocoa powder (with some of the fat removed) contains the highest amount of magnesium as food with 414 mg/100 g; however, it is much easier to rectify a magnesium deficit with brown rice. It contains 157 mg/100 g but is eaten in considerably larger amounts (Table 14).

Vitamins
Vitamins can be manufactured by the body itself. They are necessary enzyme components and are catalysts influencing energy metabolism (carbohydrates and fats), protein metabolism and mineral metabolism both directly and indirectly. Additional vitamin doses cannot increase capacity. An excessive amount, especially of vitamins A and D, can even be dangerous. In contrast, an overdose of vitamin C or of the vitamin B complex are safely carried off by the kidneys and urinary tract. However, tennis players, particularly, lose considerable amounts of vitamins C and B through comprehensive training and many competitions. Because today's sophisticated diet

contains a considerable variety of foods that offer only "empty" calories (molecules with no material that is necessary for life, such as vitamins, minerals, and trace elements), players are especially at risk of a vitamin deficiency who prefer fast food restaurants and inferior processed products. The need for vitamins can also increase two- or four-fold as the scope of stress increases. Because the B-complex vitamins play an important role in protein and carbohydrate metabolism, and vitamin C can protect against infections in the upper throat passages, the (water-soluble) vitamins B_1, B_2, B_6, niacin, and C, as well as E (which is soluble in fat) are most important for tennis players. Besides vitamin tablets, vitamins can be ingested via the following foods:

Vitamin B_1 (thiamin)
Wheat germ, whole-grain products, oatmeal, peas and beans, pork

Vitamin B_2 (riboflavin)
Milk, meat, grains, yeast, wheat germ

Vitamin B_6 (pyridoxin)
Poultry, beef and pork, wheat germ, soybeans, potatoes

Niacin
Pork, yeast, potatoes

Vitamin C
Fresh fruits and vegetables, paprika, potatoes

Vitamin E (tocopherol)
Wheat germ and sunflower oil, kale and peas

Because cooked or warmed-over food loses most of its vitamin content, a certain amount of fresh food is absolutely necessary for a healthy diet.

Nutrition Before the Tennis Tournament

During this period, which usually lasts a few days to a week, the carbohydrate supplies are topped off and increased, so that enough reserves will be ready for the competitive phase of the tournament (weekend). For this, a carbohydrate-rich diet (for example, grain products, rice, pasta, potatoes, legumes, and dried fruit) should be emphasized, so that approximately 60 percent of the ingested calories can be absorbed as carbohydrates.

Because the buildup of the muscle glycogens requires potassium and water, and vitamin B_1 plays an important role in carbohydrate metabolism, potassium-rich foods (with fluids) and vitamin B_1 carriers should also be included.

The following measures are recommended to enrich the glycogen levels in the working musculature before exhausting demands on stamina (for example, tennis tournaments with daily action lasting several hours):

- Intensive or very intensive training sessions with corresponding glycogen buildup at the latest 2–3 days before the performance peak;
- Reduction of stimulus duration and density in training in the last 2–3 days before the performance peak;
- Increase the carbohydrate components in the diet to 60–70 percent 2–3 days before the performance peak. A competitive player weighing 155 lbs. should have 600–700 g of carbohydrates per day.
- Eating a carbohydrate-rich diet in the regenerative rest periods immediately following the training sessions.

In this regard, the following dishes are especially appropriate:
Rice dishes: fried rice, rice pudding, rice dishes with vegetables;
Potato dishes: mashed potatoes from fresh potatoes, potato dumplings, layered potato casserole, or potatoes boiled in their skins;
Noodle dishes and pastas: spaghetti, noodles, cannelloni, lasagne, pizza;
Legumes: lentils and potato casserole, lentils with noodles, etc.;
And also: cereals such as oatmeal, corn flakes, muesli with fresh fruit and/or milk, yogurt or fruit juice, etc., and various sweets, such as semolina pudding with fruit, waffles, crepes with fruit or fruit yogurt.

Nutrition Immediately Before a Competition

Because the glycogen supply (supercompensation) is locked, it is enough to eat an easily digested carbohydrate-rich main meal (with protein as a supplement) of approximately 1200–1500 kcal approximately 2–3 hours before the beginning of the match. Particular attention should be given to taking in minerals, trace elements, vitamins, and also fluids. Customarily, competitive tennis players must also be able to tolerate a small carbohydrate-rich (main) meal 60–90 minutes before the beginning of the competition or training session.

Above all, on the day of the competition, the digestability of the food should always be a major concern. Examples for such foods include:

- Steamed fish (filet of rosefish, plaice, or sole) with potatoes boiled in their skins (or fresh mashed potatoes or parboiled rice) with fresh vegetables or salad; pureed fruit as dessert.
- Roast beef (or beef goulash, etc.) with a large portion of noodles (or potato dumplings, etc.) and fresh carrots or beans; fresh fruit salad (or yogurt with fresh fruit or vanilla pudding with frozen fruits, etc.) as dessert.
- Large portion of (whole grain) spaghetti with tomato-herb sauce or macaroni with ham and cheese au gratin (or spinach-cheese sauce) and fresh salad (with fresh herb or yogurt dressing); as dessert: fruit salad with wheat germ or waffles with sour cherries.

In the case of an unforeseen delay in the start of the competition or intense demands in the training session or match that has just finished, an additional intake of a <u>carbohydrate-rich snack</u> is advised. Depending on individual taste and the current situation, the player might have rice pudding with fruit, rice pudding with cinnamon, yogurt with oatmeal and fruit, instant muesli, whole-grain muesli or dried fruit (for example, dried bananas or apricots). Ready-made products such as (whole-grain) cookies, muesli bars or marble cake are also acceptable, but only as a second choice, because of their limited nutritional value.

Immediately before or during the warm-up training session and shortly before the competition (5–10 minutes before), the player should have a pure fruit juice or a mixture of carbohydrates (for example, orange juice or a banana) and a mineral drink.

Nutrition During the Competition

A specific competition regimen (in the sense of a specific carbo-hydrate supply) is not normally necessary for a single tennis competition under 2 hours. However, after comprehensive training with longer-lasting singles matches, as well as when several matches are played in one day, we recommend taking in carbo-hydrates during the competition as well. This holds also if someone has a sudden hunger.

High levels of perspiration in climatic conditions such as high humidity, strong sunshine, or high levels of reflection from the court surface, necessitate an abundant intake of water and electrolytes (especially magnesium and sodium). Especially those players who tend to have muscle cramps should take more aggressive measures (magnesium-rich food or special mineral preparations in their basic diet or at least before the competitive phase).

Examples of Nutrition for Tournaments

For the changing of sides, small portions of the following are suitable:

- Mixture of fruit juice (fruit juices contain approximately 9–12 percent of carbohydrates, as well as vitamin C and potassium) and mineral water in 1:1 proportions. Mineral water is recommended, because it tends to be rich in magnesium and low in salt; separate drinks of both types are also a possibility.

	Gatorade	PowerAde	Isotar Orange	Snapple Iced Tea	Hi-C Fruit Punch
Sodium Potassium [mg/100 ml]	110 mg 30 mg	55 mg 30 mg	95 mg 28 mg	10 mg —	150 mg —
Carbohydrates [g/100 ml]	14 g (14 g sugars)	19 g (15 g sugars)	17 g (15 g sugars)	25 g (23 g sugars)	31 g (30 g sugars)
Calories [kcal/100 ml]	50	70	60	100	110
Additives	Vitamins & Minerals	Vitamins & Minerals	Vitamins	—	Vitamin C

Table 15 Comparison of common "sport drinks" per 8-ounce serving

- Various electrolyte drinks (Table 15), such as Gatorade (14 g of carbohydrates), PowerAde (19 g of carbohydrates), Isotar (17 g of carbohydrates, and Snapple Iced Tea (25 g of carbohydrates).
- One's own drink mixture, consisting of various types of carbohydrates (for example, maltodextrin 5–6 percent) and simple sugars (for example, fructose 2 percent) and with a fluid base, depending on the individual's taste (for example, tea, mineral water, or tap water).

If one gets hungry during a match, higher levels of carbohydrates in a handy format that can be tolerated by the stomach are necessary. These have proven their worth among tennis players:

- Ripe bananas (approximately 100 g of bananas contain 22 g of simple and complex sugars, 382 mg of potassium, and 36 mg of magnesium, among other things). Ripe bananas contain significantly more quickly available carbohydrates than green bananas (approximately 5 percent simple and complex sugars, as well as 18 percent starch).
- Granola and grains bars.
- Sports-energy bars from various manufacturers (see Table 16).

- Dried fruit such as bananas (approximately 85 g carbohydrates and 1400 mg potassium per 100 g) or apricots (approximately 65 g carbohydrates, 1100 mg potassium, and 5 mg iron per 100 g) contain higher levels of carbohydrates than fresh fruit.

Nutrition Immediately After the Competition

Nutrition immediately after the competition mainly serves to achieve the prematch level or to improve it (supercompensation), in order to manage the requirements for an efficient training session or renew the optimal competitive capabilities. Immediately after the competition, the body is especially ready for the necessary nutrients because of high enzyme activation (for example, glycogen synthesis).

Depending on the previous specific type of stress and its scope, this primarily concerns carbohydrates, minerals, fluids, and protein (especially for children and young people). In this situation, "empty" calorie carriers (such as french fries or ice cream) or considerable amounts of second-level drinks (such as soft drinks, Table 17) should not be

Table 16 Nutritional content of various sports-energy bars (per 65 g bar)

	Power Bar (chocolate)	Power Bar (PB)	Balance Bar	Zone Perfect (Honey Peanut)	Zone Perfect (Choc. Alm. Fudge)
Calories Carbohydrates	230 45 g (20 g sugars)	230 45 g (20 g sugars)	205 40 g	200 22 g	200 20 g
Sodium Potassium Protein	120 mg 145 mg 10 g	120 mg 180 mg 10 g	110 mg — 12 g	150 mg 220 mg 14 g	150 mg 350 mg 14 g

	Coca-Cola	Diet Pepsi	Apple Juice	Cranberry Juice	Gatorade
Cal. [kcal/100 ml]	100	0	110	140	50
Carbohydrates	27 g	0	26 g	26 g	14 g
Sodium	35 mg	25 mg	35 mg	35 mg	110 mg
Features	Caffeine	Sweetener	Vitamins	Vitamins	Vitamins & Minerals

Table 17   Content of various refreshments (per 8 oz. serving)

consumed frequently. If they are, the compensation that will increase individual performance will usually slip away because the player starts to feel satisfied.

As examples for tennis, we recommend:
- An extensive carbohydrate-rich dinner (potato dish, rice dish, noodle dish) for the purpose of quick and extended refilling of the glycogen reserve in the working musculature.
- Sufficient intake of protein and correspondingly reduced fat intake (skim milk products, low-fat meat), especially for children and young people.
- In the case of loss of appetite, especially after exhausting competition or intensive training sessions, the players should start with balancing fluids, of course, according to their own desires (for example, apple juice with carbonated water, mineral water, and in some cases, even Coca-Cola, or beer).

The Pedagogical Responsibility of the Trainer

The aspects of training and competition treated earlier were presented primarily with the functional intention of improving performance and the long-term development of capability.

However, especially in training children and young people, the trainer has the task not only to teach tennis but also to be effective as an educator. While gearing her teaching to tennis, she must be able to motivate and to help the students deal with winning and losing, as well as valuing self-control, responsibility for health, fairness, and collegial behavior. Pedagogical responsibility extends beyond playing tennis to the overall development of the young person. In doing so, all expectations and demands are considered which the young tennis player must work out in training and competition, as well as beyond the tennis court. Such expectations and demands come from parents, other trainers, club and league officials, sometimes from sponsors and media representatives, and, finally, from school. They concern children and young people who have very general needs, for example, the need for:

- diverse experiences and adventures,
- praise and recognition,
- emotional warmth,
- personal responsibility (as they get older).

Next to the relationships between trainer and student, it should also be noted that students form relatively stable relationships among themselves, especially in the course of group training. Students learn not only to know themselves, but also to develop emotional relationships among one another. Such relationships determine the structure of the training group.

The Responsible Athlete

Children in competitive sports should be given increasingly more independence as they develop from youth to adulthood. In the end, the "responsible athlete" should determine his own athletic goals and should participate in planning his training and tournaments.

Taking Advantage of Opportunities and Avoiding the Risks in Competitive Sports

According to a statement by the German Tennis Federation on competitive sports for children, sports offer the child a range of opportunities:
- Fostering physical, mental, and spiritual development;
- Experiencing one's own performance limits;
- Building self-confidence;
- Experiencing community adventures;
- Using free time wisely.

The trainer must be careful that the child is aware of these opportunities, while carrying out the following activities:
- Consideration of how the child or young person is able to withstand stress, depending on age and level of maturity (see p. 156),
- Guaranteeing a diverse development of coordination and conditioning instead of early specialization (see p. 106),

- Allowing sufficient time for family, recreation, and social contacts,
- Making room for supplementary team competitions to foster social interaction,
- Avoiding premature pressure to succeed,
- Securing possible school and professional development, even after the end of competition,
- Including abilities that develop over a long period as one takes part in local and league group activities,
- Organizing regular sports-medical check-ups,
- Maintaining close contact with parents; regular, repeated evaluation of opportunities and risks for the individual child, perhaps slowing down the parents' overzealous expectations of performance and success.

Professional Future

The young person in training should learn to consider the competitive sport as an important part of her life, but not the most important. She must learn that some day, depending on age, the part of her life occupied by the sport will come to an end.

The job of the trainer is to help his youthful player to envision a professional and private life for herself after the sport and to prepare for it. That means that the trainer must be vigilant that school and emotional development do not suffer under the pressure of training and competition. Children and young people cannot expect to be given preferential treatment; however, they may not be put at a disadvantage because of their engagement in the competitive sport.

Summary

To assume pedagogical responsibility for the overall development (that is, not only the athletic development) of young players, therefore, means that trainers must embed training and competition into the overall world of the children and young people in such a way that at the end of their athletic careers, they can say "The sport has enriched my life."

Index